ON THE COUCH

ON THE COUCH

*Writers Analyze
Sigmund Freud*

*Edited by
Andrew Blauner*

PRINCETON UNIVERSITY PRESS
PRINCETON & OXFORD

Published by Princeton University Press
41 William Street, Princeton, New Jersey 08540
99 Banbury Road, Oxford OX2 6JX

press.princeton.edu

All Rights Reserved

ISBN 9780691242439
ISBN (e-book) 9780691242446

British Library Cataloging-in-Publication Data is available

Editorial: Anne Savarese and James Collier
Production Editorial: Sara Lerner
Text and Jacket Design: Katie Osborne
Production: Erin Suydam
Publicity: Julia Haav, Carmen Jimenez, and Jodi Price
Jacket Credit: aluna1 / Adobe Stock

This book has been composed in Arno

Printed in the United States of America

10 9 8 7 6 5 4 3 2 1

CONTENTS

v

PREFACE

In his poem "In Memory of Sigmund Freud," written shortly after Freud's death in 1939, the poet W. H. Auden described Freud as "a whole climate of opinion. / Under whom we conduct our differing lives."[1] Freud—the father of psychiatry, the pioneer of psycho-analysis—is the figure we associate with such concepts as transfer-ence, the Oedipus complex, repression, the unconscious, and a model of psychic structure comprising id, ego, and superego. Many consider his writings, from *The Interpretation of Dreams* to *Civilization and Its Discontents*, among the classics of Western lit-erature. He is also a polarizing figure, sometimes portrayed as a cartoonish persona, a caricature, with controversial ideas about women and sex—his story is one that many people think they know. To his defenders and detractors alike, however, his influence on twentieth-century thought is undeniable.

In this book, twenty-five writers engage with Freud and his legacy in a variety of ways. I invited them to analyze the great analyst: to reflect on who he was, why he did what he did, and the impact he made. Together, they present a reassessment of one of the most important and controversial figures in our history.

The pieces are loosely organized by theme. The essays in "Inter-pretations" examine Freud through a particular critical lens: some writers discuss their own encounters with Freud's ideas, while others consider Freud's work in relation to works by others. "The Talking Cure" collects essays that focus on psychoanalysis and related topics. "Personal History" provides different perspec-tives on Freud's personal history, including reflections by some of his descendants. The final section, "After Freud," addresses Freud's legacy and influence—on literature, on science, and on the authors of these essays—in the twentieth and twenty-first centuries.

The contributors embrace a wide range of perspectives, from the skeptical to the appreciative. I hope that the book leaves you with a sense of Freud as a fully realized person: not an anachronism or a punch line, but instead a gateway to better understanding ourselves, one another, and our world.

Andrew Blauner

ACKNOWLEDGMENTS

"No good deed goes unpublished." Or so I slip and say, accidentally, periodically. A Freudian slip? Who is to say?

Is Sigmund Freud having "a moment"? Somewhat of a sudden, it seems, he is manifesting like never before in my adult life, at least—in mainstream media, publications, movies, television, and articles with titles such as "Why We Should Keep Reading Freud," "Why Freud Still Matters," and "The Greatest Modern Writer."

Is it, though, a moment, per se, something in the zeitgeist now, a confluence of things conspiring, contributing to that? Or, really, more, has it been one, long, virtually continuous century of moments, uninterrupted?

I wanted to help get and share a better understanding of the person who has helped us understand ourselves perhaps more than anyone in history.

None of this could have or would have happened without a whole host of people. Starting with Jim Gibbons, an editor extraordinaire at Library of America, where he was my editor on my penultimate anthology, before this one, *The Peanuts Papers*. (While this book features, arguably, the greatest psychiatrist of all time, that one treated, perhaps, the worst, in Lucy Van Pelt.) This is the first—and probably last—of the nine books that I have edited the idea for which was not mine; the idea for this one was Jim's.

Often, it is the idea that is my main contribution to these endeavors, coming up with it, and just trying to execute it mostly by not getting in the way, the way a coach of an all-star team might.

"Editor," at least in this context, then, is a misnomer.

That moniker is more aptly ascribed to Anne Savarese, who was my editor of the Thoreau collection *Now Comes Good Sailing.* Very safe and suffice to say that, without Anne, this book would not exist. She puts up with a lot of disorganization and so many short-comings in me and, yet, stays the course, steadies things, in seam-less, selfless ways, brings out the best in books.

"Contributor" is another misnomer, of a kind. In the vernacu-lar, it's the nomenclature that we have come to use to describe those whose words make up the book itself. Yes, assuredly, they do contribute, but really, more, they do much more than that; they are the book. The best-selling book of all time, the Bible, is an anthology, with a multitude of—in that case—anonymous con-tributors. Here, I'm happy not just to name those who've contrib-uted to this volume, but to give them their due, my deep gratitude and profound admiration.

Princeton University Press, as a publisher, has been great to me, and I am grateful. Specifically, I thank Sydney Bartlett, Bob Bettendorf, James Collier, Christie Henry, Kathleen Kageff, Sara Lerner, and Jodi Price.

My assistant, Natalie Lucas, was simply invaluable again.

Thanks to Bruce Breimer, Larry Byrnes, Robert Coles, Jona-than Franzen, Jill Furman, Carl Kawaja, Stephane LaFarge, Robin Lippert, Janet Malcolm, Gil Mason, Adam Phillips, Matthew Saal, Steven Shainberg, Jim Solomon, John Solomon, and Meg Wolitzer.

Thanks to my entire family, going back to earlier generations, one side of which came from Austria, and which includes six relatives, still among us, who, at one time or another, have been therapists.

Special, ineffable, unconditional love and gratitude and more, everything, to my son, Sam. And a ceremonial throw of the bone to our dear dog, Smiles.

And a final hat tip to any and all others who provided encour-agement, inspiration, support, and more, along the way to make this, what I hope will be a meaningful book. Sometimes a book is just a book . . . (?)

INTERPRETATIONS

IT'S COMPLICATED

Sarah Boxer

Freud is family, my family. Not literally, but dreamily. I first awakened to Sigmund Freud's presence in my crib. When I was a year old or so, just lying there, my father approached me. I saw him walk toward me from the hallway. He stuck his pointer finger through the bars and said, "Bite!" And I, toothless, did bite. Nothing weird, right? In retrospect, though, this innocent scene seems kind of kinky. Thank you, Sigmund Freud, for warping my very first memory.

On the other hand, thank you, Sigmund Freud, for putting me in a class with Leonardo da Vinci. As I learned much later, Leonardo had a similar remembrance, which he recounted in the *Codex Atlanticus*: "it comes to my mind as a very early memory, when I was still in the cradle, a vulture came down to me, he opened my mouth with his tail and struck me a few times with his tail against my lips." Freud loved this vulture "memory" so much that he wrote a book about it, *Leonardo da Vinci: A Memory of His Childhood*, in which he said, Leonardo's "phantasy conceals nothing more or less than a reminiscence of nursing—or being nursed—at the mother's breast," and when Leonardo grew up, his infant vision became "a passive homosexual phantasy."

———

In the house where I grew up, everything had meaning—unconscious meaning, double meaning, hidden meaning, manifest meaning, latent meaning. Thanks to Freud, nothing was what it seemed. The finger might well be a phallus or a bird; the mouth, toothless, might be a threatening abyss. Hakuna Matata? Never. Vagina Dentata? Could be.

My dad had a shelf of Freud's writings, which he applied liberally to our daily lives. He labeled his wife's and his daughters' emotional outbursts "hysterical." (They weren't.) We were trained to be on the lookout for unconscious motives. (Always there.) We were schooled in sussing out the latent criticism behind remarks, jokes, even compliments. (We're not paranoid; we're realists!) When I took up rock climbing I was diagnosed with a "death wish." No dream went unanalyzed, no gift horse's mouth went unlooked-in. My childhood was a world of fizz and buzz, toil and trouble. Anyone who didn't see all the stuff churning under the surface of everyday life was a damn fool.

By age sixteen, I began to grapple with Freud's writings. Looking for a topic for an English paper, I ran my finger along my father's Freud shelf as if shopping for clothes on a discount rack. I grazed the paperbacks—*Beyond the Pleasure Principle, The Interpretation of Dreams, Moses and Monotheism, The Future of an Illusion, Civilization and Its Discontents*—finally landing on one, untouched and thin, that pleased my eye and my ear: *The Ego and the Id*. It wasn't really the best choice. I liked the exotic title, but the insides were a scientistic mess. At the kitchen table I pored over Freud's incomprehensible diagram of EGO, ID, Repressed, acoust., Pcpt.-Cs., and Pcs., staring at the menagerie of terms, some abbreviated, some in italics, some in ALL CAPS (only crazy people use ALL CAPS!), all linked together by an oval representing a brain.

Then something on the next page caught my eye: Freud noted that the EGO sported a little "cap of hearing," an acoustic helmet, and wore it "awry." How jaunty! At this point Freud plunged into one of his best metaphors: The ego "in its relation to the id . . . is like a man on horseback, who has to hold in check the superior strength of the horse. . . . Often a rider, if he is not to be parted from his horse, is obliged to guide it where it wants to go; so in the same way the ego is in the habit of transforming the id's will into action as if it were its own."

I was hooked. Freud's jockey metaphor won me over. I wrote my English paper on *The Ego and the Id*, or, as Bruno Bettelheim later renamed it, *The I and the It*. I had no idea what I was talking about. I got an A because the teacher couldn't understand what I was talking about either.

By the time I went to college, Freud was largely passé, at least at Harvard. The only Freud book I read there, *Three Theories on Sexuality*, was for a course on intellectual history. Meanwhile, the Harvard department of psychology and social relations was, as far as I could tell, populated by sadists. Lurking somewhere in that department was the behaviorist B. F. Skinner, the king of controlled environments, so-called Skinner boxes, where pigeons, rats, and even people were coaxed, by positive and negative reinforcements, to do whatever they were conditioned to do.

I never took a psychology course. It all seemed god-awful. Nonetheless, I came pretty close to being part of that world when I interviewed for a summer job in the Harvard lab of Torsten Wiesel and David Hubel, who were already famous (and soon to be Nobel famous) for their work on the visual processing systems of kittens. Now they were moving on to monkeys. The job I interviewed for was taking care of the monkeys. But when I found out that the new experiment entailed forcing monkeys, heads immobilized, to stare at a visual stimulus for hours on end every day for the rest of their lives, lives that would end with a beheading and an analysis of what all that torture had done to their brains, I bailed. As I left the lab, Wiesel told me that although the monkeys' lives would not be pleasant and would inevitably end with a decapitation, "at least their lives will be a little better if you care for them." Was he guilt-tripping *me*?

—

I fled psychology, psychiatry, and every associated field. But not forever. I moved to New York and found work as a science journalist. I had roommates. I had boyfriends. I had problems. I needed therapy. So once I finally managed to earn a living wage, with benefits, I went looking for a therapist. I tried many. I rejected many. Finally, one stuck.

He was a Freudian. He told me I'd have to kill a dozen shrinks before finding the right one. I think he was number six or so. He was older than my dad. He walked crookedly, like he was about to fall over. He had a sense of humor, but I worried that he was a crackpot. Once a week I went into his darkened room and lay on a couch and talked. He often steered the conversation to rage. When I looked into his background many years later, I learned that he had a horribly tragic history (captured in the 1984 movie *Bay Boy*). His parents were murdered in their home in 1941 by an anti-Semitic policeman who lived in the building they owned. No wonder my therapist was examining my rage! I'd be examining my rage too if I were him. Which didn't mean that I didn't have any.

Anyway, psychoanalysis was not dead, at least not to me. I resumed my Freud reading (*The Interpretation of Dreams*) and kept a dream journal. Then, in the late 1980s, while enjoying a brief period of unemployment and some severance pay from Time, Inc., I moved to Berkeley and started doodling. I daydreamed and I drew. Maybe I could start a comic strip. I'd always drawn a bunny and he always looked troubled to me. I tried to get him to talk and move. He wouldn't. I placed him in a bar and got him drunk to see whether he'd talk. No. Then, suddenly, a lightbulb! This bunny was totally neurotic. Why not send him to a psychoanalyst? He desperately needed help.

—

Thus Bunnyman, my neurotic superhero, was born. And he quickly found a quack analyst, a bird, Dr. Sigbird Floyd. In the mold of Dr. Freud, Dr. Floyd, the bird analyst, was only interested in Bunnyman's psychic life. Although Bunnyman came running to Dr. Floyd because he was being chased by a wolf, Dr. Floyd assured Bunnyman that the wolf was just a fantasy. But then, at the end of the very first episode, just as Bunnyman left the safe haven of Dr. Floyd's office, a wolf walked in the door for his own analysis with Dr. Floyd. It was Mr. Wolfman! This was how my first comic, *In the Floyd Archives: A Psycho-Bestiary*, began.

To research my comic, I dove deep into Freud's case histories. I studied the Wolf Man and Daniel Paul Schreber (who would merge to form some of the details of my bipolar, cross-dressing Wolfman); the Rat Man (who would become my obsessive-compulsive hoarder, Ratma'am); Dora (who would become Lambskin, the fleece that was sometimes worn by the cross-dressing Wolfman); and Little Hans (who would become my Oedipal star, Bunnyman).

By the time my comic really took shape, in the 1990s, I had a new job as an editor at the *New York Times Book Review*. There I was in charge of all books about science, nature, psychology, and psychoanalysis. Dumpster-size containers full of books came in every week. I got to decide which ones would get reviewed and who should review them and then I would edit the reviews. For a few books (*On Kissing, Tickling, and Being Bored* by the child analyst Adam Phillips being one), I did the reviewing myself.

One of my first—and scariest—editing assignments was handling the review of *Final Analysis: The Making and Unmaking of a Freudian Analyst* (1990) by Jeffrey Moussaieff Masson, who was infamous for his battles with psychoanalysis. In the 1970s, Masson, a charming and dogged Sanskrit scholar who was also a psychoanalyst in training, befriended the founder of the Freud Archives, Kurt Eissler, as well as Freud's daughter Anna Freud, keeper of her father's flame. Shockingly, the two of them handed Masson the keys to the psychoanalytic kingdom in 1980: Masson was named the project director of the Freud Archives and thereby gained access to all of Freud's letters and interviews. Eissler came to regret it, bitterly. When Eissler died in 1999, I wrote his obituary and quoted what Gwen Davis had written about him in the *Nation*: Eissler was like "old Geppetto, who had carved himself a son, only to discover, to his profound chagrin, that Pinocchio was a naughty boy."

Once Masson had access, beginning in the early 1980s, to Freud's letters, he zoomed in on what he considered the most scandalous and amoral turn in Freud's life—his abandonment of the so-called seduction hypothesis. In 1895, Freud wrote a letter to his friend Wilhelm Fliess stating his belief that *all* neurosis was caused by child abuse. Then, less than a year later, Freud scaled back his hypothesis, arguing that *some* neuroses might be caused by the *fantasy* that one had been abused. In a 1983 *New Yorker* essay titled "Trouble in the Archives," the journalist Janet Malcolm described the revision: Freud "never doubted that seductions and rapes and beating of children sometimes do take place," she wrote, but he "came to believe that many or most of the seductions reported by his patients were 'wishful fantasies.'"

To orthodox Freudians, this shift away from historical reality toward so-called psychic reality was the very key to psychoanalysis. To Masson it was a horrible abandonment of abused children and a disaster for psychoanalysis. In her *New Yorker* piece, Malcolm quoted Masson's 1981 address to the Western New England Psychoanalytic Society, in which he damned Freud's revision: "By shifting the emphasis from a real world of sadness, misery and cruelty to an internal stage on which actors performed invented dramas for an invisible audience of their own creation, Freud began a trend away from the real world that, it seems to me, has come to a dead halt in the present-day sterility of psychoanalysis throughout the world."

Masson was promptly removed from his throne at the Freud Archives. And then he had a royal tantrum that lasted years. By the time I handled the review of his 1990 book *Final Analysis*, in which he chronicled his own terrible psychoanalysis and his ejection from the Freud Archives, his antitherapy rampage was famous. He had already written two other books against psychoanalysis, *The*

Assault on Truth (1984), detailing his case against Freud, and *Against Therapy* (1988), arguing that "abuse of one form or another is built into the very fabric of psychotherapy." Most ominously (to me), he had sued the *New Yorker* in 1984 for Janet Malcolm's reportage about him, which had become, in 1983, a book, *In the Freud Archives*. His case went all the way to the Supreme Court, where he ultimately lost.

———

Even after I left the *New York Times Book Review* to become an arts and ideas reporter at the *Times*, psychoanalysis remained one of my regular beats. In 1997 I wrote a piece titled "How Oedipus Is Losing his Complex," and an article on the history of hysteria. In 1998 I wrote about pupaphobia, the fear of puppets, and also covered the heated debate among psychoanalysts about Freud's abandonment of his seduction hypothesis. By the late 1990s, when the so-called Freud Wars had reached a fever pitch, I was embedded more or less with the Freudian troops. I understood their lingo and seemed to care more than anyone I knew on the *Times* staff about the past and future of psychoanalysis. I felt it was my duty to report honestly about the Freud Wars from the front.

Nonetheless, I had plenty of doubts about Freud and his methods. The comic I was drawing made hay of Freud's mania for fantasy over reality. I had also modeled the most sinister character in my book, Dr. Fleece, who threatens Lambskin with a fleecing, on Freud's quackiest friend, Wilhelm Fliess. But, despite my skepticism, I felt no kinship with the anti-Freudians. They struck me as humorless, petty, and mean.

On December 17, 1995, for instance, I reviewed Paul Roazen's book *How Freud Worked: First-Hand Accounts of Patients*. His main point was that Freud had no boundaries with his patients, which sure seemed true. Among Freud's analysands were his own daughter, his daughter's friend, his translator, and his caregiver. As I noted in my review, "He was personable to the point of being meddlesome and indiscreet, he was more than willing to ask favors of his patients and give them advice, and he vacationed, played cards and spoke unguardedly with his favorites." But when I, after agreeing with Roazen's main argument, took issue with his tendentious quotation marks and his questionable logic, finding his book a "minefield of shattered quotes and non sequiturs," he sent me hate mail. And when a new Italian translation of the book came out he sent me jauntier hate mail.

—

By the end of the twentieth century, Freud's attackers seemed to have gained the upper hand in the Freud Wars. At the *New York Review of Books* the critic Frederick Crews often published long essays on Freud's faults (which he then collected in a 1995 book titled *The Memory Wars: Freud's Legacy in Dispute*). And when, in 1995, the Library of Congress first announced plans for an exhibition on Freud's legacy, the anti-Freudians, so the rumor went, managed to get the show postponed until a more critical take on Freud could be found.

Three years later, in 1998, when *Sigmund Freud: Conflict and Culture* finally did open, the Freud bashers seemed to have won some concessions. As I wrote in a 1998 essay for the *Times*, "When Verbal Resists Visual: Freud's Defense Against Art," the exhibition's greatest claim for Freud was merely an irrefutable and obvious point: "Freud, like it or not, has had an extraordinary influence on our culture, from Thurber to Popeye." Still, a lot of Freud's bashers were unhappy; they seethed that such a man got to be honored with such a show in such a venue. As the British historian and philosopher John Forrester put it in his 1998 book *Dispatches from the Freud Wars*, Freud's harshest critics had a "heartfelt wish that Freud might never have been born or, failing to achieve that end, that all his works and influence be made as nothing."

Were the bashers going to get their way? Was the ship of Freud sinking? Were there any lifeboats? Could psychoanalysis be saved?

The Freudians seemed to be on their heels. I wanted to know what would happen. So I gathered all the Freud-bashing books I could find and reviewed them in an essay for the *New York Times Book Review*, "Flogging Freud" (August 10, 1997). My tone was fairly breezy, as if Team Psychoanalysis would sail on no matter what, with a cigar-smoking Freud on its prow: "Freud has proved to be a great whipping boy for our time. He has been blamed for turning children against their parents (Frederick Crews) and for excusing parents who seduce their children (Jeffrey Masson), for being a crypto-biologist (Frank Sulloway) and a crypto-priest (Richard Webster), for believing patients too little (Jeffrey Masson) and too much (Mikkel Borch-Jacobsen), for hiding his faults (Henri Ellenberger) and flaunting them (John Farrell)." But deep down I was worried. Freud wasn't exactly my personal hero, but he was, after all, family.

At the height of the Freud Wars, I was putting the finishing touches on my spoof of Freud's case histories, *In the Floyd Archives: A Psycho-Bestiary* (2001). By this time my main characters were so closely tied to Freud's famous patients, the Wolf Man, the Rat Man, Dora, Schreber, and Little Hans, that I felt compelled to add some seventy-five endnotes to my comic. And I decided to name my book after *In the Freud Archives*, Malcolm's book about Masson's undermining of the Freud Archives. My comic was neither tribute nor hatchet job. It was . . . Freudian. I turned Freud's ideas on themselves, sometimes making fun of them. In one review, titled "An Analytic Casebook Full of Animal Instincts" (*New York Times*, September 6, 2001), the playwright Jenny Lyn Bader wrote, "If Freud had a bad dream, it would probably be Floyd." Fair enough.

Freud's case histories, his most vivid and dramatic material, captivated me, but I knew they were treacherous territory. In the Wolf Man case, Freud totally overreached in claiming to know with certainty what his patient really had seen as an infant and how it affected him. Was the Wolf Man's dream of wolves silently sitting in a tree really proof that as an infant he saw his parents having sex doggy style? And the infamous Dora case was Freud at his worst.

This was ground zero for "No means yes." When Dora, a teenager, told Freud that his old friend "Herr K" had tried to seduce her, Freud demurred, saying that her report merely showed her wish to be seduced by Herr K, and by Freud too. Talk about unexamined projection! In dealing with this infuriating and almost absurdly awful material (and, by the way, Herr K later confessed to Dora), I still was awed by Freud's ability to be both maddeningly literal minded and beautifully metaphorical in almost the same breath, his talent with puns and slips, and his great ease with unconscious life. Sometimes he used his gifts atrociously. But what gifts they were!

———

I won't say that the *Floyd Archives* ended the Freud Wars, but I will say that the Freud Wars ended abruptly and dramatically on the day of what was supposed to be my first New York book party for *Floyd*, originally scheduled for September 11, 2001. (Needless to say, the party was canceled.) On that day, the Freud Wars came to a screeching halt. Freud was worse than dead; he was totally beside the point. Who cared about psychological reality when actual reality—airliners used as weapons, collapsing towers, three thousand dead, a smoke-filled city, the threat of future terrorism—was so clearly present?

However, not everyone got the memo. To some people, or at least those who attended my book talks, Freud still mattered. At one of my talks for *In the Floyd Archives*, a few audience members voiced outrage that I was using Freud's ideas at all. Someone asked: If Freud has been discredited, why would you spend so much time on him? Another asked: If Freud hated women so much, why would you, a woman, pay him any mind? I was on the defensive. I imagine I said something unwitty about Freud's wit.

Closer to home, I faced opposite challenges. From Freudians and psychoanalytically inclined persons, including some from my family, came questions about the critical tone of *In the Floyd Archives*. Why do you mock Freud? At a meeting of the American Psychoanalytic Association, I had a little friendly back-and-forth with Harold Blum, who had become the executive director of the Freud Archives in 1986, after Masson was fired from that post. In a conversation called "Dr. Freud and Dr. Floyd" Blum and I compared what was in the Freud Archives with what was in the *Floyd Archives*. Apparently I was still welcome among the psychoanalysts, but I could tell that my audience, battered and bruised by the Freud Wars and September 11, was in no mood for Freudian fun and games. Everyone with a psychoanalytic bent wanted to know what my real attitude toward Freud was. Once again, I was on the defensive. If I recall correctly, my answers boiled down to one rhetorical question: Wasn't I honoring Freud by engaging him, playing with him, fighting him on the very playground that he himself built? I'm not sure anyone bought it.

——

Several years later, I wrote and drew a sequel to the *Floyd Archives*, titled *Mother May I? A Post-Floydian Folly*. There I played with some of the wild ideas that Freud formulated at the end of his life—the father-fearing, father-killing, father-worshipping foundations of civilization as he outlined them in *Totem and Taboo* and *Moses and Monotheism*—as well as some of the mother-centric ideas of the post-Freudians, namely the breast-obsessed object relations theory of Melanie Klein and the play therapy of Donald Winnicott. My new comic turned out to be a much broader comedy than the *Floyd Archives*. So when International Psychoanalytic Books wanted to publish *Mother May I?* (along with a new edition of *Floyd*) I was both pleased and surprised.

In *Mother May I?* I was as tough on late Freud and the post-Freudians as I had been on early Freud in my first book. By turning Melanie Klein, the great analyst of rage and envy, into an intrusive and bossy little sheep named Melanin Klein (which means "Little Black"), I literally belittled her. And if that weren't

enough, I gave Klein, the prime theorist of the infant-mother bond, three disturbed animal children: Melittle Klein, a kitten who hates her mother with a passion (true to life); Little Hans (aka Hans Klein), a happy but violent little bunny named for one of Freud's sweetest cases; and Squiggle Piggle, an indignant pig who speaks only when someone pulls his tail. (I modeled him after the so-called Squiggle Game that the child analyst Winnicott used to play with his patients.)

In 2019 I gave a slide talk at 192 Books in New York titled "How to Psychoanalyze a Bunny." (The title of my talk was a nod to a short documentary about the artist Ray Johnson, *How to Draw a Bunny*.) There I presented the brief and sometimes tragic true life stories behind each of the characters I drew in *Mother May I?* After my talk one die-hard Freudian I knew asked: "Why are you so hard on Freud?" And I responded: "Why are you so easy on him?" He never spoke to me again.

I do not hate Freud. I grew up with him. Sure, he had deep faults, which are especially evident in his case histories, the works I drew on most. But there is so much brilliance in his leaping logic. When Freud, whose study was cluttered with antiquities, was once struggling to get his favorite patient, the obsessive-compulsive Rat Man, to open up, to unearth his real thoughts, he told the Rat Man that if he kept all his disturbing unconscious thoughts to himself, buried, he would actually be preserving them, keeping them alive and powerful, just as antiquities are protected from air, hands, accidents, and soot as long as they are left buried underground. It is a beautiful, deep, and complicated metaphor that I think of often. Without Freud, it would not exist.

Without Freud: No Freudian slips. No Oedipus complex. No latent content. No repression. No wish fulfillment. No death drive. No unconscious life. No ego. No id. As I think now on my long engagement with Freud, back to the crib, I keep returning to Freud's words and metaphors. It is magical stuff. The world would be worse without it. I do not hate Freud. Nor do I worship him. I am conflicted, which is a feeling from Freud, who defined the psyche as a field of conflicts. My ambivalence is Freudian. Which is not to say, as Freud might, that my resistance to Freud is a defense against my attraction to him. My "no" is not a "yes." Nor is my "yes" a "no." Rather I would say that after all the love and war, Freud is still the air we breathe, the language we speak, and the finger we bite.

PENIS ENVY

Jennifer Finney Boylan

On the way home there was a dispute in the car about whether I had a big one, or not. I didn't think it was anything special. But Dan had seen mine one night the boys in our comedy group got naked at some radio station, and so he held his ground. For their part, Maggie and Tom were curious, I guess. I don't remember Peter weighing in, but it was a whole thing, the conversation rising and falling. I kept hoping they'd move on to something else, but you know how people are with a thing like that.

Finally I told them to pull the car over, and I whipped it out in the breakdown lane. This was on Route 101, the two-lane road that leads from Olympic National Park to Bainbridge Island, where we were going to catch the ferry back to Seattle. We'd been in the wilderness.

Everybody got a good look. Then I pulled my pants back up and climbed back into the back seat, where I was jammed in between Peter and Maggie. We got back on the highway. Nobody said anything for a while.

Dan said, "I think it looked cold."

Everyone nodded. Maybe it *had* been cold. That could have explained a lot of things.

—

Freud figured everybody wanted one. "It consists in attributing to everyone, including females, the possession of a penis, such as the

Fort Mitchell, Kentucky, 1982.

boy knows from his own body. And: the boy's estimate of its value is logically reflected in his inability to imagine a person like himself without this essential element."[1]

There's a lot, as they say in grad school, to unpack there. But the phrase that I come back to is "a person like himself." Freud assumes that men and boys are the *default human*. If you're female, you must spend your days in lamentation that you somehow arrived on earth without the factory settings, and that penis-wise, we're like the playthings in *Toy Story*. "If you don't have one," counsels cowboy Woody, "get one!"

That women might consider *ourselves* the default human, or, God forbid, that in fact there might not even *be* a single way of being human, seems not to have crossed Freud's mind.

Since penis envy is a concept with its supposed roots in childhood, though, it is worth noting that the only default humans I ever encountered in elementary school were bullies and assholes. Most of these were boys, but there were a few girls in that cohort too. They always got their way, those characters.

I didn't hate the one I had. It was pleasant enough if you wanted one, which I didn't. I guess the thing I would compare it to, really, was like having a St. Bernard dog for a pet. There were times when it made demands, and then there was the problem of what we might refer to as the *drool*. Other times, it was adorable: a big, sloppy, goofy presence that merely wanted, as they say in Ireland, "to live a life given over totally to pleasure." In the years since, I've known a lot of men, and more than a few women, who have wanted to live their lives like that too: like penises. They do just as they please. Are they happy, people like that? I don't know. A lot of them *look* happy, anyhow.

Anyway, most of the time mine just lay there like a St. Bernard puppy, exhausted, sated, fast asleep.

"All this seems to show," Freud writes, "that there is some truth in the infantile sexual theory that women, like men, possess a penis." And: "They develop a great interest in that part of the boy's body. But this interest promptly falls under the sway of envy. They feel themselves unfairly treated."

I *did* feel myself unfairly treated. There I was, with a penis that I did not want. I didn't hate it, or write it angry poems in which I told it *you are a caul that blinds my sight.* It just didn't make any sense. I was clearly a girl; I mean, as they say in psychoanalysis, *duh.* I'd known this from the age of five or six, from the languid afternoon when I lay beneath my mother's ironing board, and she said, as she steamed my father's shirts, "Some day you'll wear shirts like this," and I thought, *What? Seriously?*

Unlike lots of trans girls today, it never occurred to me back then to say out loud the thing that was in my heart. These days, I look at young girls out and proud, taking puberty blockers, wearing dresses to school, buying *My Little Pony* lunch boxes. It just amazes me. The closest I ever got to that was one time when I got frozen, sledding at Woojee Trousdale's house, and I started crying because of the cold. Her mother took me in, set me down by the fire, dressed me up in her daughters' clothes until I warmed up. When at last I'd thawed, she suggested it was time for me to go home.

But I didn't want to go home.

I guess it would have been easier for me if I'd been born later, or if I'd had the courage to state the truth when I was a child. But what's the point of this kind of thinking? It's kind of like saying, *Life would have been different if I had a time machine.* Maybe that's true, but I don't know if it would be better. Mostly I'm grateful for the life I've had, even with all the trouble.

Sometimes, I'd see men naked in locker rooms or skinny-dipping in a pool, wreathed in careless contentment. When I lived in Ireland—this was in the late 1990s, when I taught at University College Cork—I remember huge men standing nude before the mirrors at the gym, shaving the thick cream from their pink faces as steam from the showers drifted around them like fog. On these and so many other occasions I would look on in wonder, and try to imagine what it might be like to be a creature such as this.

I don't know cis women who've ever experienced penis envy as Freud described it. But as a woman born with one, all I can say is, I know exactly what he meant. Why yes, I did feel myself *unfairly treated.*

In the movie *Zelig*, the title character says, "I worked with Freud in Vienna. We broke over the concept of penis envy. Freud felt that it should be limited to women."

———

We stood backstage at the Met Breuer museum, the poet Sharon Olds and I. This was just a few years ago. We were part of a festival called "The In-Between," which the Met was staging in the museum that had formerly been the Whitney, and which the Met was now taking over. The festival was taking place after the Whitney moved downtown, but before the Met moved in. Everywhere you looked there were sawhorses, ductwork, big piles of trash. The place was in transition.

That title, "The In-Between," had irritated me a little bit, given that, posttransition, I didn't feel particularly liminal. Still: it was good company—not just Sharon and me, but Isabella Rossellini, too. They'd wired us all up with those remote headphone microphones, so we could hold forth wirelessly at the podium. As we waited to go onstage, it occurred to me to ask Sharon about the poem she'd written some years before, "Outside the Operating Room of the Sex-Change Doctor" from the collection *The Gold Cell*, a work in which a tray of displaced penises take the measure of their situation. "I was a dirty little dog," one says. "I knew he'd have me put to sleep."

Another: "I am safe. Now no one can hurt me."

It's got a wow finish, that poem: "Only one is unhappy. He lies there in terrible grief, crying out, Father! Father!"

I'd always revered her work. She was my favorite poet. But that piece hurt my feelings. Even now, I get sad just thinking about it.

I imagined myself clearing my throat and saying, *Sharon, listen, can I ask you about something?*

Onstage, we heard the person before us wrapping up his speech. I think this was Ricky Jackson, a man who'd spent thirty-nine years imprisoned for a crime he did not commit. I've never been behind bars, but sure: his story spoke to me, as a transgender person. I hadn't committed any crimes, either.

Maybe, I thought, if Sharon heard the piece I was going to perform, her heart would open. It was a story about that time I drove to Nova Scotia to take my life. At the last second I'd been blown back from the precipice of a cliff by a fierce gust of wind. I'd lain there on the moss, looking up at the blue sky. A voice had whispered to me. *You're going to be all right*, it said. *You're going to be okay.*

In the auditorium, the audience applauded, and the stage manager pointed to Sharon and said, "You're on!"

The third penis in that poem says, "I am a caul removed from his eyes. Now he can see."

She stood up.

"Break a leg," I said.

—

We'd wound up in Olympic National Park, my friend Peter and I, at the tail end of a long road trip that had begun at my parents' house in Devon, Pennsylvania. We'd taken the blue highways the whole way, stopping en route at places of interest to stoned-out goofballs, which, let the record show: we were.

At Vent Haven, a museum for retired ventriloquist's dummies, I stood in a room full of carved figures, all of their voices fallen silent. This was in Kentucky. "Ventriloquists get very attached to their figures," our guide explained. "After they die, they want to make sure they have a good home." She laughed nervously. "They don't want anybody else's hands working the controls!"

I laughed, too, although it occurred to me then that this was exactly what it was like, being a man. You had to waggle the eyebrows, use the deep voice. On certain occasions you even had to make the penis do its thing. Sometimes this was easy for me, and sometimes not. It all depended on whether I could forget myself. On a good day, the woman I was with filled my thoughts: how much I loved her, how much I wanted her to feel happy. Other times, it was impossible not to look at her and wish that she was a mirror, rather than a human.

One time, after I had tried and failed to forget myself, I'd just rolled over on my pillow in exasperation. "Darn these things!" I said, like my penis was a temperamental Model A Ford that had failed to start, even though I'd turned the crank. The girl that I was with thought that was very funny.

"Don't worry," she said. "It happens to everybody."

I thought, "Yeah, well. Not to you."

Before I went out west with Peter, I'd spent June of that summer house-sitting my mother's house, back in Pennsylvania, while Mom was off in Germany, where she'd been a child. It was the first time she'd been back since the war. I spent those weeks *en femme*, day after day. It was the first time I'd really been able to be myself without interruption for a long time. It had been glorious, and deeply frightening.

I'd shaved my legs for the first time that June, a process that turned out to be a whole lot less fun than you'd think. A month later, I was faced with the awkward experience of having to keep my friend Peter from noticing the fact that I'd shaved my legs. One day, in Yellowstone, I'd jumped into a swiftly moving stream, and found myself briefly borne off by the current. When I got myself back on land, I was afraid Peter was going to notice, all at once, that his friend had legs like Sharon Stone.

But Peter didn't notice. The hairiness of my legs wasn't a topic that concerned him.

———

I'd broken things off with my psychoanalyst just before I left New York to house-sit Mom's place. He had a practice in one of the tenement buildings on Broadway and 125th Street, right where the number 1 train emerges from the tunnel. Once a week I'd walk up there and lie down on his couch. The very first time I went there it took me virtually the whole session to say this sentence out loud: *I have juh juh juh juh gender issues.* Sweat poured off of me. My whole body shook, like I was riding the Wild Mouse in Ocean City.

It was just like in the cartoons, me lying on a couch, my analyst—let's call him Dr. Fernweh—staring at his notepad from his chair adjacent. He held a pen to his lips. Sometimes he licked its tip. Dr. Fernweh had cold blue eyes and a gray goatee. I wish I could say he had a Viennese accent, but he didn't. Actually, there were long, long minutes in which he said nothing at all. He did that thing where he waited me out, like someone fishing for marlin. Eventually I just started talking, but only because I was embarrassed. I felt bad for him, not having anything to say.

Was my mother overbearing? he asked. No, she was sweet and literary—a bookseller in the days before she met my father. *Would I describe my father as remote?* No: he was an all-around good guy, gentle and loving. "Would you describe yourself as depressed?" *Not really. Only when I'm sad.*

My psychoanalyst's ears pricked up when he heard about my sister, who rode horses. Our family's lives revolved around her when I was young. *Were you jealous of your sister?* he asked. I said *yeah, I guess.* I could almost hear him thinking, *Aha!*

Did you ever feel like you wanted to be *your sister?*

I lay there, dumbfounded. Be her? Why would I want to be my sister?

Perhaps you wanted her life?

Even now, forty years later, I would like to push a baked bean up his nose. My sister is a lovely person; she lives in England now, a scholar on the history of the book. But I have never wanted her life. The life I wanted was my own.

But I was convinced by Dr. Fernweh that this was my problem; somehow, bereft of love, I wanted to be my sister.

How could I have known back then that being trans isn't the result of envy, or loneliness, or you know: *polymorphous perversity.* It is, instead, a thing that God has given us: like the blue potato, or the duck-billed platypus. As such it is not a complex for theorizing. It is a wonder of nature.

That's what makes me sad about psychoanalysis. My doctor didn't want to make me happier; he wanted to lower a complex superstructure of behavioral speculation over my head, like I was a toucan and he had the world's most fascinating birdcage. Never once did he say, *Well, here's what you might do in order to find solace.* Maybe that wasn't his job; I don't know. But that's the thing I needed. Instead, in so many ways, psychotherapy set me back years and years.

Once, in frustration, I asked him, well what *about* transgender people? What are some of the paths people have followed in order to find their happiness? He licked his pen. Then he suggested I might take out some books from the library.

In 1854 Drs. James Bovell and Edwin Hodder injected a forty-year-old man with twelve ounces of cow's milk. They had a theory: milk would transform, within the body, into white corpuscles. Dr. Henry Cotton, a half century later, also had a theory: mental illness was the result of infected teeth. In order to help his patients, he pulled them all out.

History is full of bright ideas: bloodletting with leeches, drilling holes in the skull.

My thought is that if you have a theory that does not bring kindness and compassion to people who are suffering, what you really need, more than anything else, is a new theory.

Maybe the problem wasn't psychoanalysis as a whole so much as Dr. Fernweh himself. But what do I know about psychiatry? I'm probably the wrong guy to ask.

—

After the long trip west, Peter and I wound up at my sister's house in Portland, Oregon, for a few days. She was then living in an apartment one floor above a guy who played the bass for Frank Zappa and the Mothers of Invention.

After a few days at my sister's, Peter and I headed up to Seattle, where we met up with friends from college: Tom, and Maggie, and Dan. Tom had worked in a factory that made replicas of old flintlocks; Maggie played the mandolin. Dan, with whom I'd had a radio show back in the late 1970s, was just getting started now in the world of video production. We were all twenty-five, plus or minus: a bunch of misfits casting around for whatever came next. One day, in Seattle, Tom and I wound up at a grocery store, where the video game Frogger was brand-new. Hour after hour we poured quarters into that machine, making the frog leap from lily pads onto the swiftly moving logs. When the frog died, a big skull and crossbones appeared on the screen.

In the evenings, we went to a place called Dick's for hot dogs.

Then we went out to Olympic National Park. We hiked in on a boardwalk through the tropical rain forest: huge trees, shiny moss, slugs the size of hamsters. As we walked, blackness descended on me. It was clear enough that I was never going to be able to do anything in this world unless I dealt with the transgender business: I would never be able to write, I would never be able to be in love. But what could I do? I'd tried psychoanalysis, and it had left me more miserable than when I began.

What I thought, as we trudged west through the deep forest, was that I'd gone about as far as I could go.

As we walked, somebody came up with a funny bit of business about the size of the one I had. They slapped their inner thighs to indicate its length. They spoke my name: *James—slap! slap! Boylan!* Then, my friends would laugh, but only because it was clear, maybe, how much I hated this. I guess it was pretty funny, if you were not me.

At a ranger station in the lush wilderness I saw a young woman in a ranger's uniform, a Smokey the Bear hat. She looked so much like me, if I had been born female, that I was stunned into silence. Even my friends noticed it. *She looks more like your sister,* Peter said, *than your sister!* The ranger showed us a hand-drawn map of that part of the park. There was a place on it marking the location of an old cemetery on the banks of a lake. The location was marked with the same skull and crossbones we'd seen in Frogger a few days before, after the frog died.

Some of the early settlers were buried in that graveyard. "Could we go and see them?" I asked. The ranger girl looked at me funny. "Why would you want to see the cemetery?"

"To see where they wound up," I said. "Those early explorers." Considering that she looked so much like a nether me, that ranger girl was strangely oblivious to the way I identified with those people. But they'd come all this way. Then they couldn't go any further.

My friends weren't interested in finding any overgrown graveyard, either. And so we continued walking west.

We arrived on the beach near sunset. The Pacific Ocean crashed before us.

Peter and I pitched a tent not far from the North Ozette River, a broad creek that emptied out onto the sand. Later, as I lay in my sleeping bag, I heard the sound of its clear waters, rushing toward the sea.

———

The average penis is between 5.1 and 5.5 inches. Eighty-five percent of people who have one think that the average size is bigger.

In 2015, a man named Roberto Esquivel Cabrera was certified by something called the World Record Academy as having a penis 18.9 inches long. "Look where it goes, it goes beneath the knees," he said miserably, after the official measurement. Mr. Cabrera said his penis had ruined his life. "I cannot do anything," he said. "I cannot work."

He had hoped, in going public, that he'd be certified by the more prestigious Guinness World Records. But Guinness had told him it had no category for penis size.

———

In June 2020, author J. K. Rowling posted an essay in which she explained her reasons for speaking out about gender issues. "Woman is not a costume," she wrote. "Woman is not an idea in a man's head. Woman is not a 'pink brain,' a liking for Jimmy Choos, or any of the other sexist ideas now touted as progressive." She concludes: "Biological sex is real."[2]

I agree with all of that. I am not female because of an idea or a costume. I don't own any Jimmy Choos, which I am told is a kind of shoe. And my brain is gray, same as hers. The thing that makes me female is the same thing that makes her female: a sense of self, deeply rooted in neurology and experience. Being female is not an idea for me; it is a fact. But it is a fact that cannot possibly be understood without imagination.

Which is a thing you'd think that the person who came up with the idea of a three-headed dog named Fluffy, for instance, would have in good measure.

Is being female about having ovaries and a uterus? Well, sure, except that the world is full of women who've had hysterectomies.

Is being female about having breasts and a clitoris? Well, sure, except that the world contains women who've had mastectomies, or clitoral circumcisions.

Is being female about two X chromosomes that you can't even see? Well, sure, except that the world contains women—like those afflicted with androgen insensitivity syndrome—who have Y chromosomes and never even know it, humans whose genetic makeup contains as many variations as a fugue by Bach.

It would be nice if the line between male and female were simple. But gender, like the universe itself, is all gnarly. Clownfish can change their sex. So can reed frogs, green sea turtles, slipper limpets, and central bearded dragons. These creatures—like me— do not change sex in order to hurt Ms. Rowling's feelings. We do so because nature demands it. Because we are, like so many things on this earth, wonders of God's creation.

I'm going to believe in a better J. K. Rowling, not the one that she is, but the one she might still become. As one of my favorite authors once wrote, "It matters not what someone is born, but what they grow to be."

Who wrote that? J. K. Rowling, of course.[3]

—

In the morning I woke to the sound of the ocean and crawled out of the tent to find the horizon gray in the early light of dawn. I had lived on the East Coast almost my entire life; the Pacific Ocean filled me with wonder. It still does, actually.

The ocean was filled with crags; off to the right was a huge out-cropping of rock with a cave in one side. The waters of the North Ozette River glided across the sand.

I stepped into the water. It was cold. A few steps in, the ocean floor disappeared beneath me, and now I was swimming in those blue waters. I headed straight out, toward Japan. Big swells lifted me up then fell again. I banged my knee on a submerged rock. It hurt.

I treaded water for a moment and turned to face the shore. All my friends were standing there, watching me. Dan gestured with his hands. *Come in, James. Why don't you come in.* Another wave picked me up.

When I finally got back on land, Maggie gave me a towel. "I don't think it's safe to swim here, James," Dan said. "The undercurrents. You might get swept away."

I couldn't tell him that getting swept away would have suited me just fine.

Later that day we got high and waded out to the crag with the cave. It was a big womblike space, with an arching ceiling, tide pools on the floor. Dan and Tom and I sat down on the rocks and looked at the sea anemones and hermit crabs. Everything echoed in the cave. Now and again a wave would crash through the entrance. Light rippled on the ceiling.

"The anemone of my anemone is my friend," I said.

"Hey," said Tom, in glee. "I made a hermit crab change its shell!" He was a small man with merry eyes, his head shaved nearly bald. Tom and Dan sat there for a long time playing with the anemones and the hermit crabs. They watched the crabs scamper around; they tricked them into wrapping their pink tentacles around their own fingers.

They were so entranced, those boys. What would it be like, I wondered, as I looked upon my friends, to be able to lose yourself in something other than yourself? Was Dan or Tom so much happier than I? I was pretty sure they didn't spend hours privately agonizing over the fact of their own embodiment. But what did I know? They had problems of their own.

The thing they had, and I did not, was not a penis; it was the ability to be in love. Dan once told me that, when he was single, having sex was just about the best way he could imagine of getting to know someone. But that was the very problem: I was too frightened to allow myself to be known.

I was twenty-four and, for all intents and purposes, still a virgin. It was pretty clear by now that the thing that was wrong with me was not a thing that could be solved.

The tide was coming in. If we waited long enough, it was possible the entrance to the cave would be underwater. But Dan and Tom weren't concerned. They were exactly where they wanted to be. Their voices echoed in the cave. *Yo*, said Tom, with delight. *It has a mouth in the middle!*

I looked at those men with envy and sadness, and an anger burned in my heart.

Later, as I walked on the beach with Peter, we ran into a ranger, an Indian from the Ozette Reservation just a few miles to the south. "What do you do?" Peter asked the ranger.

"I control the tides," he said, matter-of-factly, and then roared. It was a deep, hearty laugh. I had never heard anything like it.

"Did you see the eagle?" he asked us. "There was an eagle flying."

I shrugged. I hadn't seen any eagle. "I was looking down," I said. What I was kind of thinking, actually, was *fuck you. Fuck the eagles. Fuck the tides.*

"Well," said the ranger. "If you always look down, you won't see the eagles."

I wanted to tell him, I don't always look down. But then I wondered whether this was true. I was so consumed with trying to solve the mystery of my own impossible life that I was pretty much blind to everything.

In the meantime, the ranger had turned and walked away. A moment later he'd faded into the forest and was gone.

———

Twenty years later, I was wheeled off to surgery on a gurney. My wife and my friend Rick were at my side. "I'm going to wash that man right out of my hair!" I sang. "I'm going to wash that man right out of my hair!"[4]

The intern wheeling me away looked entertained. "She's singing," he observed.

"Is that—typical?" asked Rick.

The intern shrugged. "We get all kinds of reactions," he said.

A few years later I was watching some movie on cable TV. I forget which one. But all at once, there was a naked man on television. I hadn't seen one for a while. I looked upon his junk and thought, *Will you look at that!* It struck me with wonder: the penis, and the scrotum, swinging around like the giblets you'd yank out of a Thanksgiving turkey.

I did not, at that moment, feel myself *unfairly treated.* What I felt more than anything else, was a vast sense of relief. It seemed like a long, long time ago, when I was sad.

—

We struck our tents and hiked back through the rain forest to our car. We didn't see that ranger girl again, although as we passed the lodge, I looked around. I thought to myself, Someday I'll come back here, as a woman, and I'll hike through those woods and find that cemetery. I'll stand by those graves and say *Thank you.*

I said that to myself that summer, August 1982. But I've never been back.

—

Twenty-five years later, walking through Morningside Heights, I saw Dr. Fernweh walking south on Amsterdam, not far from the Hungarian Pastry Shop. He hardly seemed to have aged a day: same black glasses, same gray goatee. I was thunderstruck. Here he was, after all these years! I wanted to rush up to him and say, *Doctor! Doctor! It's me, Jenny Boylan! I did it! I'm happy!*

Which I am, most of the time. Although, like anyone else, I have my bad days too. But most of the trouble I find in the world doesn't have anything to do with being trans. It comes from being female, a soul who, even now, some individuals see as something other than the *default human*.

It is hard being around people without imagination. But it's not really my problem that I am someone for whom others have no theory.

"The programme of becoming happy," Freud writes in *Civilization and Its Discontents*, "which the pleasure principle imposes on us, cannot be fulfilled, yet we must not—indeed, we cannot—give up our efforts to bring it nearer to fulfilment by some means or other."

Dr. Fernweh looked at me.

I waited for him to find the spark of recognition, for him to see his former patient, now an older woman, at peace at last.

But he just walked on. It didn't matter to him whether I was happy, or not. What did he care? I was no one he had known.

ON "MOURNING AND MELANCHOLIA"

Rick Moody

Dreams Having Served Us as the Prototype
You would hear a lot about him in the 1970s, this Sigmund Freud, back when I was an inquisitive teenager.[1] But rarely did this hearsay involve a direct interaction with the texts. I was a committed reader of light psychology in those days—*I'm Okay, You're Okay*, and similar products. My mother subscribed to *Psychology Today*, too, which I often perused when it was on the coffee table. I searched there for answers to the larger questions. I can remember Fritz Perls, in *Gestalt Therapy Verbatim*, which I read in a class in high school, referring to "all that Freudian crap." I looked there, in Perls, and I looked everywhere else, like *Stranger in a Strange Land*, and *Zen and the Art of Motorcycle Maintenance*. I read the stuff that did not seem intellectually rigorous, but which had the value of informality, or a lack of prejudice. Nowhere in this mulch of substandard therapeutic solutions did I ever encounter the actual work of Freud.

And then I went to college.

The Brown University of circa 1979–83 was nothing if not a hotbed of Marx and Freud, and all that came after, continentally speaking, like Foucault, Barthes, Deleuze and Guattari, and Derrida, and of course French psychoanalysis, lots of French psychoanalysis (Lacan or Laplanche and Pontalis, e.g.), and so it seemed the Freudian crap was *good fertilizer* for the young minds of the Northeast. And therefore at my university I first encountered *The Interpretation of Dreams*.

In recollection, which is unreliable (memory being perturbed as the site of longing), the occasion of this encounter was the creative writing workshop of Angela Carter, the great British novelist and short-story writer on a short-term appointment at Brown University, who seemed to both love and resist Freud, perhaps not an uncommon position. Carter was fond of saying she didn't believe in a subconscious, only a "preconscious." I think we read *The Interpretation of Dreams* alongside Borges (*Labyrinths*), García Marquez (*100 Years of Solitude*), Calvino (*Invisible Cities*), and of course the ultimate example of a dream-informed fiction, *Sanatorium under the Sign of the Hourglass*, by Bruno Schulz. One student sometimes slept through class (imagine his dreams). The image that I most remember from all the monumental reading of that semester was when the father in Bruno Schulz's opus turns into a crawfish.

When I say that I encountered *Interpretation*, I mean that I remember reading *Interpretation* on an Amtrak train platform over a vacation that semester, waiting for the train, thinking over and over about whether the absence of a dream could be interpreted as a dream, thinking about interpretation and whether it was free-floating, or oriented toward a "correct" result—Thanksgiving, maybe, in a rather bad year of college for me, in which, for instance, I punched out a friend's window, at one point, and sliced my wrist badly enough that I had to go to the infirmary and get stitches. (I left a trail of blood down the corridor of the dorm.) Lots and lots of drugs and alcohol, lots of romantic failure. I remember reading *Interpretation* and marveling at the adroitness of Freud's readings of all these dream texts, especially when my own dreams seemed composed entirely of anxieties and self-recrimination.

The Correlation of Melancholia and Mourning Seems Justified by the General Picture of the Two Conditions
I mean: it had been not going well, the college time, pretty consistently. In addition to the copious drugs there were lots of feelings of isolation, but the part that was broken was even more broken

than is described here. A perception of failure exceeded the facts at hand, exceeded the reasoning about failure, exceeded the naming of failure. Freud asks, in "Mourning and Melancholia," "whether an impoverishment of ego-libido directly due to toxins may not be able to produce certain forms of the disease," the disease being melancholia, and in my experience, well, maybe, yes.

Note the word *disease*.

Would my particular set of complaints look, from this remove, like the recoiling action of grief, as Freud describes mourning, or more like the recoiling action alongside an abundance of self-loathing? I did have a crumbling relationship with a Yale student, some sixty miles away, and there were my divorced parents and their various escapades, and the siblings who aimlessly landed back at home without finishing college, everyone blowing it a little bit. These are explanations for my trouble that are in no way reasonable if considered anything but ordinary. These explanations were just what was at hand.

I came upon "Mourning and Melancholia," the essay in question, on the differences between the two, in my sophomore year, after reading *Interpretation*, during this time of mixed outcomes. My experience with "Mourning and Melancholia" was different from that with *Interpretation*, with which I had engaged in a fragmentary way. Incompletely. I think "Mourning and Melancholia" was perhaps on the syllabus for my class in existentialism, which I disliked because it didn't have enough Sartre and Camus. We read Dostoevsky. We read Frantz Fanon. I think I made my term paper about Satan in *Paradise Lost*, from an existentialist perspective, because I think I was also taking a class in Milton. I liked the topic so much, Satan and existentialism, that I used it twice, two different drafts of term papers for two different courses, with "Mourning and Melancholia" as the place for leaping off in each.

Let me then speak directly to the effect of "Mourning and Melancholia" on me, which was in the area of revelation. There was a clearing out of detritus, of intellectual nonsense, and a feeling that something authoritative was being said, that I needed to be here, hearing this, reading this. There was a shining of the light on some murk, on some persistent concealment; there was an accurate appraisal, and it had the effect of conferring on me that very popular formulation: I was being seen.

Maybe there are two registers to "Mourning and Melancholia." One register is diagnostic (there are people who are mourning a death, and there are people who are mourning nothing in particular but still seem to have many of the symptoms of mourners). The other register is etiological (how did they get this way?). I loved the Freud who cared about this subject, the diagnostic Freud, because in the observing he seemed to care, in some way, about a community I knew and loved well, the losers, the bereft, the outcasts, the failures, those in states of dread and angst. But I thought his etiological approach was, well . . .

It is Merely That He Has a Keener Eye for the Truth
You probably remember the lines from *Paradise Lost*, book 4, concerning the rebel angel who would not reside in heaven:

> Me miserable! which way shall I fly
> Infinite wrath and infinite despair?
> Which way I fly is Hell; myself am Hell;
> And, in the lowest deep, a lower deep
> Still threatening to devour me opens wide,
> To which the Hell I suffer seems a Heaven. (IV, 75–79)

What Satan had lost—by his own devices, by his own refusing, as it were, to bend the knee—was the love that Milton describes, "free love dealt equally to all," and in such a condition, which is to say the condition of exile, of fury, of estrangement, of refusal, Satan sounds a lot more like a regular down-to-earth character than does God in *Paradise Lost*. He also seems a lot more human than Adam and his consort. Those two, Adam and Eve, are like yoga instructors, spa customers, Instagram influencers.

I had to take the Milton class to fulfill an area requirement, a class in pre-nineteenth-century literature. I was prepared for the class to be dull, but it was electrifying, really, in that it turned out that Satan had a lot to say to the contemporary college student. Maybe Satan was the most like a contemporary college student of any character from any book we read in those times. Milton, like Freud, was startling as a diagnostician.

I was wrestling with *Ulysses*, too, because back then, which would-be writer did not wrestle with it, and it was in that context that I learned about *non serviam*, which Stephen quotes in the Nighttown section of *Ulysses*, and which he alludes to in *Portrait*, the allegedly Satanic remark that occasioned Satan's casting down into the infernal regions. "I will not serve" is the translation. It was a good sentence to describe the lingering, in 1980, of revolutionary activity from the counterculture period, which found its place in fiction writing, in filmmaking, in the arts. The dislike of authority, the suspicion of authority, the Oedipal angst, if that's what it was, the rage to be free from perceived control, the *resistance*, to use the Freudian word.

I made my Milton term paper out of this thought, that Satan was an existentialist hero, and that he was a *melancholic* in his resistance. Because who was not?

Loss of the Capacity to Love, Inhibition of All Activity, and a Lowering of the Self-Regarding Feelings
The Freudian reading of Satan's problem, perhaps, the Satan of the Miltonic epic, would be that "object-choice has been effected on a narcissistic basis," that Satan elects *not to serve* because Satan is, after a fashion, a narcissist, maybe the first, and not because he (Satan) has a valid critique, arguably, to mount against an authority that requires perfect loyalty. But is Satan not accurate, in some way, by insisting that the subservience should *not* be essential, but rather freely engaged in, based on circumstances, on rational engagement?

From the point of view of the undergraduate exegete, Satan had a good point. In Stephen Dedalus, the mourner, who invokes *non serviam* to a figment of his dead mother, we can see how the loss characterizing melancholia is prefatory, and how it emerges from a kind of estrangement from a prior generation that is not easily resolved: "myself am hell," after which, of course, art gets made.

My encounter with the melancholia as described in Freud's essay "Mourning and Melancholia" was first of all an encounter with intense identification; I understood and felt something, something that had not been described elsewhere in the same way. But I also felt a curious nonidentification with the etiology of the Freudian essay, the "object-cathexis regressing to narcissism" part. That is, my identification with "Mourning and Melancholia" had about it the succor of exactitude, followed by a disappointment.

One might argue, from this great distance (I am writing now from my own sixties), that the individuation that causes one to wish to pronounce *non serviam* is the inevitable course of youth. The melancholy, the aloneness that follows, is a natural outcome of this process, to love our parents and grandparents, our teachers and coaches, our mentors, our priests, our gurus, the figures who had a hand in who we are emotionally, to separate from them, to strike out on our own, to require this striking out as the beginning of being adult, of being intellectual, of being fully formed, of being, is natural, and just as natural is the feeling that accompanies this process: loss.

It Is This Sadism Alone That Solves the Riddle of the Tendency to Suicide Which Makes Melancholia So Interesting
To put it another way: notwithstanding the *being seen* of encountering "Mourning and Melancholia," therefore, and its etiology of narcissistic fixation as a beginning point for melancholic experience, I continued to have features of the "melancholic" as described in the essay by Freud, during my college years, despite having contact with the essay. I didn't get better for having terminology or awareness; I got a bit worse. I got worse for at least five or six years, culminating in a six- or eight-month period of acute

depression that ultimately landed me in the psychiatric hospital, in 1987, from which, incrementally, I began to improve.

If Freud's essay feels inclined to elucidate a set of causal properties in the melancholic, perhaps, it is in part because—as I learned in the fall of junior year in Brown's famous course Semiotics 12: The Foundation of the Theory of Signs—Freud's work, especially in the case histories, was ultimately indebted to the shape and form of the nineteenth-century novel. Freud had to have a *big ending*. A cure! They, the semioticians, used to say stuff like this all the time. Freud was corrupted by Romanticism! His obsession with result was not empirically necessary (empiricism being just another phenomenology), but the result of a Romantic orientation, in which stories ended happily like in the nineteenth-century novel. The "feminine hysteria" is remediated! By men!

I loved taking this class, Semiotics 12, which, I think it's fair to say, featured many of the most brainy students on the humanities side at my university in those days. It was sort of an intellectual hot spot. I did not allow its being a hot spot to get in the way of my aggressive program of self-destruction, however, and was often reading Derrida or Barthes, and then going out, just about every night, to annihilate my youthful supply of neurons, and somewhere in the midst of this class I did more than that: I very intentionally took about sixteen quaaludes (if that was the right name for these pills—that's what they were *called* by the dealer in question) and washed them down with something whiskeyish, slept for fourteen or fifteen hours, and then got up, groggy and disoriented and still alive, and went to that week's discussion section for Semiotics 12. I passed out, in class, too, not waking up until people were shuffling out the door. It is true that someone had broken up with me. Which might make my actions a sign of mourning, of Romantic crisis, of object-cathexis. Though it's also true that I was broken up with, arguably, because of counterproductive amounts of melancholia, a condition that always has a kind of halitotic or antisocial aspect to it, a nonpartnering aspect. In any event, this seemed a fitting occasion on which to end it all, which in truth

I was always thinking about anyway, thus the drugs and alcohol, but it all did *not* end, because that would have been a cheap way to go, a Romanticist way. There was more to learn about "Mourning and Melancholia," while exhibiting the classic narcissistic symptoms, perhaps, while also reading about *The Sorrows of Young Werther* (in Roland Barthes's *A Lover's Discourse*), or watching Douglas Sirk films. My wish to attend class prevailed, and I told no one, no parent or person in authority (*non serviam*), what I had done. (And, I should say, in the context of Semiotics 12, I came to love *Dora*, and the Little Hans case history, and, then, I really loved *Civilization and Its Discontents*, which has some genuine overlap with "Mourning and Melancholia.")

He Has Lost His Self-Respect and There Must Be a Good Reason for This
It seems to me now, after the waking up in Semiotics 12, that part of what was missing from Freud's account of "Melancholia," by which we probably mean *depression*, or major depression, or clinical depression, was the possibility that this illness was a *physical* complaint, like smallpox or SARS-CoV-2. If Freud enacts, performs, certain Enlightenment ideas in which there is the thing called "mind" (or, in Lacan, there is a "language," of which the "mind" or the "self" is an effect), then it is part and parcel of this Enlightenment reasoning to see the "mind" as the driver of certain forces, and rarely, at the same time, to see what we call "mind" as a collection of physical facts, or emanating from the physical, emergent therefrom. To look at depression (or melancholia) as a crisis of letting go, a failure of relinquishment, an "object-crisis," is perhaps to invalidate, in some respect, the complaint itself, the physical course thereof, and to see the physical course in some way as secondary, an effect of an effect, a mental condition that can simply be alleviated by programmatic rhetoric of the etiology, the putative causes, when, generally, this is not what a person with depression feels unless they are, in their crisis, casting the failure to improve as an example of their all-around human weakness.

Even if you are willing to accept only that depression is a dynamic system in which "mind" and "body" interact, you are still, to some extent, admitting to the theory that brain chemistry or other physical facts have a role to play, are essential mechanisms of the dynamic of so-called mental illness. The pharma industry of course subscribes to this hypothesis as regards neurotransmitters. An astute observer can also see how clinical depression can run in families, which means either that it is inherited, genetically, or that family is the perfect hothouse for causing it. Or both. And: almost any observer will see how addiction can cause depression, reifying the will-to-unconsciousness that the addiction then affords, in a kind of hamster wheel of circularity (I feel like shit, I will try to make myself unconscious, and now I feel *more* like shit because of what I did last night, just before the unconsciousness, or during, and thus I further require more unconsciousness). These are kinds of recognition of the "physical" set of facts about depression, which facts liberate the sufferer from the icky morass of feeling responsible for it, the *disease*.

His Illness Must Become an Enemy Worthy of His Mettle
A psychoanalyst acquaintance of mine was talking through this problematic with me, recently, and her articulation was this: Even if Freud is correct about etiology, antidepressants may, in some cases, improve symptoms in certain patients enough that they can then make it to the session to talk through where they are, whereas in the absence of such treatment, their symptoms are sometimes too aggravated to make psychoanalytic engagement possible. If a treatment of the physical symptoms is available—a treatment of the sleeplessness, the anorexia, the compulsive overeating, the anhedonia, the drug abuse, the complete physiognomic loss of will—might not this treatment exist coincidentally with an analytical or therapeutic approach, such that proceeding on both fronts is a more effective approach to what people with "melancholia" actually experience?

A more direct way of saying this might be that I felt "seen" by "Mourning and Melancholia," as long as it was describing melancholia as a set of emotional tendencies, even if I disagreed with Freud's etiological reasoning, but in a later moment when I became a person acquainted firsthand with *depression*, I felt just the opposite way. Not understood at all. Blamed, even, in a way. Does that mean that a change occurs in the conception of "melancholia" when you instead use for it the word "depression?" Does it mean that *renaming* reframes an illness? Or that history changes the perception thereof, so that earlier schematic descriptions seem quaint? Might we now be in a period in which *melancholy* is no longer an adequate frame to put around anhedonia, anorexia, sleeplessness, cognitive impairment, obsessive thinking, and the package that contains an admixture of them all?

We Cannot Conceive How That Ego Can Consent to Its Own Destruction

My friend the analyst is especially fond of Freud's remarks and perceptions about repetition compulsion. In this I could not agree more. (See, e.g., "Remembering, Repeating, and Working-Through": "We have learned that the patient repeats instead of remembering, and repeats under the conditions of resistance. We may now ask what it is that he in fact repeats or acts out.")[2] Why the human repeats, always hoping, in a way, to resolve the crisis that generates them, in the act of repetition, is at the heart of how the human is human, a wrestler with motif, with hopefulness and regiment, as if the self is protagonist in a sonnet, circulating toward a couplet. The human is an effect, in this way, of certain kinds of processes, forged in reiteration, and until she/he/they incorporates in the solution to the emotional problem that engenders repetition she is destined to fail to grow. And thus destined to repeat.

In this way we might pause over "Mourning and Melancholia," as evidence of the suppression of its author's own repetitions. Freud, the cocaine user, the guy who smoked his way into oral cancer, and who refused to give up smoking during his oral cancer treatment, could have himself been suppressing the theory of addiction in "Mourning and Melancholia," the better to practice the kind of repetition he schematized so effectively, namely a scripto-therapeutic compulsion, an analytic duplication, a repetition of theoretical purposes, especially psychosexual ones, for the greater glory of academic legitimacy. Easier to call "Melancholia" a variety of *sadism*, or *narcissism*, than to call it sheer physical repetition that will not brook being examined, the same repetition that the author of "Mourning and Melancholia" practiced himself, as did the author of these lines (in college times).

In addiction studies, these days, it is common to see addiction as *an illness*, and indeed there are many studies on the subject, which describe what it would mean for addiction to be a physical dependency, a crisis of the endorphins or the deployment of endorphins, or of the monoamine neurotransmitters, or an allergy to specific chemical pollutants. In this regard, we might, in fact, embark on a study of melancholia and addiction in which alcoholism, for example, features melancholia as a natural or predictable outcome, a human outcome, in which we might, as do those who intervene on behalf of its sufferers, treat them with the same respect and sympathy with which we treat the "physically" ill. Not morally deficient, not psychically deficient, but physically ill.

The Analyst Again Attempts to Bring a Particular Moment into Focus
Burton, in his monumental treatise on the subject of melancholy, the *Anatomy of Melancholy* of 1621, finds the origin of the problem in the organs of the human animal:

> A humour is a liquid or fluent part of the body, comprehended in it, for the preservation of it; and is either innate or born with us, or adventitious and acquisite. The radical or innate, is daily supplied by nourishment, which some call cambium, and make those secondary humours of ros and gluten to maintain it: or acquisite, to maintain these four first primary humours, coming

and proceeding from the first concoction in the liver, by which means chylus is excluded.

More specifically, melancholy in Burton is owing to a specific effluent from the spleen, "cold and dry, thick, black, and sour, begotten of the more feculent part of nourishment, and purged from the spleen," and there is ample reason, in our empiricist present, to find this description wanting, though the same rationale gives us our contemporary *affairs of the heart,* and our *sanguine* dispositions. Wrong, perhaps, according to our current understanding of the spleen, but wrong in the right way.

For example, what if Burton is right in finding an origin for depression in the physical? And, what if Burton is historically bound, in exactly the same way "Mourning and Melancholia" is, a thing of its time, as our own description of neurotransmitters and addictive illnesses may be approaches to treatment that flatter the ideological chemistries of the twenty-first century, but not the ideas about "body" and "mind" that are yet to come?

Such an approach, a historical approach to human psychology, is plenty valid, but it leaves me wanting to go back to the dorm room of the young person with a fistful of pills in front of him, and some stronger ethanol distillate right beside, at the advent of mortality: the feelings of the moment we could easily catalog, the not having a reason to stick around, the feeling of being without the consolations of love, the lack of desire for food, the inability to sleep, the numbness, the loss of self, the helixing of compulsive thoughts of a punitive kind, and the desolation of it all, the blackness, the darkness made visible.

Should our purpose as a community at this moment be to speak theory to human anguish? In my own moment of agon, the language of Freud's description of melancholy would scarcely have been comprehensible, notwithstanding having read it in a class on existentialism, and this was the case on an accelerated basis, progressive imperviousness in my anguish, until I gave up drugs and alcohol, which I did, not long after, by consulting a clinical social worker, and through group support. There was, in therapy, occasional discussion of my object-cathexis, and my occasional narcissism, at least in the early days, and then not so much.

Perhaps I would call this a humanistic result, in the Rogerian sense of the word "humanist." Perhaps I would say that what was required, for me, in coming to an awareness of the limitations of the Freud of "Mourning and Melancholia," was the need for *unconditional positive regard*, with respect to the symptoms I experienced, and the anguish that they caused myself and others. Maybe the intellectual hothouse of undergraduate education was not made that way, for *unconditional positive regard*—in those days. And thus education failed in some ways to educate.

In my journey since, as a writer, as a person in recovery from depression and addiction and attendant difficulties, the quaint humanist impulse in the psychological treatment of human beings has come to seem more imperative. I mean love and respect. And according to this variety of consideration, it's more common for me to think of "Mourning and Melancholia" as a great piece of art, more so than as a meaningful description of the origin of one kind of psychic pain. It is a great piece of art through which history and its ripples can still so keenly be felt.

DREAMS OF THE DEAD—IV

Alex Pheby

A psychoanalytically informed piece of short fiction

Her room, in its disposition, was an exact mirror of his. Indeed, if he had taken a plan of the asylum and folded it in half down the middle—along the road that ran up to the administration building—the outline of her room would have overlapped exactly with his. They were identical, even in the slight alcove that seemed to serve no purpose in either place.

Unlike his room, though, hers was decorated. The walls were draped with an oxblood linen phoenix damask, spotted black where damp had come through from the walls. It was heavy and musty, and to it had been pinned portraits in flaking gold frames of men and women he did not recognize. There was a chair and table on one side of the room, and an iron bed on the other.

She was on the bed.

She was breathing slowly, turned away from him, covered by a patchwork quilt. On the table there were piles of paper and in the middle of them, dwarfed, a blown-glass pen and a bottle of ink.

He stood in silence, watching.

There was another smell beneath the damp and the paraffin from her lamp. Of incense. He watched the rise and fall of her outline under the quilt and listened to her breathing—it seemed in keeping, somehow, with the smell.

There were books on the table: two, laid open, side by side, with paper and the glass pen beside them. He stepped forward, silently, to take a closer look. The lamp was wicked low, and it was not until he was over the table that he could make much out. The first book was a professionally published volume bound in leather, while the second was sewn by hand from coarse paper. The words were identical, in both works, except that the second stopped in midsentence two-thirds of the way down the recto. Though the hand in the second was clearly done with a pen, it mimicked almost perfectly the typeset of the first, down to the serifs and curves of each letter. He had to lean closer and closer to make out any imperfection in the copying—perhaps the occasional blurring of a stroke, caused by the coarseness of the pulp in the paper of the copy. Here and there were places where the paper had failed to absorb the ink, a splinter having been left unfiltered in the stock, on which she had scratched the line of the letter with a sharp nib.

He read the words but did not understand them.

"Do you like books?"

He stiffened. Her hand was on his shoulder; her long fingers, stained around the nails, pressed into his jacket. Her breath was on the skin behind his ear. The closeness of her voice—the way she whispered—it made his jaw clench.

"I should introduce myself . . ." he said, and he tried to turn. She went with him, so that she was still behind.

"Do you write?"

She put her other hand on his shoulder.

He turned more quickly, but, regardless of which way he went she stayed behind him. She stepped closer. He tried to move away.

"Do you write?"

He stepped to the side and succeeded in putting the chair between them.

She turned away when he looked at her, beautiful, except that she had a squint. One eye looked constantly off into the distance, while the other flicked around, apparently attempting to make up for the idleness of its sister. She put on a loose silk cap and slanted it so that her eye was covered and she came forward again.

"My father was a writer. A great writer. I am a writer, too. I write what he wrote. This, I think, makes me a great writer too, doesn't it?"

As she came nearer, he backed away.

"Do not touch my desk!"

In a flash she was behind him again, but this time she paid him no attention. She bent over her desk with her hands hovering— they moved as if she was rearranging everything, but her fingertips were always a few inches above the objects. When she was convinced everything was correct she turned to him.

"Would you like to see my writing?"

"I am . . ."

"I know who you are, Sam. Would you like to see my writing?"

He moved over to the door.

"Would you like to see my writing? I have it here."

She indicated the desk with a graceful swing of her arm and smiled. She was young, perhaps not even twenty.

"Miss, I am not sure why I have been brought here . . . my doctor . . ."

"He's a fool. Do not believe a word he says."

"He said you would cure me."

"You are not ill."

"My parasite . . ."

"Your doctor wants me to perform a service of which he is incapable. It is a simple thing."

He stopped.

"The parasite . . ." she said, "even when it is black, it can produce the white excreta. I can make it wither. Look at me."

He did as he was told.

"What do you see?"

"I don't understand . . ."

"Would you like to see my writing? I have it here."

She held out her hand, and he took it. She pulled him gently toward the table, and when he was close enough she ran her hand over the back of his head and directed his vision, very gently, toward the page.

"Words have power," she said, "not in what they mean—that is not it. It's in their shape, in their line, their shapes as they rest on the page. Hieratics, sigilics, glyphics. It's in the hand and in how they are written. Even the worst writing has it. Does this make sense to you?"

"Please call me by my name."

"Does this make sense to you? Do you feel it too? When you look at it, from a distance? When you lie in your bed, undressed, just before you sleep? When you can see the pile of papers on the desk where you left it and you sit up before you snuff out the light? Though you can't see the words, can you feel them there? Can you sense their power? Can you see it, leaking up into the air from the page?"

He stepped away, and she let him go. He followed the curve of her neck, a shallow "j," and from where the jaw joined it he traced the outline of her face until he reached the crown of her head.

"You say nothing? You are a clever man, though? They said so. They said you were a writer. You can't have missed it, can you? I will show you. The shapes and colors and the ways they interweave with the letters and the meanings—this is what I use for my work. I write about losing. Have you lost?

"I see it written in your face. In the way that you hold your hands. They are empty where they wish to be full. You hold them as if something is about to be delivered. Or has recently been taken away. It's as clear as if you were holding up a sign."

She took the pages from her desk and placed them on the bed, face down so that he could see nothing except perhaps, faintly, the traces of ink reversed on the backs of the pages—nothing he could read.

"I have one wish, Miss, and that is that I should return home. Can you help me?"

"Your parasite, the breach—I can fix it all. But you must do something for me?"

He looked away.

"I am not in a position to do anything," he said.

She laughed.

"Lock the door. They will not return until the morning. They are in the doctor's quarters, f——g. He goes and does what he pleases. He goes into the handmaid as he pleases. I give him money, and he brings you here. What does he take from you? Spite? His brother was hanged. Did he tell you that? He hates you. He spits in your porridge. And worse. That is the way things are, below. Will you look at my work?"

She sat and patted the bed by her side. He came and sat, and between them she placed a single page of roughly cut paper.

"Paper is like the landscape where something happens: a hill-side; snow; a forest; a battleground. It has an effect. To say that it is only there to show the ink is wrong. The paper is like the land, and it changes what is written on it. When the nib touches the paper for the first time it is the most difficult thing to take the pen around a single letter. I have to learn the paper as I work, and I only begin to understand it when the first word is finished. It doesn't stop there. The paper comes to life as I work. Do you understand?"

Before he could answer she took another page, this one written on, and she put her stained fingertip at the beginning of the first word, hovering over the page so that she did not touch it and she traced it in its entirety, speaking it silently on her lips.

"You see the curve of the 'a'? Lowercase because this is the middle of a sentence. The sentence is in the middle of a paragraph, and the paragraph is in the middle chapter of the book—so, I make the semicircle more perfect than it should be, because it is in the middle, and I press the nib harder than I sometimes do, so that it bites the page. I want to show how important the letter is. The rising shaft of the 'a'—the thickness of the line—do you see how it is not quite even? The paper. An accident, but a good one. It clashes with the curve, makes it look fuller. Pregnant. When my father wrote this scene he wanted it to be the pivot—that was what he said—'the central moment in the plot' where the threads he uses come together. He wanted it to hint at the events to come. So, on this page, you can see many of the vowels on the page are very round, the vowels being the internal life of the book, what it says, and the consonants being more active, more superficial and obvious, the vowels contained and expressed by them. Do you see? How much is written in a single letter! And all because the paper was uneven . . ."

She waited for him to say something.

"You use crimson ink?"

"This page is fresh. The ink gets darker. Brown, eventually, and then black. I don't usually let people see my pages so soon. I don't usually let people see them. The next word, four letters this time and each letter is altered a little from the normal, the first is wider, the third narrower, taller in the second and shorter in the fourth. That way, each letter gets the same space, to be fair. The ink is even and I keep the pressure constant. The next word is the fifth in the sentence, an adjective. It alters the mood, pinching something inside the eye, giving a shock. At first it looks as if I have written it that way; it looks as if my hand has wobbled and I've put down the nib with too much ink on it. Do you see the way it wells up and rises off the page? Do not touch! Here, if I hold the page at an angle you can see it. A hemisphere . . . do you see? It looks as if I lost control of the pen, but only to begin with. Faith, I hope, is restored by the end of the stroke. Or I hint at it. I allow the letters to join up. Usually I write them apart, but not here. Here I let them flow together. At the end of the second letter, there is another hemisphere, matching the first perfectly, even under the eye glass, do you see? Do not let the glass touch the page! It might be wet. The ink is not quite congealed. When we are finished, we will attend to your business, and I will put this page on the window sill. The breeze that comes through the cracks in the glass will harden the ink and then, if you wish, I will let you run your fingertips over them and you will feel what you can now only see, the perfect smoothness of them and their glassiness and, if you have—let me see . . . yes, delicate fingertips—you will understand what I mean."

She held his hand and looked into his eyes.

"I am forgetting myself. The word is half finished."

She let his hand drop and returned to her page.

"So, you see that first the letters presume to agree with the use of the word, and then, so that the reader understands control has not been lost, the effect is reduced, and faith is returned, and by that point it is possible for me to do what you see next, to overturn everything; do you see it? You must see it!"

He looked at the word, and there was nothing in it that meant anything to him beyond that which a child might understand from reading the dictionary.

"The substitution? The near substitution? The pulling down of the curve of the center letter, transforming it? The effect is so obvious, so daring, that it can only be used once the ground has been prepared for it, the relationship of trust established from its first having been put in jeopardy. Do you see? This is what I have done!"

"What you have done is very beautiful."

Her face fell, and the room darkened. She took her pages and returned them to her desk. When she returned to the bed she was angry.

"It is more than that. I have created something entirely new. What is a word, after all, but a replica of another word, heard or seen before, pulled down from the shelf and eaten, like a pie, or a piece of bread. With no effort gone into its making, it is just taken from the stove and laid out on the plate to be read and eaten, and for my father to assume any different is ridiculous. To lord it about the house. Why? Because he can put one word in front of another? Put a pie down with a piece of bread on a plate and call it creation? Genius? If he was a cook, perhaps, but he is not! To eat something, no matter how complicated, is not to create. Not as I create. And he is a great writer, and I am what? Locked up in a hole servicing all comers so that I can at least work! And he talks of sacrifice? He knows nothing. It is time. Undress."

He did not move.

She let her gown fall to the ground.

"What are you waiting for? Do you not want to be released? You think that I am not willing to do this? You feel embarrassment? Ridiculous! This will be an exchange, nothing more. You have something I need, and to get it I will give you my body. I have no attachment to it. You, on the other hand, like all men, like him, you have a fetish for the flesh, for my flesh, even him, the great intellect. You are pathetic, all of you. You think it embarrasses me, to stand here undressed? You think I have an investment in this skin. It is nothing. It allows me to work; that is its function. Take it. I insist. No? You do not want release? You are shy? You wish to be taken then? It is all the same. You wish to play the woman's part and I the man's? It is all the same."

She came over to him, flowing more than walking, emerging from the shadow an inch at a time, her eyes wide.

"You would have me be the father. Is that it? Come," she said and wrapped her hands behind his neck.

"Please. I want nothing of this."

"You do not wish to be released? You are laughed at. Do you know that they mock you? In Heaven. On Earth. You are a laughingstock."

"I want only to return home."

She drew him closer.

"Then submit to me. The parasite will understand it has made a mistake. It will shrivel and die. The nerve connection will be undone."

She put her lips so that they were almost touching his.

"My flesh is nothing. These breasts might as well be hard and flat. Yours might as well be round. That is the way it is now. Do you believe me? Could you believe anything else now the candle is blown out? And this thing between your legs, it is nothing and my hand feels inside you? Are you not a woman?"

"Please!"

"You see, it is easier than you thought. It is perfectly easy. And now you will have your wish, will you not? To submit to me."

"What do you want from me?"

"That comes next. There is no need to disrupt the order; all will come in good time. You feel that hardening? That is me and that softness? The wetness? That is you. It is all the same. You have no choice but to succumb to me, to my desire. Can you feel me becoming stiffer? You should understand, my girl, that your existence, your body is nothing but an adjunct of my desire. You exist only for me. That realization thrills you, doesn't it? It pricks against your insides. Burns there. You can feel it. My pleasure moves you. Can you hear it, child? Can you hear your womb singing out to me? As I push myself inside you, can you hear it? I can feel that you can. That is the slave's song. It is the love song of debasement."

She bit him hard on the cheek. He pulled away, but she was stronger, so much stronger and unbowed by this asylum, where he was withering. She held him even closer so that he was not sure which part of himself was her and which was him and who was where. She bit him again and pushed so that she was hard inside him. He felt everything that she had told him he would, and now it lived a life of its own, inside his body, and though the higher part of him was outraged, mortified to the heart of his masculine pride, this was only fuel to the fire that he felt in his belly, in his bowel, wherever that place was that women gave themselves over to, and that heat rose up to his face so that his skin flushed, across his chest too, his breasts swelling and heaving. He struggled, but there was no escape, and she held him like a snake does, wrapping herself around his limbs and preventing his movement, barely restraining from suffocating him. His futile efforts were like water splashed on hot metal, having no effect other than to add sound and splatter and steam, and when his struggling ceased, in its place came a higher pitch of pleasure, piqued by the knowledge that he had tried, but that he was trapped in spite of it all. She was harder and harder inside him, and she bit, deeper and deeper, and there was a moment when her teeth punctured his skin, it giving suddenly and she went hard up inside him, and the pain was like pleasure to him, and he was like a girl, taken for the pleasure of someone she hardly knows, against her will, and it ground inside him until he could hardly bear it, and he whispered.

"God save me!"

And she replied in a quieter whisper still.

"My son," and with that he was overtaken entirely with pleasure.

When he recovered himself he was alone on her bed, and she was at her desk, her back to him, her face inches from the paper, pen in hand, fingers bent like a crab's legs, pressing down, the other hand dipping her pen into a filled inkwell.

"It is your blood I use," she said.

There was a small mirror in front of her, set into a frame decorated with blue flowers, and her eyes were in it. She returned her gaze to the paper in front of her.

"I wish to be returned to my cell . . ."

He moved away from her and went to stand at the door. He peered through the peephole but could see nothing but the wall on the other side of the corridor. He tried the door, but it was locked.

"I want the doctor to take me back."

She turned to him.

"Is that all you have to say?"

He stood and stared.

"What should I say?"

She turned back to her work, shaking her head.

"You are cured—don't you think that deserves something more?"

He said nothing.

He stood and said nothing and it was silent in the room.

Silent except for the gliding of her nib on the paper.

FREUD AS A FICTION WRITER

Sheila Kohler

My intention in this essay is to demonstrate Freud's skill as a writer of fiction. I will use his essay "Fragment of an Analysis of a Case of Hysteria," commonly referred to as the Dora case (written in 1901, not published until 1905) as an example of his expertise in this role. For better or for worse—I'll come back to this question at the end—the young woman escaped Freud's clutches after only three months of treatment. Because of its brief duration, Freud was able to wrap up all the elements of her story neatly, something that in his other four case histories proved, understandably, more difficult.

First, a personal note: I initially read Freud's case histories on an airplane, traveling through the night to visit my mother back in Johannesburg, South Africa. This was the 1970s, and I was a psychology student at the Institut Catholique in Paris. As I read about Dora, a girl of seventeen, not many years younger than I was, who was suffering from a plethora of symptoms—a hoarse cough, fainting fits, breathlessness, pains in her side and leg—I began to feel ill. I turned the pages fast with sticky fingers, drawn in by the direct voice, by the drama of the girl's story, and feeling increasingly faint, myself. Was I, then, just as hysterical as Freud felt this young girl to be? Was my illness provoked by an identification with her? Was I just reflecting her symptoms as through a glass darkly? How could I differentiate my own feelings from hers or, indeed, Freud's own? He, too, had experienced hysterical symptoms, and he—to give him his due—was one of the first to admit that men, too, could be hysterics. I felt that someone familiar was talking directly to me. But it was more than relief I felt when, upon landing, I was diagnosed with a typical case of measles.

Freud wrote all five of his case histories toward the start of his career (1901–14), shortly after his book on the interpretation of dreams appeared. The sequence was not incidental: once he had published the extensive account of what he considered his single most important discovery—namely, that dreams had meaning and that they could be made to yield to interpretation—he was at pains to show that they, like neurosis itself, were ubiquitous. Along the way, he demonstrated that real patients could be made to come alive as much as could fictional characters—something that none of his successors would ever match, not even the British pediatrician-turned-psychoanalyst D. W. Winnicott, his closest competitor in this skill.

Though Freud's aim in presenting the Dora case, he tells us, is to provide material to buttress his theories on dreams, my own is to show how he uses mystery and suspense, along with other writerly skills, to engage the interest and acquiescence of the reader. We have here all the necessary, surprising reversals in one shocking, high-stakes story, one in which we come to believe, however reluctantly. He uses a direct voice that rings true, while creating characters of considerable complexity, with whom we identify, who remain with us over the years, and in whom we find reflected not only their foibles and failures, but also, perhaps our own.

Freud comes through to us loud and clear in these pages. The voice is direct and without unnecessary obfuscation. He is forceful and persuasive. I was taken by his tale. Like the best Victorian writers, such as Thackeray or Charlotte Brontë, he addresses his readers directly just when they begin to doubt or question him. In a sense we, the readers, become his patients, too.

We might ask where Freud had learned his craft. Like so many bourgeois Viennese of his time he was extremely well read. As an adolescent he had read *Don Quixote* in Spanish with a friend. As

Erich Auerbach wrote in his landmark work of literary criticism *Mimesis*, "The theme of the mad country gentleman who undertakes to revive knight-errantry gave Cervantes an opportunity to present the world as play in that spirit of multiple, perspective, non-judging, and even non-questioning neutrality, which is a brave form of wisdom." Freud seems to have learned from Cervantes's attitude toward his characters this capacity to listen carefully and to suspend judgment, until he has sufficient information from the patient to come to his own conclusions.

After Cervantes it was Charcot, chief neurologist of the Salpêtrière clinic in Paris, who taught Freud to observe and to listen carefully to his patients, and, above all, to suspend judgment, thus allowing us to enter, at least for a moment, into each one's individual point of view.

From the first few lines of the case Freud immediately makes us aware of his control of the material, revealing the heart of the matter only gradually, letting the information emerge at just the precise moment when we are about to raise a question. The case history starts at the end, or anyway, in the middle, with the patient and the mystery of her symptoms that are to be discovered by our Sherlock Holmes, while the patient herself gives us our Watson.

Freud has a great sense of timing. Like Dostoevsky at the beginning of *The Brothers Karamazov*, when speaking of the father's death "which I [i.e., the narrator] shall relate in its proper place," Freud gradually leads us through the intricate unraveling of this tightly tied and complicated knot. Like Nabokov in the preface to his *Lolita*, Freud captures our interest, in his case by telling us that "sexual questions will be discussed with all possible frankness, the organs and functions of sexual life will be called by their proper names, and the pure-minded reader can convince himself from my description that I have not hesitated to converse upon such subjects in such language even with a young woman." Who among us could resist such an invitation to read on?

Both Nabokov and Freud speak of the necessity of hiding the identity of their characters. Nabokov announces that "save for the correction of obvious solecisms and a careful suppression of a few tenacious details that despite H[umbert]H[umbert]'s efforts still subsisted in his text as signposts and tombstones (indicative of places or persons that taste would conceal and compassion spare), this remarkable memoir is presented intact." Freud tells us of his attempts to hide the identity of the real Dora: "I have picked out a person the scenes of whose life were laid not in Vienna but in a remote provincial town, and whose personal circumstances must therefore be practically unknown in Vienna." Is the purpose of these statements only to respect privacy? Or is it also—primarily, even—to make us curious? How much truth do they hide? Regardless, mystery is created, and questions are aroused in our minds.

It is Freud's ability to create mystery and, at the same time, to give us precise details that make us see, hear, and understand Dora's dilemma that had kept me turning the pages through the night, finding myself completely caught up in the text and seeing myself disconcertingly mirrored in many of Dora's symptoms. Like her I felt the wish to attend lectures rather than concern myself with housework, and I could understand the despair contained in the letter she left, saying she could no longer endure her life. We wonder from the start what is troubling her so deeply.

Freud chose here a high-stakes story. One might even equate it with a soap-opera quartet. Dora's father had been successfully treated by Freud for syphilis. Now he had brought his young daughter, seventeen years old, an intelligent girl "in the first bloom of youth" to Freud, telling him that his goal was to get her to be reasonable, and maintaining that she had been led astray by unsuitable reading, such as Mantegazza's *Physiology of Love*. It was most likely, he had added, that she had merely fancied the whole scene.

———

But the scene she reported was by no means a fancy. Rather, it was an accurate report of Herr K's crude attempt to seduce her. Herr K, we learn, is, in fact, the husband of the woman Dora's father is having an affair with, and whom her father covers up for, along with, in effect, offering him his daughter, in compensation. Though he was brought in for the purpose of suborning this behavior on the part of both men, Freud at least maintains neutrality, explaining that "I had resolved from the first to suspend my judgment of the true state of affairs till I had heard the other side [i.e., Dora's], as well."

Steven Marcus, a literary critic well versed in psychoanalysis, writes in his essay "Freud and Dora" in *Freud and the Culture of Psychoanalysis* that "if we try to put ourselves in the place of this girl between her sixteenth and eighteenth year, we can at once recognize that her situation was a desperate one. The three adults with whom she was closest, whom she loved the most in the world, were apparently conspiring—separately, in tandem, or in concert, to deny the reality of her experience." Freud makes us listen, too, to this story, which remains shocking, even to us today. Who would not empathize with this vulnerable young girl, treated as a pawn in her father's adultery, part of a diabolical quid pro quo: "You take my daughter, and I'll take your wife."

Like many skilled writers of fiction, Freud often uses a binary structure with reiteration and reversals. We learn of two seduction scenes: the first, in Herr K's office, when Dora is only thirteen, where he has proposed to meet her along with his wife. Instead, he comes alone and informs her he needs to close the shutters. He then asks her to wait for him near a staircase. There he clasps her to him and begins forcibly to kiss her. Revolted, she wrenches herself away and flees, not mentioning the scene to anyone.

The second such scene takes place two years later, by a lake where the family has a house. Dora has previously learned from the governess to the Ks' children that he, Herr K, while "ardently courting" the governess, had complained, "I get nothing out of my wife." He uses the same sexual allusion with Dora in a similar overture of love. Insulted and traumatized by this crude approach, she slaps him in the face and flees and ultimately tells her father of his behavior. That same afternoon, when she awakens from a nap, she finds Herr K again beside her, insisting that he can enter her room whenever it suits him.

We are presented with two dreams, around which the case history is organized, like any successful novella. Only occasionally, in Freud's account, are we privileged to hear the direct voice of the patient. The notable exception is her dreams, which are reported in the first person.

Wanting to convince his readers that dreams are the "royal road to the unconscious," he lets Dora speak to us directly. How wonderfully suggestive these dreams are is reflected in the fact that they have been used again and again as inspiration by various writers, such as in D. M. Thomas's *The White Hotel*.

Henry James once said, "Tell a dream, lose a reader." But that is not what happens here. Who could forget Dora's first dream of a burning house and the jewel case that must be saved? Or her second one, which involves a train station, a letter, and the death of her father? These two dreams conjure up many mysterious dangers: of fire, of death, of voyages.

Freud also introduces mystery by using an obfuscating, third-person narrator. This device allows him to claim he is protecting confidentiality but also frees him up to introduce convincing arguments.

He rarely took notes during the session, explaining that he wished to avoid "shaking the patient's confidence." One wonders how much he could have remembered. Even had he wanted to, could he have reproduced the words of the session in direct dialogue? How dull that might have been for us! Rather, his method allows him to make a selection, to pique our curiosity, to prepare us for his often-startling revelations, to foreshadow the ultimate outcome. According to James Strachey, who edited the *Standard Edition* of Freud's works, his details were famously unreliable. "He constantly contradicts himself over details of fact," Strachey writes to Ernest Jones, Freud's biographer, as Jones tells us in *The Life and Work of Sigmund Freud*.

Mainly, Freud gives us his own version of what his patients have told him. Here, he describes Dora's dragging her leg after that famous kiss: "That is how people walk when they have twisted a foot. So she had made a 'false step,' which was true indeed, if she could give birth to a child nine months after the scene at the lake." One supposition, namely that pregnancy could result from a kiss, leads him to the next, namely "the false step." Does Dora accept all of this? We have only what Freud's third-person narrator tells us: "And Dora disputed the fact no longer."

His need to curtail and at the same time to select the essential in the exposition of his analysis is reinforced, he tells us, because of the patient's "resistances and the forms in which they are expressed." This resistance, of course, was useful to Freud as a writer, although it might have made his task as a therapist more difficult. Resistance enables him to create conflict. For example, when he likens the jewel box in her dream to her vagina, Dora, in one of the few moments we are privileged to hear her voice directly, says "I knew you would say that!" We immediately agree with her because, indeed, what else would Freud have said!

Similarly, whatever "resistance" may mean clinically, it enables Freud to delay his revelations until the right moment not only for the patient but also for the reader. We are held in suspense and brought along gradually like Hansel and Gretel trying to find the lost crumbs in the forest to accept as reality what might otherwise have seemed unbelievable.

Nothing is what it seems: behind every object, every gesture, every word, lies its opposite. Ultimately, Freud leads us on with reiteration and reversal like a wily orator. What Dora feels as disgust Freud assures us is desire. Love and hate are juxtaposed: this is the best and the worst at the same time, as in a Dickensian world. Truth remains elusive, but what matters here are the skill of the writer, our pleasure in this well-told tale, and, above all, the deeper truths about human nature we find scattered here like gold, which are to be extracted by our unreliable narrator, Freud, himself.

At the same time Freud allows himself the freedom to tell us the truth as he sees it. He does not hesitate out of prudery to give us all the small details that are necessary to create real life in all its complexity on the page. He writes in his prefatory remarks to this case history: "If it is true that the causes of hysterical disorders are to be found in the intimacies of the patients' psycho-sexual life, and that hysterical symptoms are the expression of their most secret and repressed wishes, then the complete exposition of a case of hysteria is bound to involve the revelation of those intimacies and the betrayal of those secrets."

Another technique he uses to draw us in, is to suggest that the theory behind this case history is hermetic. He suggests that, to understand his reasoning, it is necessary, first, to read his *Interpretation of Dreams*, published shortly before. This is more likely a piece of self-promotion, because the case history remains today an engaging read, needing no prequel. As Freud himself wrote to his great friend (and, in effect, his psychoanalyst) Wilhelm Fliess (*Letters of Sigmund Freud*, selected and edited by Ernst L. Freud), "It is the most subtle thing I have ever written and will produce an even more horrifying effect than usual."

Nor does he disappoint us: behind each revelation there is always an even deeper one. The fourth major character we discover in this quartet, after Dora, her father, and Herr K, is Herr K's wife. All three of the adults betray Dora in varying and horrifying ways. We learn, early on, that Frau K has shared a bedroom with Dora, knowing that her husband is sleeping elsewhere. She has shared the secrets of her troubled marriage with Dora, who is taken with her "adorable white body." As it turns out, Dora is in fact attracted to Frau K rather than to her husband. Thus, Freud gives us a much more interesting and unusual triangle, surely a more believable one for such a young girl. He thereby introduces the theme of bisexuality, much on his mind at that time, as revealed in the letters to Fliess, whom he himself may well have been in love with. His cleverly divulging at the right moment what might be called today "the reveal" still seems modern to us, today.

Thus far, I have tried to enumerate many of the literary devices Freud used to win us over, to convince us of the reality he saw in what his patients told him. These have included comparisons to his own literary and medical models, the qualities of mystery and suspense, the use of revelations and reversals, his varieties of structure, his varieties of points of view, his methods of selection of details, and his methods of persuasion. In all these he was clearly successful, as shown by his being the recipient of the Goethe Prize, awarded for literary style.

I close by returning to the beginning. This case history is not only a literary story; it is also the report of a treatment—or at least, the initial phase of one. Was it, in the end, successful in this aspect, as well?

Years later, I was to return to the case history, though as so often happens I read the story quite differently. I was appalled by the role of the therapist here, Freud's bullying tone, his insistence on his assumptions. How dare he, I asked myself, insist this girl was in love with Herr K, the husband of her father's mistress, a man, like Freud, in his forties, who had repeatedly attempted to seduce her since she was thirteen? How much of what Freud speculated was based on this girl's life and feelings and how much lay simply in his own mind? How to differentiate the two?

These gaps in Freud's narrative, the lack of Dora's point of view, all the gaping spaces in Freud's fascinating text, led me to dare to write my own version. Freud leaves so many questions unanswered, so much that "Dora," or Ida Bauer, never gets a chance to explain, that I was tempted to fill in the cracks. As Felix von Hardenbourg says, "Novels arrive out of the shortcomings of history." This is Freud's gift to all of us.

Inspired by his text, I set about writing a historical novel of my own in an attempt to fill in what seemed to me to be missing: Dora's voice. And here I am guilty of self-promotion if I tell you my novel is called *Dreaming for Freud*. Here, I tried to enter into the mind of both my characters: the analyst and the analysand. I came up with two narrators: Freud was there but as an equal, struggling to feed his family, to solve the meaning of dreams, to find fame. I even allowed Dora to read his dream book and to make up suitable dreams for him. The strategy allowed Dora to speak directly, and through her, the women of her time and place, 1900 Vienna, and, I hoped, young women of all time and place, surrounded by the often narcissistic desires and incomprehension of their elders.

The text and my interest in Ida Bauer led me, too, to find out what had happened to her in later years. The story of a sick father who has a sick mistress who has a sick husband who proposes to a sick daughter as her lover has been written about extensively. What happened to her afterward is less well known.

Four years after Freud treated her, he tells us, his young patient whom he called Dora (Ida Bauer) moved on. A significant change had taken place in her life.

She had, indeed, married a would-be musician and given birth to a little boy.

I have traced her path from the days of penury, when her father's fortune and Austria's power were lost at the end of the First World War, through her escape from Vienna during the Second World War, first to France, then through Casablanca to America.

This woman, who seems so often to have aggravated and annoyed the male doctors who tried to treat her, showed considerable intelligence, resourcefulness, and pluck.

She met up with Frau K, who was really Frau Zelenka, her father's mistress, and together they started a bridge school, teaching rich Viennese ladies how to play bridge, in order to make sufficient money to survive.

A fierce and formidable mother, she obliged her gifted little boy to study music and to learn the foreign languages that would enable him to leave Austria at the right moment and flee to America, where he became the head of the opera in San Francisco, finding some of the world's greatest singers such as Pavarotti.

Was all of this because of, or in spite of, her brief exposure to Freud? I leave the answer to you.

Whatever the answer to these questions, Ida Bauer provided Freud with the necessary material to write up a case history that would be read and read again, emulated, analyzed, turned into plays and films and books. He wrote an unforgettable story with all the necessary mystery and the significant detail that novelists can only envy and emulate.

SIGMUND FREUD, PRIVATE INVESTIGATOR

David Gordon

You are shown into the study. It is a gloomy autumn day at the beginning of the last century, or the end of the one before, and you are a well-dressed bourgeois, outwardly respectable, hat, gloves, umbrella, but burdened with a desperate secret. You smell smoke. That's the first thing you notice before you even have time to look around. It is a comfortable, well-proportioned room, if a bit cluttered and dusty: books, carpets, a lounge, a big desk, a fire in the grate, but also sculptures, trinkets; ancient, broken objects; a chess set, a microscope, perhaps a violin. You introduce yourself to the imposing but polite gentleman dressed and groomed impeccably, but with a penetrating gaze and a famously original mind, capable of rare leaps of connection and startling depths of insight, as well as radical, even outrageous ideas. Puffing away, he invites you to tell him your problem, and with a deep breath, haltingly, you begin: Perhaps something is missing? Or there has been an injury or a loss? A crime. Or else it is a haunting, a ghost, a monster, a beast. In every case, it is a mystery, with the cause and the solution unknown. And so the investigation begins.

There are at least two figures I could be describing here, of course: Sherlock Holmes and Sigmund Freud. I say *figures* because Holmes, while obviously created by Sir Arthur Conan Doyle, has long ago escaped the confines of those books and become a living, thriving being in the culture. And Freud, in a sort of reverse process, has gone from a mere mortal to an archetypal cultural presence, a being who is still very much alive in many domains of the culture, including his own writings. He has become a literary character, most especially in his case studies, which I am thinking of here and which struck me, from the first time I read them, as detective stories.

I am certainly not the first to notice this, but as someone who has ended up spending much of the last couple of decades writing crime novels—while also nurturing an ongoing obsession with Freud's writings and psychoanalytic theory in general (for a while we hosted a Freud discussion group in the loft where I lived)—I suspect I have given the matter more thought than most and from a particularly, perhaps peculiarly, "literary" perspective.[1] In other words, it is as natural for me to read Freud as literature as it is to consider his work's clinical effectiveness or usefulness in other critical fields or academic disciplines. And whatever anyone thinks or does not think of his writings as theories or treatments, one thing is for sure: the man is a literary genius. And as a character? As great as Sherlock Holmes, with whom he has this uncanny resemblance.

Uncanny. A loaded word when fired anywhere close to Freud. But the parallel emergence of these two figures, one real, one imagined, at more or less the same time is too odd to be a coincidence; and now that we have crossed over into the world of both detectives and psychoanalysts, we must accept that there is no such thing as coincidence. Perhaps it was timing: this era—when the old world was crumbling, and the modern emerging, in technology, science, urban development, industrialization, art, and culture, and finally in an unprecedented modern war—demanded a modern urban hero, the detective.

Be that as it may, they are contemporaries, more or less, and develop their practices on parallel tracks, despite seeming to be opposites: Holmes the ultimate rationalist, using icy logic, and Freud the explorer, developing a kind of science of the irrational.

But—and this is why I say *seeming*—their methods are strangely alike. They are both materialists, penetrating into the state of things as they are. They are realists.

The symptom is the clue. In this way, both detectives proceed in precisely the same way, by noticing and then interpreting the signs that we unknowingly provide. For one, it might be Afghani dust on our boots, cigar ash, an accent. For the other a slip, a denial, an oddly strong emotion, a seemingly random association. In either case, we give ourselves away. This is the main thing: Once the detective has you in his sights, you always give yourself away. You cannot do otherwise. As Freud says in *Introductory Lectures*, "He that has eyes to see and ears to hear may convince himself that no mortal can keep a secret. If his lips are silent, he chatters with his fingertips; betrayal oozes out of him at every pore."

2

Indeed, dreaming is another kind of remembering, though one that is subject to the conditions that rule at night.

—THE WOLF MAN CASE

The trail of clues always leads us into the past. That is, after all, when the crime occurred, back before our story begins, or at least before the entrance of the detective on the scene. *Something* happened, and we are living with its consequences, even if no one knows, or remembers, or can even bear to admit what it was. And that is where the detective must go, to solve the case and identify the offender. Often, of course, the offender turns out to be us— we wished something terrible, and now we are punishing ourselves. Freud's own origin myth—*Oedipus Rex*—is sometimes called the first detective story, with the first twist ending—the killer was the hero all along. (Also, I am struck by how central the role, in their time, of nannies and housekeepers was, seeding obsessions by bending over in aprons to do their chores, tucking future neurotics in for nap time, forging fetishes by blithely walking around in stockings and heels. This is a whole book someone else can write.)

With or without a magnifying glass, the inspection of the primal scene will hopefully yield some clue, some tiny fragment that, however meaningless, even ridiculous, it seems to the rest of us, will lead the detective on. As in a fairy tale, we have all left a trail for ourselves, but time has passed, the path is overgrown, the birds have eaten our crumbs, and we are lost in the darkest part of the forest.

For me, inevitably, this summons up another literary figure, also roughly contemporary, and also engaged in a quest for what has been lost: Marcel Proust. Once again he is both author and character, Proust and Marcel. Once again, he is victim, detective, and criminal. (He breaks his grandmother's heart; he steals his mother's kiss; he takes Albertine captive; he fails to save Gilberte from her fate; etc.) But most striking—considering the dates, the roughly analogous social strata, the bourgeois and aristocratic setting, though in Paris, rather than Vienna or London—is that the methodology and ultimately, the solution, are very much the same: something has been lost or stolen—in this case it is life itself, time: where did it all go, my childhood, my youthful loves? We know it is missing; the ache of the loss is always there, what Proust (as quoted by Walter Benjamin in "The Image of Proust") calls "the incurable imperfection in the essence of the present moment."

Of course it is in the past, but where? This is not memory as we understand it, since so much of it, the most vital part, is beyond our recall. This is a kind of memory that (as Benjamin noted) seems very much like forgetting, a forgetting that forever preserves the forgotten. Lost time is sleeping, as it were, waiting for us to awaken it, with a kiss or a nibble—just as Freud, in a stunning paradox, informs us that it is that which is never experienced (the trauma, the crime) that lives on as "memory."

Here the clue is just as minor, inane, even silly as Holmes noticing a bit of fluff or Freud grasping hold of a twitch or pun. It is, famously, a cookie. Or an uneven bit of paving. Or the sound of cutlery ringing across a boring dinner party. It is the nature of the clue to be small, modest, and without signification, except to the detective. It is meant only for him. It is there for him to discover. And if Holmes never notices the ash, the thread, then it blows away unread, crumbles into nothingness like a forgotten cookie.

But once tasted, it unlocks everything. The past is trapped inside it, as though under a spell, transformed into a tree, or a flower, or a wolf, waiting for the one brave enough, wise enough, childlike enough to find and free it—"for my own observations show that we have rated the powers of children too low and that there is no knowing what they cannot be given credit for," Freud tells us in the case of the Wolf Man. It is one of the most touching characteristics of the great doctor that, like the creators of fairy tales, he has the utmost respect for children. (The only two things that I've seen enrage him are religion and narcissistic parents.)

And so, as if on a parallel track, Proust too withdraws into his dusty, old-fashioned chamber, a cork-lined, shuttered room where he reclines (both analyst and patient) under many thin, worn blankets, and turning his nights to days, he dreams wide awake, employing neither deduction nor free association but "memoire involuntaire," and discovers what in Vienna they will come to call the unconscious.

This is the great conclusion of the search: at first Marcel thinks it is a matter of sheer luck—if you never eat the cookie you will never unlock the past. But then, in the end, he understands that the book itself is the treasure, that writing his own story will be the solution. This makes *In Search of Lost Time* a masterpiece of sad redemption, an act of hope, that all is not lost after all, that even the most misspent life is not wasted—though Proust is a pessimist, a realist like Holmes and Freud, and his truths are the hard truths of a detective: the dead do not live again, the lost loves will not love us again, understanding will not save anyone.

3

But I don't want to forget to mention how funny Freud's writing is.

He is a great comic stylist as well, and in rereading the case studies, as I lie on my couch (of course) in my own book-lined room, I am laughing out loud at the poor Rat Man: when he loses his pince-nez on maneuvers and sends for a new pair and he is told by Lieutenant A he must reimburse Lieutenant B for the 3.80 crowns, or whatever, and becomes obsessed with doing this, even though it turns out that he must simply pay the postal clerk, and frantically beseeches the bemused A & B to come to the post office with this minor sum so he can pay them and have them pay her, and gets so worked up relating this inanely logical and insanely precise idea to Freud that he says, "the patient behaved as though he were dazed and bewildered. He repeatedly addressed me as 'Captain.'" (and if you don't do this properly of course, rats might eat your (dead) father's anus, by the way); or when he becomes convinced he is mishearing or failing to catch what is said and torments his fellows by asking them to repeat and explain. "He forced himself to understand the precise meaning of every syllable that was addressed to him, as though he might otherwise be missing some priceless treasure." (But isn't this what Freud himself does, poring over every word in the dream like Holmes collecting dust?) "Accordingly he kept asking 'What was it you said just then?' And after it had been repeated to him, he could not help thinking it had sounded different the first time, so he remained dissatisfied."

To me this reads like the greatest farce, a presentation of human life at once so real and so absurd that, despite his doctorly demeanor and dry, wry delivery, I picture Freud here as Groucho, wiggling his eyebrows and twiddling his cigar. No doubt Freud's writings are comedy as well as mystery (just as Proust's great work is a comedy deep in its broken heart), the saddest and silliest of all. And, it should go without saying, it is always a love story too.

Marcel has Albertine to lose; Holmes meets his match in Irene Adler. Who is the femme fatale for Freud? Dora, of course. She comes to the doctor having literally lost her voice, and this mystery is swiftly solved. The detective believes her account of the crime—Herr K, the father's friend, had made advances, earning a slap in the face, while her father looked the other way to pursue his own affair with Frau K—and she is restored.

But when Freud pushes further, insisting that Dora herself was jealous of her father and Frau K and ambivalent about Herr K, she breaks off treatment on 1/1/1901—a date that might symbolize new beginnings or relate (silly clues) to Freud's own address, Berggasse 19. Freud would bitterly regret this failure all his life: he had missed the transference—poor Dora's anger, her resistance, he came to suspect, were in fact the acting out of the drama that needed to be analyzed—and the countertransference, the unconscious interference of his own emotions. Although she did come back to visit a year later, she would haunt him for the rest of his life. She was the victim he failed to save, the one whose predicament his own resistance blocked from his always penetrating view. He helped her regain her voice but was unable, in the end, to hear what she told him.

I'm reminded of a chart a therapist once drew for me, a simple cross forming four boxes, with C above and U below, duplicated on either side, roughly depicting the therapeutic scene, two people face to face, each with a conscious and unconscious mind. Of course the two consciousnesses can converse. And the trained analyst can consciously detect much that I did not see myself, my unconscious on display across the room. But there might also be things I notice that he is unaware of, my conscious mind, an amateur detective, noting his unconscious at play, in fidgets, say, or in moods. But there is more—and here my therapist drew a line across the bottom of the page, connecting U to U: the unconscious meeting the unconscious, with neither of the two conscious participants knowing a thing. "This," he said, "is the therapy."

4

This is the twist in the mystery, the late plot turn. Even after the evidence is found, the crime solved, the violator named, there is the final reveal: We, the victims, are a mystery too, unsolved and unsolvable, for the same principle that allows the detective/analyst to know us—this endlessly confessing and testifying unconscious, alive in our speech and stutters, our tics and gestures, our silly fears and odd desires—this principle also guarantees that we will not, cannot know, or even meet ourselves. We are strangers. According to Freud, this unconscious that contains our deepest truths, that determines who we are, that drives us and explains our motives, is off-limits to us and will forever recede to the dark side of the horizon as we endeavor to approach it:

> Humanity has in the course of time had to endure from the hands of science two great outrages upon its naive self-love. The first was when it realized that our earth was not the center of the universe, but only a tiny speck in a world-system of a magnitude hardly conceivable. . . . The second was when biological research robbed man of his peculiar privilege of having been specially created, and relegated him to a descent from the animal world, implying an ineradicable animal nature in him. . . . But man's craving for grandiosity is now suffering the third and most bitter blow from present-day psychological research which is endeavoring to prove to the ego of each one of us that he is not even master in his own house, but that he must remain content with the veriest scraps of information about what is going on unconsciously in his own mind. (*Introductory Lectures*)

Or, as Jacques Lacan puts it: "The Unconscious is the discourse of the Other."

This fundamental insight—that we are, at bottom, alien to ourselves, and must remain so—is so extreme that I still don't think we have digested it, all these years later. Even analysts seem to have a hard time actually integrating it into daily life. I myself have benefited hugely from therapy—and from one therapist in particular who is now a close friend—but I also have found that some days I am having the same conversation I have with a friend or neighbor about weather or student loans or airline tickets. Even my personal, private, painful stuff, the matter that brought me there, is worked over in the most mundane way, a litany of complaints that I myself am tired of hearing, since I've already told my friends everything, and even the therapist, rather than a detective cracking a case, or interrogating a suspect, sounds like a bored family friend: Why don't I just get out more often and meet people? Get a better job? Stop blaming myself and cheer up! I nod politely and think, is this what Freud would say? Maybe so. He was a nice old Jewish grandpa after all. But the irony is that, while Freud's theories have necessarily come under wave upon wave of critique and revision and rejection and revival, he is, in many ways, still too radical for us. He is not only too old; he is also still too new.

Were there times when these truths, these glimpses beyond the veil, were too much for Freud himself, this view of ordinary bourgeois as haunted, possessed by the ghosts of their dead ancestors, their lost loves, their infantile desires and fears? Or maybe we are the ghosts, projections of a sleeping unconscious that we never meet by day? He analyzed his own dreams as assiduously as anyone's, but remember Dora? At times even he missed the clues that were right there in the room.

And so we have the detective who is haunted by both the crimes he's solved and those left unsolved, the hard-boiled noir detective who, even in victory, knows that every case successfully cracked is a tiny glimpse, a flashlight shone into a limitless darkness. The detective's trail of clues always ends at the edge of the abyss, and there he must pause and go no further, lest he plunge in himself and be lost.

This brings to mind another writer, in yet another genre, also roughly contemporaneous with the others, living and dying during that century's turn, though here in America, not in old Europe.

Unlike the others he toiled in obscurity, struggling with ill health and possessed by the demons of his country—racism, anti-Semitism, class struggle—dying young, but nevertheless leaving his own mark, or stain perhaps, like a seeping damp, on literature. I mean, of course, H. P. Lovecraft:

> The most merciful thing in the world, I think, is the inability of the human mind to correlate all its contents. We live on a placid island of ignorance in the midst of black seas of infinity, and it was not meant that we should voyage far. The sciences, each straining in its own direction, have hitherto harmed us little; but some day the piecing together of dissociated knowledge will open up such terrifying vistas of reality, and of our frightful position therein, that we shall either go mad from the revelation or flee from the deadly light into the peace and safety of a new dark age. (*The Call of Cthulhu*)

To misquote Nietzsche: Dr. Freud, psycho-detective, explorer of the dark and primitive unconscious, did indeed stare into the abyss, every day, in hourly sessions, and the abyss did stare back, and it did indeed have a cost—persecution, notoriety, exile—but he slayed no monsters, nor did he become one. Rather he recognized us, under our everyday human masks, for the monsters we are. And like the child in *Frankenstein*, he took the monster gently by the hand and tried to make it a friend.

5

Or maybe that is too much to hope for. Not every case has such a dramatic climax. Maybe, in my case for example, all the unconscious finally contains, like an unearthed trunk or stolen suitcase, is a few old notes from lost loves, a faded family picture, a canceled ticket or two. Maybe that's why detectives are such a melancholy lot, walking off alone in the rain at the end of every episode, or folded in the wings of their chair, smoking. They are, in the end, not heroes, just workers on the night shift, doing what they can.

And perhaps here is where Inspector Freud parts ways with Holmes and the other great detectives. They restore order and punish the wrongdoer. Freud just accepts the crime and learns to live with it, as best he can. As he writes in *Studies on Hysteria*, "But you will see for yourself that much has been gained if we succeed in turning your hysterical misery into common unhappiness."

6

Or perhaps not. That is both the hope and the curse of the unconscious: there is always more. Love might win in the end, desire stage a rebellion, life refuse to die. As the good doctor wrote, toward his own end, in *Civilization and Its Discontents*, when gazing sadly at the coming victory of Thanatos, the death drive, and the darkness falling all around: "And now it is to be expected that the other of the two 'Heavenly Powers,' eternal Eros, will make an effort in the struggle. . . . But who can foresee with what success and what result?"

FREUD AND THE WRITERS

Colm Tóibín

In his biography of Freud, Peter Gay wrote about the general response to the outbreak of the First World War: "The most extraordinary thing about these calamitous events was less that they happened than how they were received. Europeans of all stripes joined in greeting the advent of war with a fervor bordering on a religious experience. Aristocrats, bourgeois, workers, and farmers; reactionaries, liberals, and radicals; cosmopolitans, chauvinists, and particularists; fierce soldiers, preoccupied scholars, and gentle theologians—all linked arms in their bellicose delight."[1]

In his "Thoughts in Wartime," written in 1914, Thomas Mann wrote: "How the poets' hearts caught fire when the war broke out! And they had thought they loved peace—really loved it, each according to his humanity, some like peasants, others out of meekness and German education. Now they sang of war as if in a contest, extolling it as though nothing better, more beautiful, or happier could have happened to them and the people they give voice to than that a desperate, overpowering enmity finally raised itself up against them. Even the most accomplished and famous were grateful for the war and welcomed it no less heartily than the good soul who in a newspaper began his war song with the cry 'I feel born again.'"[2]

It is not merely that sane, sensible, and rational people appeared to lose all reason. But writers such as Thomas Mann himself, known for his irony, his calmness, and his sense of history, and Henry

James, known for his subtlety and his nuanced concern with the private life, appeared to take crude delight in the war, especially during its early months. In December 1914, the German critic Wilhelm Herzog asked: "What reason does a writer like Thomas Mann have to express thoughts in wartime that during peacetime at least he always suppressed?" Hermann Kurzke, one of Mann's biographers, writes: "Mann's behavior at the outbreak of the war belongs to the great riddles a biography must solve."[3]

In 1915 Mann embarked on his book *Reflections of a Nonpolitical Man*, in which he attempted to tease out his own relationship as an artist to the German tradition and his own heightened response to the war. In the same year, Sigmund Freud wrote *Reflections on War and Death*, a pair of essays in which he deplored "the lack of insight that our great intellectual leaders have shown, their obduracy, their inaccessibility to the most impressive arguments, their uncritical credulity concerning the most contestable assertions."[4]

The war gave Freud a chance to consider the relationship between intelligence and emotion and report on the ways in which emotional life can regress, under pressure, to an earlier stage of development. "The transformation of impulses," he wrote, "upon which our cultural adaptability rests can . . . be permanently or temporarily made regressive. Without doubt the influence of war belongs to those forces which can create such regressions; we therefore need not deny cultural adaptability to all those who at present are acting in such an uncivilized manner, and may expect that the refinement of their impulses will continue in more peaceful times."[5]

Freud's two essays help us to interpret bellicose, patriotic, and unthinking passages in the correspondence of writers such as Mann and James, and indeed Edith Wharton, in 1914 and 1915.

On September 22, 1914, with the war only a few weeks old, Henry James wrote to his old friend Lilla Cabot Perry in New Hampshire of "the uplifting and thrilling side to it." A month later, he wrote to his niece: "I have been finding London all this month exactly what

I knew it would be, agitating and multitudinously assaulting, but in all sorts of ways interesting and thrilling—such a reflection of the whole national consciousness."[6]

Although in some other letters, James deplored the war itself and was sickened by the carnage, its outbreak caused him to feel not only patriotic and excited, but also useful.

In London, he began to visit the wounded, writing to the novelist Hugh Walpole in November 1914 that he had "almost discovered my vocation in life to be the beguiling and drawing-out of the suffering soldier. . . . The British influx is steady, and I have lately been seeing more . . . of *that* prostrate, with whom I seem to get even better into relation. At best he is admirable—*so* much may be made of him; of a freshness and brightness of soldier-stuff that I think must be unsurpassable. We only want more and more and more and more, of him, and I judge that we shall in due course get it."[7]

James, in that same letter, singled out a Russian soldier: "I met a striking specimen the other day who was oddly enough in the Canadian contingent . . . and who was of a stature, complexion, expression, and above all of a shining candour, which made him a kind of army-corps in himself."[8]

It is significant that James wrote in this tone to Walpole, who, he knew, was the type of young man likely to remain a bachelor. Five years earlier, he had written to Walpole, forty-one years his junior: "I dream of the golden islands with you there, along with me, for my man Friday."[9] The war gave James an excuse to describe young men whom he liked to Walpole, who would see the point.

In France, in 1915, as she toured the front line, James's friend Edith Wharton wrote of the troops: "It is not too much to say that war has given beauty to faces that were interesting, humorous, acute, malicious, a hundred vivid and expressive things, but last and least of all beautiful." She found the armaments as alluring as she did the soldiers themselves: "And near each gun," she wrote, "hovered its attendant [French] gunner, proud, possessive, important as a bridegroom with his bride."[10]

In a letter to Wharton in March 1915, James wrote of an account of British troops in battle that "did me a kind of unholy hideous good. . . . It appears to have been an absolute massacre for our advance, the Germans surprised, fleeing, hiding terrified in every corner. . . . It overwhelmed and annihilated, to an appalling tune of numbers, while our losses were 'comparatively' small. . . . I declare it quite wreathes me in smiles again . . . to repeat it to you."[11]

Of the Germans, James wrote to Lilla Cabot Perry in June 1915: "they really believe that it's a sweet privilege for the British and Belgian and other civilians to be variously massacred by them, and that they do us an honour thereby that it's in shocking taste of us not to appreciate. It's the sublimity of their bloody fatuity that leaves one staring."[12]

He also wrote of "a world squeezed together in the huge Prussian fist and with the variety and spontaneity of its parts oozing in a steady trickle, like the blood of sacrifice, between those hideously knuckly fingers."[13]

In June 1915, when James decided to apply for British citizenship, he wrote to Mr. Asquith, the prime minister: "I find my wish to testify at this crisis to the force of my attachment and devotion to England, and for this cause for which she is fighting, finally and completely irresistible."[14]

On August 7, 1914, Thomas Mann wrote to his brother Heinrich about "the upheavals, especially the large-scale psychic upheavals, which war must necessarily bring. Shouldn't we be grateful for the totally unexpected chance to experience such mighty things? My chief feeling is a tremendous curiosity—and, I admit it, the deepest sympathy for this execrated, indecipherable, fateful Germany." The following month, when war had actually broken out, he wrote to his brother of "this great, fundamentally decent, and in fact stirring peoples' war."[15]

Mann wrote to a friend serving in the German army in December 1914: "One wonders how it will all turn out. The anxiety and curiosity are tremendous. But it is a joyful curiosity, isn't it? It's a feeling that everything will have to be *new* after this profound, mighty visitation, and that the German soul will emerge from it stronger, prouder, freer, happier. May it be so. Hail and victory, Herr Doktor."[16]

In his biography of Mann, Donald Prater writes that "Thomas held firmly to the conventionally patriotic line," which he outlined in an essay, "Thoughts in the War," written in 1914: "In it, he saw the conflict as an honorable defence of 'German' values (Lutheran, romantic) against the insults being hurled from all sides at his Fatherland."[17] In this, he was not alone. Mann's patriotic fervor in 1914 was shared by writers such as Gerhard Hauptmann and Rainer Maria Rilke, even if it was not shared by Mann's own brother.

With Mann, even in peacetime, it was often difficult to disentangle his erotic dreams from his other imaginings. In wartime, his support for militarism had, as with James, a distinct homoerotic edge. In 1919, a year after the publication of his *Reflections of a Nonpolitical Man*, he noted in his diaries: "I have no doubt that *Reflections*, too, is an expression of my sexual inversion." The literary scholar Hans Mayer interpreted the nonpolitical world of the book as "the author's declaration of love for a certain blond and blue-eyed type of German male."[18]

What the war offered Mann and James was simple and primitive emotion and a chance to glorify male strength. As writers, they worked alone, and, as men whose sexuality was ambiguous, they had reason to be careful. Now, with the war, they were no longer outsiders, no longer watching themselves. They might have seemed at one with their nation. But nothing was as simple as that. In truth, they were both somewhat as confused by the war as propelled into certainty by it.

Freud's *Reflections on War and Death* offer us some clues to their confusion. The essays provide a context, but also a tentative exploration of the jumble of unstable feelings that overtook Mann and James in 1914. Freud does not formulate a theory of what happened to the mind and the unconscious as war broke out. Rather, as he says in *Beyond the Pleasure Principle*, he sought to throw himself "into a line of thought and follow it wherever it leads."[19] Freud, in this way, came close to imagining the pressures felt by these writers; he understood how the evasions and strategies that had previously nourished them became useless to them and left them helpless and strangely hysterical once war drums began to beat.

Part of the reason Freud made some sense of the less refined impulses that were let loose by war was that he felt such impulses himself. In 1912, he commented to a friend that "the expectation of war takes our breath away." In July 1914, he said: "Perhaps for the first time in thirty years, I feel myself an Austrian, and would like just once more to give this rather unpromising empire a chance." He was rather surprised at himself speaking "of the success of 'our' war loan" and discussing "the chances of 'our' battle of millions."[20] He was having the primitive feelings and then studying them with care, as though he were his own best patient.

Although Freud, like James and Mann, did not take part in the war, his three sons and his son-in-law saw action. (When his sons came home on leave, they posed in their uniforms for family photographs.) His nephew was killed in 1917. Freud was constantly in a state of deep anxiety. Also, potential patients were now in uniform, and his practice was suffering. And many of his colleagues, including the most eminent, had been drafted.

At Christmas 1914, Freud wrote to his colleague Ernest Jones in London—he had refused to chance to have Jones as his enemy: "I do not delude myself: the springtime of our science has abruptly broken off, we are heading for a bad period; all we can do is to keep the fire flickering in a few hearths, until a more favorable wind makes it possible to light it again to full blaze."[21]

But he still saw himself as an Austrian who could use the word "our." Early in 1915, he wrote to a colleague: "Our mood is not so brilliant as in Germany; the future seems to us unpredictable, but German strength and confidence has its influence." In November 1914, irritated by Ernest Jones's support for the British side, he wrote to his brother: "He writes about the war like a real Anglo.

Sink a few more superdreadnoughts or carry through a few landings, otherwise their eyes won't be opened."[22]

But Freud's patriotism was tempered by a great melancholy feeling that, as Peter Gay writes, "people were behaving precisely the way that psychoanalysis would have predicted." In November 1914, Freud wrote to a friend: "I have no doubt that humanity will get over this war, too, but I know for certain that I and my contemporaries will see the world cheerful no more. It is too vile."[23]

As the conflict went on, Freud moved between such feelings and his support for the Central Powers. In July 1915, for example, he gave "our beautiful victories" credit for his own "increased capacity for work."[24] Such work, in 1915, included *Reflections on War and Death*. While much material in these texts is rational and analytical, the tone is tempered by a dark knowledge that Freud, too, had had his own imagination stirred by patriotism, that his own impulses in late 1914 and early 1915 had been less than refined.

There are passages in which Freud seems to be studying his own confusion as the war broke out, how he himself was implicated in the pathology suffered by newborn patriots all over Europe: "Seized by the whirlwind of this wartime, tendentiously informed, lacking distance from the great changes that have already taken place or are beginning to take place, and without having wind of the future that is in the process of forming, we begin to be confused about the significance of the impressions that intrude upon us and the value of the judgments we form."[25]

———

In his *Reflections of a Nonpolitical Man*, published in 1918, Thomas Mann pondered on the relationship between the individual and the state: "It is the state that sets definite limits to human activity, to all human life and striving, and only within these limits can the human being prove his worth. It is the state that attempts to settle social conflicts, brings them *closer* to a reconciliation, and here it shows itself to be a necessary condition of culture."[26]

In his book, Mann held "that democracy, politics itself, is foreign and poisonous to the German character. . . . I am deeply convinced that the German people will never be able to love political democracy simply because they cannot love politics itself, and that the much decried 'authoritarian state' is and remains the one that is proper and becoming to the German people, and the one they basically want."[27]

What is curious about this passage is its resort to the word "love," as though politics were a matter of deep emotion. Mann was seeking to analyze the inner life of the German people. The German character appeared here as opaque, hidden, almost neurotic. In his "Thoughts in Wartime," Mann would go further, like a man inviting psychoanalysts into his realm as necessary interpreters of his own hysteria. He wrote that "depth and irrationality suit the German soul. . . . It is the Germans' 'militarism,' their ethical conservatism, their soldierly morality, that daemonic and heroic something that resists accepting the civilian spirit as the highest human ideal. . . . The Germans are truly the most unknown people in Europe. . . . You wanted to catch us, constrain us, wipe us out. But as you have discovered, Germany will defend its deep, hated self like a lion."[28]

———

In the opening pages of his essay on war, Freud was concerned about the state; he expressed disappointment at the ways in which "the great ruling nations of the white race, the leaders of mankind" had behaved. These same nations, he wrote, "set a high moral standard to which the individual had to conform if he wished to be a member of the civilized community."[29]

Above all, Freud noted, the individual "was forbidden to resort to lying and cheating," and "these moral standards" were "the foundation of its existence." Now, in wartime, the state forbade the citizen to do wrong "not because it wishes to do away with wrongdo-ing but because it wishes to monopolize it, like salt and tobacco."[30]

Freud wrote with great beauty and idealism about the idea of "a newer and greater fatherland" to which people from outside could travel, to which there would no paranoid feelings about be-longing. He wrote of "the blue and grey ocean, the beauty of snow-clad mountains and of the green lowlands, the magic of the north woods and the grandeur of southern vegetation, the atmosphere of landscapes upon which great historical memories left, and the peace of untouched nature."[31]

He outlined this sweet dream before he returned to the night-mare of the present. And this nightmare happened first in the pub-lic sphere. "The great nations themselves," he writes, "one should have thought, had acquired sufficient understanding for the quali-ties they had in common and enough tolerance for their differ-ences so that, unlike in the days of classical antiquity, the words 'foreign' and 'hostile' should no longer be synonyms."[32]

But the nightmare was also being enacted in his own mind, in his own language. He was writing about Germany when he re-ferred to "one of these great civilized nations" that "has become so universally disliked." And he went on: "We live in the hope that impartial history will furnish the proof that this very nation, in which language I am writing and for whose victory our dear ones are fighting, has sinned least against the laws of human civilization. But who is privileged to step forward at such a time as judge in his own defence?"[33]

Freud was thus writing in a time when both the state and indi-viduals had joined one another in giving in to base impulses. "Two things have roused our disappointment in this war: the feeble mo-rality of states in their external relations which have inwardly acted as guardians of moral standards, and the brutal behavior of indi-viduals of the highest culture of whom one would not have be-lieved any such thing possible."[34]

Freud noted that nations seemed even more in need of treat-ment than patients. Nations "are perhaps repeating the development of the individual and at the present day still exhibit very primitive stages of development with a correspondingly slow progress towards the formation of higher unities. . . . It seems that nations obey their passions of the moment far more than their interests. At most they make use of their interests to justify the gratification of their passions."[35]

Freud found "an outer compulsion to morality," which was active in individuals, to be "barely perceptible" in nations. But, in wartime, this compulsion had given way to "the brutal behavior of individuals." This caused Freud to "wonder that evil should appear again so actively in persons who have been educated." He recognized "that the deepest character of man consists of impulses of an elemental kind which are similar in all human beings, the aim of which is the gratification of certain primitive needs." In psychoanalytical language, he found a kind of metaphor for his own state of being in two minds: "many impulses appear almost from the beginning in contrasting pairs; this is a remarkable state of affairs called the ambivalence of feeling."[36]

The war had emphasized for Freud how thin the veneer of "civilized obedience" was. Society, by placing "ethical demands as high as possible," had thereby forced "its members to move still further from their emotional dispositions. A continual emotional suppression was imposed on them, the strain of which is indicated by the appearance of the most remarkable reactions and compensations."[37]

Thoughts of war moved to thoughts of death. In July 1915, Freud dreamed "very clearly the death of my sons, Martin first of all."[38] He then learned that on the day of the dream, his son Martin was, in fact, wounded at the Russian front.

The war, he thought, had changed the response to death: "People really die and no longer one by one, but in large numbers, often ten thousand in one day." The edict "Thou shalt not kill," Freud wrote, "arose as a reaction against the gratification of hate for the beloved dead which is concealed behind grief, and was gradually extended to the unloved stranger and finally also to the enemy."[39]

Now, because of the war, "civilized man no longer feels this way in regard to killing enemies. When the fierce struggle of this war will have reached a conclusion every victorious warrior will joyfully and without delay return home to his wife and children, undisturbed by thoughts of the enemy he has killed either at close quarters or with weapons operating at a distance."[40]

Freud wrote about primitive man's ambivalent attitude toward death. "On the one hand he took death very seriously, recognized it as the termination of life, and made use of it in this sense; but, on the other hand, he also denied death and reduced it to nothingness." Now, with war, primitive man had returned: "War strips off the later deposits of civilization and allows the primitive man in us to reappear. It forces us again to be heroes who cannot believe in their own death; it stamps all strangers as enemies whose death we ought to cause or wish; it counsels us to rise above the death of those whom we love."[41]

—

By the time the war broke out, Freud's work was, indeed, known to writers such as Thomas Mann; one of Freud's disciples had even treated Henry James. In a lecture given in 1936 to mark Freud's eightieth birthday, Thomas Mann wrote: "The close relationship between literature and psychoanalysis has been known for a long time to both sides."[42]

In the lecture, Mann described his own relationship to psychoanalysis: "It would be too much to say that I came to psychoanalysis. It came to me. Through the friendly interest that some younger writers in the field had shown in my work . . . it gave me to understand that in my way I 'belonged'; it made me aware, as probably behoved it, of my own latent, preconscious sympathies; and when I began to occupy myself with the literature of psychoanalysis I recognized, arrayed in the language of scientific exactitude, much that had long been familiar to me through my youthful mental experiences."[43]

In 1911, after the death of his brother William, Henry James consulted two doctors in the United States after he had a kind of nervous breakdown. One of them was James Jackson Putnam, a close friend of his brother's, who in 1911 became the first president of the American Psychoanalytical Association. In 1909, Putnam was among those instrumental in bringing Freud to America. He wrote the introduction to the translation of Freud's *Three Contributions to the Theory of Sex*.

After his consultations with Putnam, James wrote to him about his efforts "to grasp the real clue to the labyrinth." He went on: "However, I am boring you to death (if I am not really interesting you!) and I only risk the former effect to possibly invoke the latter. It's a flood of egotism—but what are the Patient class but egotistic, especially in proportion as it's grateful? You tided me over three or four bad places during those worst months."[44]

In his letter to Putnam, James mentions a visit to another, less reputable doctor, Joseph Collins, in New York, "after the last time of my seeing you. I had a bad crisis again there—and beyond being very kind and interested he did nothing for me at all."[45] Collins, in fact, prescribed "baths, massage and electrocutions." After James's death Collins wrote about him in a book called *The Doctor Looks at Biography*: "He put himself under my professional care and I saw him at close range nearly every day for two months, and talked with him, or listened to him, on countless subjects." Collins concluded that James "had an enormous amalgam of the feminine in his make-up; he displayed many of the characteristics of adult infantilism; he had a singular capacity for detachment from reality and with it a dependence on realities that was even pathetic. He had a dread of ugliness in all forms."[46]

Some of James's work and, indeed, some of Mann's, can be read as secret script in which the unconscious mind sought an outlet. Beneath the text, there is another one that if read carefully can make the text above seem like a set of poses and disguises, or indeed a set of traces and clues. In figures such as Hanno in *Buddenbrooks*, Aschenbach in *Death in Venice*, and some of the characters in *The*

Confessions of Felix Krull, Mann drew veiled self-portraits, just as James did in figures such as Ralph Touchett in *The Portrait of a Lady*, John Marcher in *The Beast in the Jungle*, and Spencer Brydon in *The Jolly Corner*.

In 1915, when asked about his novella *Death in Venice*, Mann wrote in a letter: "Certainly it is in the main a story of death, death as a seductive antimoral power—a story of the voluptuousness of doom."[47]

It is also, of course, a story about repressed desire; it is notable that Mann will use the word "voluptuousness" and then apply it to Thanatos rather than Eros. In 1915 he had reason to shift the emphasis, to make the story fit into the theme of death and do so in a time when death was everywhere.

—

When Freud sought to describe the precepts used by the state to induce self-restraint and a marked renunciation of primitive impulses, he used the ban "on lying and cheating" as his primary example, the "lying and cheating," he wrote, "which are so extraordinarily useful in competition with others."[48]

Both Henry James and Thomas Mann would have taken an interest in this. James's best work, for example, dramatized the power of lying and cheating. By avoiding any treatment of lying and cheating in the commercial realm and confining his drama to the personal sphere, James intensified the drama. He made it seem more rooted, more essential. In *The Portrait of a Lady* (1881), the primitive impulse is given to the most ostensibly civilized people. The more evolved their manners and the more developed their style, the more intense their lying and cheating.

In James's last three novels—*The Wings of the Dove* (1902), *The Ambassadors* (1903), and *The Golden Bowl* (1904)—some of the characters, usually a pair who are bound together by heterosexual passion, manage to deceive and trick other characters. The cheating ones portray themselves as sophisticated and cultured. In their manners, in their ways of speaking and moving in society, they are quite advanced. But in their appetites and their slyness, in their willingness to pounce and retreat, in their base greed, they have instincts that are primitive.

In 1911, Thomas Mann wrote a story called "Felix Krull," penned as a confession by a trickster, a chancer, a liar, a cheat, a hotel thief. Feeling it was incomplete, Mann abandoned it to write *Death in Venice*. Forty years later, however, in California, he resumed work on what became *The Confessions of Felix Krull*, his last work of fiction. "It is truly curious," he wrote to a friend, "to take up the old fragment again after four decades and all I have done in between. I have actually resumed on the self-same page of Munich Manuscript paper (from Prantl on Odeonsplatz) where I stopped at that time, unable to go on."[49]

Like many figures in the picaresque tradition or the tradition of fake confessions or fictional memoir writing, Krull is untrustworthy, but he is not ashamed. Instead, he is amused, amusing. He will always manage to escape. He will not be punished for his crimes. Mann's task is to lure the reader into Krull's amoral, subversive space, all the more to beguile the reader, remove the reader from a sphere in which lying and cheating are viewed as primitive and must be left behind.

Thus, Mann and James, despite their advanced narrative methods, were holding the fort for images of the primitive instinct, the instinct that preachers deplored and legislatures sought to criminalize. James's untrustworthy and duplicitous characters— Madame Merle, Gilbert Osmond, Kate Croy, Charlotte Stant, to name but some—feel free to move from the moral shadows into the amoral light. Mann's trickster can brilliantly use his intelligence and his good looks to fool anyone who comes into his orbit.

If such novels of lying and cheating had not existed, would our knowledge of what it means to lie and cheat be confined to court reports, bad sermons, folktales, and old ballads?

Mann and James, as they worked on their images of subterfuge and chicanery, were not deliberately exploring a deep unconscious.

If they had tried this, they would have failed. Their work is all the more powerful, dangerous, and telling because it is suggestive rather than prescriptive, with implications that may have been unintended.

But their work is not innocent as it sets about raising images from the lower depths to the glittering surface, thus undermining the "moral standards" that, Freud writes, "the civilized state considered . . . the foundations of its existence."[50]

Thus, Mann and James had been dealing with the primitive all along. It did not take much, as Freud would have understood, for further base instincts to emerge in them as war broke out in 1914.

THE OPEN-ARMED, BECKONING EMBRACE

Thomas Lynch

My daughter leapt to her death off the Golden Gate Bridge. It was early July in that first god-awful summer of Covid, and the last cankerous year of the Trump presidency. It was the summer of George Floyd and John Lewis and Ruth Bader Ginsburg. Whether any or all of these grim contingencies had anything to do with her suicide, it is impossible to know. Nor do we know if she acted on an impulse or planned it in advance. She had driven across the country, leaving her husband and carrying a torch for an unrequited love—a man she'd gone to a prom with decades before, hadn't seen in years, and who had unambiguously rejected her sudden advances. She'd been hospitalized and diagnosed with schizophrenia earlier in the year—a diagnosis and treatment she never agreed to or accepted. A court, on the testimony of her medicos, had determined she was, indeed, a threat to herself and to others, so supplied her husband with an order that approved her rehospitalization if she ceased to take her prescribed medication. But hospital beds for the mentally ill filled with the breathless victims of the pandemic. Her escape from husband and home and further hospitalization created a reality that tendered constricting options. She drove west to the ocean and then turned left. She never made it across the bridge.

Because her suicide happened on a holiday weekend, and because she was a couple thousand miles from home, the news was not traced back to her family in Michigan until the following week. There were few details: there were witnesses to her leap, which was filmed by the closed-circuit cameras on the bridge, a popular venue for those seeking oblivion and abyss. She was fourteen minutes in the water, and after recovery, her body was taken to the Marin County morgue under the name of Jane Doe. Eventually, authorities Googled the name on the rental car agreement they found in the vehicle left on the bridge and traced her back to family in Michigan at the funeral home that they operate in her hometown. Her brother Michael got the call from the coroner on a Tuesday afternoon. He called me up at the lake where I was quarantined against the pestilence. I called her mother, her stepmother, her other brothers, her godfather. Then I called a firm of funeral directors in San Francisco who had my long-dead mother's maiden surname and told the young woman in charge to please get my daughter out of the morgue and ready her for transport home. Michael flew out to California to escort his sister's body home. He called from the embalming room of the O'Hara Funeral Home to say it was Heather Grace, his sister, my daughter, there on the porcelain table. His brother Sean and I met him at our local airport late Thursday afternoon and waited at Air Freight to get her into our hearse and home again. We got her back, alas, to let her go again. She was laid out for a limited (by pandemic policies) visitation on Saturday. Her parents and brothers, aunts and uncles, cousins and close friends kept a quiet vigil. Her female cousins served as pallbearers, bearing her wicker coffin to the grave, where she was buried on Sunday afternoon in Oak Grove Cemetery. There's a stone there now with her name and dates on it, to wit, *Heather Grace, 1975–2020*.

———

We stand upon the brink of a precipice. We peer into the abyss—we grow sick and dizzy. Our first impulse is to shrink from the danger.

Unaccountably we remain. By slow degrees our sickness and dizziness and horror become merged in a cloud of unnameable feeling. By gradations, still more imperceptible, this cloud assumes shape, as did the vapor from the bottle out of which arose the genius in the Arabian Nights. But out of this our cloud upon the precipice's edge, there grows into palpability, a shape, far more terrible than any genius or any demon of a tale, and yet it is but a thought, although a fearful one, and one which chills the very marrow of our bones with the fierceness of the delight of its horror. It is merely the idea of what would be our sensations during the sweeping precipitancy of a fall from such a height. And this fall—this rushing annihilation— for the very reason that it involves that one most ghastly and loathsome of all the most ghastly and loathsome images of death and suffering which have ever presented themselves to our imagination—for this very cause do we now the most vividly desire it. And because our reason violently deters us from the brink, therefore do we the most impetuously approach it. There is no passion in nature so demoniacally impatient, as that of him who, shuddering upon the edge of a precipice, thus meditates a plunge. To indulge, for a moment, in any attempt at thought, is to be inevitably lost; for reflection but urges us to forbear, and therefore it is, I say, that we cannot. If there be no friendly arm to check us, or if we fail in a sudden effort to prostrate ourselves backward from the abyss, we plunge, and are destroyed.

—"THE IMP OF THE PERVERSE," EDGAR ALLAN POE, 1845

In the fifth paragraph of his story "The Imp of the Perverse," Edgar Allan Poe dispassionately describes the impulse to destroy oneself as this "imp"—a mischievous devil child—the "death wish" or Thanatos, Sigmund Freud would call it, half a century later, and fashion it the countervailing psychic energy to Eros, the life instinct.

Shakespeare puts the rhetorical question "To be or not to be?" up front in Hamlet's soliloquy, which he wrote early in the seventeenth century. Some few years earlier he had investigated the dark

imbroglios of love and death in *Romeo and Juliet,* as a harbinger for
Freud's "Mourning and Melancholia," three centuries later.

As with the English bard, so too the Irish master: "I am still of
the opinion," wrote the old poet W. B. Yeats to his former lover
Olivia Shakespeare in October of 1927, "that only two topics can
be of the least interest to a serious and studious mood—sex and
the dead."[1]

This bifurcation of the human enterprise—an impulse to be
and the contrary impulse to cease to be—accounts for so much
that undergirds our lived experience and requires that we learn
these equal and opposing gravities, to achieve a kind of balance
between opposite poles and their magnetics.

Among my first recollections around these themes involved a
young man whose funeral was handled by my father's funeral home
when I was in my teens. What was known about this poor client
was that he was damaged by a broken heart, which was the predi-
cate for destroying himself with the shotgun he pulled from the
rack of same he found in the bedroom of his former girlfriend's
father's house. She had, apparently, broken up with him the week
before, and, fraught with feelings he had never experienced before,
he kept calling her frantically on the phone. When she stopped
answering his calls, he went over to her house, ran through the
front door and up the stairs to the master bedroom, broke the lock
on the rifle cabinet, pulled a shotgun from the assorted long rifles,
and lay on the erstwhile girlfriend's parents' bed. Placing the muzzle
of the gun in his mouth, he managed to pull the trigger with his toe,
accomplishing in horrendous fashion the "overwhelming gesture"
his diary later explained he wanted to offer his former sweetheart
of his devotion to her. It was the notebook his parents brought to
the funeral home when they came to meet with my father and ar-
range the dead boy's funeral. I held the door of our emporium open
for them as they came and went on the day. They were vacant faced
in their desolation but managed to thank me coming and going. I
wore a black suit, white shirt, striped tie, and polished wingtip
shoes, and worked for an hourly wage to buy cigarettes and date

girls and put gas in my car. I'd no clue about the future or the past. I lived in the moment like the gift the present is.

I've often wondered if my father planned for me to see this poor boy's corpse in case I might, as often young men do, harbor thoughts of such convincing gestures. He could have sent the boy's clothes down to the embalming room with one of the embalmers but rather called me up to his office, after the parents left, to have me take the blue jeans and plaid shirt, underwear and cowboy boots down to the basement where the bodies were. And when I saw the body on the embalming table, unembalmed, I could see his skull split like a hapless pumpkin by the gun's dull power. Whatever else his gesture accomplished, I thought standing there, the dead pilgrim looked ridiculous, with the cleavage of his cranium, above the nose leaving him a grim cartoon of his former self. If I'd ever had any romantic notions about suicide, the sight of this poor grotesquery banished from my mind any remnant of them. And though I've had some aggressive, downright murderous designs on politicos and bad drivers, I've never thought that I should be the target of my violence. Still, the vision of that dead boy's ruined body remains alive in my imagination. A poem by which I sought to address the swithering in-betweenness of equal and opposing gravities, emblematic of my astrological sign of Libra, represented by the scales of justice, was an effort to understand my own double-mindedness and includes a reference to the horrendous suicide.

Libra

The one who pulled the trigger with his toe,
spread-eagled on his girlfriend's parents' bed,
and split his face in halves above his nose,
so that one eye looked east, the other west;
sometimes that sad boy's bifurcation seems
to replicate the math of love and grief—
that zero sum of holding on and letting go

by which we split the differences with those
with whom we occupy the present moment.
Sometimes I see that poor corpse as a token
of doubt's sure twin and double-mindedness,
of certainty, the countervailing guess,
the swithering, the dither, righteousness,
like Libra's starry arms outstretched in love
or supplication or, at last, surrender
to the scales forever tipped in the cold sky.

—from *Bone Rosary—New and Selected Poems*, 2021[2]

———

It is known that in the more serious cases of psychoneuroses one
sometimes finds self-mutilations as symptoms of the disease. That
the psychic conflict may end in suicide can never be excluded in
these cases. Thus, I know from experience, which someday I shall
support with convincing examples, that many apparently accidental
injuries happening to such patients are really self-inflicted. This is
brought about by the fact that there is a constantly lurking tendency
to self-punishment, usually expressing itself in self-reproach, or
contributing to the formation of a symptom, which skillfully makes
use of an external situation. The required external situation may
accidentally present itself or the punishment tendency may assist it
until the way is open for the desired injurious effect.

— *THE PSYCHOPATHOLOGY OF EVERYDAY LIFE*,
SIGMUND FREUD, 1901

By the time Sigmund Freud breathed his last, his dog recoiled
from the stench of his oral cancer—the toll of his addiction to
cigars. And when the Nazis came to Vienna, he fled to London,
where another refugee, Max Schur, promised to assist him, with
morphine, out of the predicament of his painful and grotesque
terminal cancer. He died on September 23, 1939, and soon after was

cremated at Golders Green Crematorium, where his urn and ashes remain these decades later when the notion of "assisted suicide" would define the context of Freud's demise.

As with the late-twentieth-century iterations by Jack Kevorkian, a.k.a. Dr. Death, Freud's overdoses of morphine were more an agreeable homicide than an assisted suicide. The outcome is the same, to wit, the former being has ceased to be but the etymology of suicide does not allow for any assistance. It refers to a killing *of and by oneself*—the operative syllable there being *sui*, or "one," much as assisted sex is more romance than masturbation.

So Poe and Freud and the poets agree: we humans hanker for a balancing between the will to live fully and the will to die, between love and grief, the longing to be and to cease to be, between intimate attachments and deadly detachments. But what is clear from each of these nineteenth- and early twentieth-century paradigms: the seed of our own demise is bred into the bone and sinew of our coming to be. Which is why *la petite mort*, the little death, commonly refers to the moment of ecstasy and lost consciousness associated with orgasmic sexual ecstasy, sung into an old folk song by Paul Stookey of Peter, Paul and Mary:

> Some girls will die for money,
> Some will die as they're born,
> Some will swear they'd die for love,
> Some die ev'ry morn.[3]

It is a haunting tune and haunting concept—that love and death belly up to the same bar. I read Freud and Poe, Shakespeare and Yeats in my late teens, and possibly the commingling of their theories took shape in my own particular curiosities about self-harm and suicide.

In her classic text *On Bullfighting*, the Scottish writer A. L. Kennedy reports that this fact—that she might look ridiculous in death (she was planning to leap from her fourth-floor window in Glasgow because she was suffering from an extreme case of writer's block)—along with the blaring of "Marie's Wedding" on a car radio down the block, were sufficient to bring her off the ledge and safely inside to live to write another day, and other books.

But whether the confrontation of suicide inoculates against the contemplation of suicide, or the choice of a soundtrack for the occasion makes a difference, it is hard to know; like much about self-destruction, whether plan or impulse is to blame, most of it remains a mystery secure behind the locked door of purpose and intention.

Freud knew as much, which may account for his reticence in addressing the issue comprehensively in text. The closest he seems to come is in "Mourning and Melancholia," where he suggests as a cause the failure to deal effectively with one's response to the experience of a "lost object," a person or circumstance or identity that has become central to someone's sense of self:

> If the love for the object—a love which cannot be given up though the object itself is given up—takes refuge in narcissistic identification, then the hate comes into operation on this substitutive object, abusing it, debasing it, making it suffer and deriving sadistic satisfaction from its suffering. The self-tormenting in melancholia, which is without doubt enjoyable, signifies, just like the corresponding phenomenon in obsessional neurosis, a satisfaction of trends of sadism and hate which relate to an object, and which have been turned round upon the subject's own self in the ways we have been discussing. In both disorders the patients usually still succeed, by the circuitous path of self punishment, in taking revenge on the original object and in tormenting their loved one through their illness, having resorted to it in order to avoid the need to express their hostility to him openly. After all, the person who has occasioned the patient's emotional disorder, and on whom his illness is centred, is usually to be found in his immediate environment. The melancholic's erotic cathexis in regard to his object has thus undergone a double vicissitude: part of it has regressed to identification, but the other part, under the influence of the conflict due to

ambivalence, has been carried back to the stage of sadism, which is nearer to that conflict.

In this work Freud finds that mourning and melancholia, grief and depression, are, to borrow an Irish bromide, "the same but different." Whereas mourning is the natural and healthy response to the loss, often the death, of a beloved person, melancholia, what we might call today a sort of chronic depression, becomes a pathology, a disease that works its way through life and time and ends, sometimes, with the final, fatal symptom of the illness, suicide.

In much the same way as the acute myocardial infarction becomes the final fatal symptom of coronary artery disease, my daughter's leap from the Golden Gate Bridge was the final fatal symptom of the depression, the melancholia, the psychological distress she'd suffered from most of her life. Her long estrangement from her family of origin, her disavowal of her paternalistic family name, her difficulty in holding onto meaningful employment and long-term relationships, the grandiosity of her plans compared to the paucity of achievements—all of these, in retrospect, seem like symptoms of a pathology, no doubt related to unmanaged loss, which nonetheless left her with few paths toward remediation. Furthermore, it might well have been exacerbated by her confinement, her hospitalization against her will just months before while in the midst of a psychotic episode, which neither she nor any of her family, myself included, had any experience with, rendering us all helpless to intervene in any corrective way. That I had spent two years and more in weekly joint therapy sessions with her does not, in hindsight, comfort much. Her troubles were outside the range of talk therapy. Mostly I believe that the suicides I have known were too cruelly permanent in their outcomes for the temporary, though intense, distress they sought to relieve. We've all had times when we did not want to be alive tomorrow, but the rate of suicide, those who wanted to be dead tomorrow, remains minuscule but convincing.

Whether the lost object that figured into my daughter's painful case was the fantasy of love with a former prom date, a disappointing marriage, or the end of her family as occasioned by her parents' divorce when she was nine years old is hard to know. Possibly her melancholia was hereditary. Her schizophrenia surely echoed symptoms her maternal grandmother had in her menopausal years. Still, all we get as bereaved survivors of suicide is the occasional glimpse at intention and motive, a momentary look into the sad heart of self-destruction.

In the months following my daughter's suicide, I would wake in the middle of the night with a sense of the acceleration of a body falling through space in pursuit of the thirty-two feet per second squared, which is said to be the speed of gravity. It was neither a fright nor comfort, only a momentary effort at knowing what my daughter's last sensations might have been. The rest, the answers, much as Freud's inconclusive writing on the subject suggest, remain just out of reach. As Tim Buckley sings in "Song to the Siren," "I'm as puzzled as an oyster / I'm as troubled as the tide."[4]

In the long years of my daughter's estrangement from her family of origin, I used to tell my nearest and dearests that a death in the family came with consolations—social, ritual observances, protocols and traditions—whereas none had developed around the predicament of estrangement, the renouncing of family connections and communications by one of its central members. In some ways, I was in the habit of saying, estrangement is more difficult than a death in the family. I was wrong.

In "Mourning and Melancholia" Freud writes:

> The analysis of melancholia now shows that the ego can kill itself only if, owing to the return of the object-cathexis, it can treat itself as an object—if it is able to direct against itself the hostility which relates to an object and which represents the ego's original reaction to objects in the external world.

To destroy oneself, according to Freud, the obsession formerly aimed at the lost and beloved object must be turned on oneself.

The pain of being seeks relief in the distant and permanent parish of ceasing to be, from which there is, alas, no return.

When I think of my daughter on the Golden Gate, I pray she saw the open, beckoning embrace of the abyss and heard the seductive song of the siren promising surcease, release, relief, oblivion. I pray the melancholia, its manic poor cousin, the paranoia, the desolation were all transformed, as love transforms the broken heart to hope.

THE TALKING CURE

THE FREUDS

Casey Schwartz

I arrived in Freud world when I was twenty-three, my possessions stuffed into two suitcases, or left behind in a thoughtless heap in Los Angeles, forfeited to the parallel life that now wasn't going to happen. By Freud world, I am not referring to the infamous Viennese address, Berggasse 19, but rather to Freud's final residence, 20 Maresfield Gardens, Hampstead, London.

Here, among these hushed, tree-lined North London streets, an imposing statue puts you on notice: at the base of stately Fitzjohn's Avenue, Freud is captured in bronze, seated but leaning forward in a posture of glowering intensity, as if to pounce on you with his discerning insight.

I had arrived, I discovered, at the very epicenter of a small but thriving psychoanalytic universe, a neighborhood complete with training institutes (two) and a devoted bookstore, Karnac, where you could acquire every text necessary to parse the local language: the highly precise vocabulary with which psychoanalysts had fitted out the human psyche. Repression and projection and reaction formation were now everyday terms. Phantasy was not to be confused for fantasy; *imago* no mere image. Here, I discovered, even in the digital hustle and bustle of the year 2006, the old analog mind was still treated as an object of wonder and reverence.

I had come for graduate school, to study psychoanalysis. I thought that I was going to work in the field of psychology, and I couldn't imagine a better entry point than on Maresfield Gardens.

Freud himself had arrived here in 1938, finally convinced to leave Nazi-occupied Vienna on pain of death, already himself dying from jaw cancer, with his wife, his sister-in-law, his housekeeper, and his youngest daughter, Anna Freud. In fact, the Freuds very nearly didn't manage it: soon after Hitler marched into Austria, they were visited by Nazi thugs, who raided their perfectly appointed bourgeois apartment. Calmly, Anna Freud led them to the safe, unlocked it, and offered them all the money inside: six thousand shillings, or about $840. ("I have never taken so much for a single visit," Freud later wryly commented, according to the historian Andrew Nagorski, who captures the whole scene in his book, *Saving Freud*.)

By then, the Viennese consulates were thronged with desperate Jews, seeking the paperwork that would let them out of Austria, and the separate paperwork that would let them in somewhere else. Most did not succeed. Because Freud had rich and powerful friends like Princess Marie Bonaparte, and the former American ambassador to France William Bullitt, he, along with the members of his household, did get out, as did his treasured possessions: the collections of statuettes from ancient Greece and Egypt, many of his books, and of course his iconic analytic couch, with its oriental carpets, and its ghosts. But his four sisters remained in Vienna. In their seventies and eighties, they would all perish at the hands of the Nazis.

Freud never learned of his sisters' fates. Safely installed in London, on Maresfield Gardens, in a three-story red brick house, drenched in sunlight, and overlooking a rose garden, he lived and worked until his death, a year later, just as the war began. And it was here, on Maresfield Gardens, where his daughter Anna lived too, and practiced in a consulting room of her own, upstairs. She hung a portrait of her father on the wall directly above the analytic couch where she treated her patients. Which tells us something, no? Certainly no psychoanalyst would overlook that detail, that portrait on the wall. Anna's devotion to her father, it seemed, was limitless.

I thought of this history often, this father and daughter. Their stories lived on in the education we received, directly across the street from their house, at 21 Maresfield Gardens. Our school was named for her: the Anna Freud Centre.

From the beginning, Anna had to fight against long odds for her father's attention. The youngest of his six children, she was born, it is often said, the same year as psychoanalysis: 1895, the year her father published his first major psychoanalytic work, *Studies on Hysteria*. She was a mischievous child with flashing dark eyes. Her older sister Sophie was considered the family beauty.

Anna learned early about the work that so preoccupied her father, that kept him in his consulting room all day with his patients, and up writing until late in the night. One evening, when Anna was fourteen, she and her father went for a walk together after dinner. As they passed the stately homes near Vienna's Prater, the public park in Leopoldstadt, father turned to daughter. "You see those houses with their lovely facades?" he asked. "Things are not necessarily so lovely behind the facades. And so it is with human beings, too." This exchange is included in Elisabeth Young-Bruehl's penetrating biography of Anna Freud.

According to Young-Bruehl, Anna longed for her father, for walks with him, trips with him, time with him. At seventeen, Anna was sent alone to Italy, to a pensione in Merano, as her family were absorbed in preparations for Sophie's upcoming wedding in Hamburg. Anna wrote every day to her father and vented that he didn't properly reciprocate. After all, she wrote, she was "the one who is soon to be your only daughter."

Unlike her five siblings, Anna never left home and never married. She was rewarded for it. By 1915, Freud was writing about her to Sándor Ferenczi: "She is developing into a charmer, by the way. More delightful than any other of the children."

"Her father was her model for group leadership and for triumph over moods, and he was her interior model, her standard setter, her ego ideal," writes Young-Bruehl. "Rationality and lucidity were her goals for both inner and outer domains, and they were her counters to anger, jealousy, rivalry."

So it was inevitable, if anything can be said to be inevitable, that Anna would turn to psychoanalysis: first, as her father's patient, unorthodox as that might seem, with all the parsing of her inner-most impulses and masturbation fantasies that that relationship implies; and then as a practitioner herself. She had first trained and worked as a schoolteacher; now, she became interested in psycho-analytic treatment of children, and theories of childhood.

Freud encouraged that in her. In fact, he famously remarked, in 1925, that "the future of analysis belongs to child analysis." Freud had written one case study of a five-year-old boy with a phobia of horses, known as "Little Hans." But the field of child analysis did not truly begin to develop until the 1920s, with Anna Freud's involvement, as well as the work of a handful of colleagues and counterparts.

As the years went by, the symbiosis between father and daughter only expanded. As his oral cancer advanced, she was the only one who was allowed to attend to her father's painful, prob-lematic prosthetic jaw. Gradually, in many ways, she replaced her mother as her father's caretaker and partner.

Her father died on September 23, 1939, mere weeks after Hitler marched into Poland and Great Britain declared war on Germany. The following year, as London braced for the Blitz, Anna opened the Hampstead War Nurseries, for children displaced by the war, the bombs, or any other kind of "billeting problem." Here, she and a handful of colleagues, almost all of them women, took in nearly two hundred babies and children throughout the war.

Anna Freud was an avid knitter and weaver—she often knit during sessions with patients—and she kept a loom in her bed-room. It was on this loom that she created net-like coverings to install around the cribs in the Hampstead nurseries' bomb shel-ters. They looked like cages, but if the German bombs jolted the babies, Anna's nets would prevent them falling on the floor.

So much was unknown about child psychology, still. There was a widespread view of children as a family's property, or that children were like weeds, destined to grow in any kind of soil. It's startling now to recognize that until the war, with all its displacements and upheavals, no one had quite understood that separating children from their parents could be an earth-shattering trauma, more so even than living through the fire of a hundred German bombs. In fact, it was Anna Freud and colleagues who helped drive home the critical importance of the first three years of life on a child's development. Seeing how disturbed the children in her nurseries were by being separated from their families, Anna encouraged parents to be involved to whatever extent they possibly could, visiting, or writing letters. After the war, nearly all the children in her nurseries were reunited with their families. She continued to follow them in the years to come, sending them cards and gifts. She never had children of her own.

The war nurseries served as a kind of observational bonanza, a close-up look at child development in extreme circumstances. "The variation in the case material made it possible to see children, almost from birth, in contact with their mothers or deprived of mother care, breast-fed or bottle-fed, in the throes of separation or reunited with their lost objects, in contact with their mother substitutes and teachers, and developing relations with their contemporaries," she wrote. "The stages of libidinal and aggressive development, the process and the effects of weaning and toilet training, the acquisition of speech and of the various ego functions could be followed closely." (Her writing is included in the psychoanalyst Nick Midgley's book *Reading Anna Freud*.)

Midgley's book shows how Anna Freud's observations of these children, and her native intuition, facilitated in her a child-centric vision of the world that was often commented on by the people she worked with. After the war, she opened the Hampstead Clinic at 21 Maresfield Gardens. Later, this building would be renamed the Anna Freud Centre. When a three-year-old girl was provoking negative feelings in the clinic's staff by relentlessly showing off, Anna Freud turned to one of them and said, quietly: "But what can we expect when this child was separated from her mother at just the time she still desperately needed to be with her?" It doesn't seem much, this remark, but the fact that it had to be made at all, and that it was made with such apparent effect, is revealing. Her words allowed the other adults in the room to access their empathy for the difficult child once more. The wartime years of close observation provided the foundation for some of Anna Freud's most enduring contributions, like her developmental lines, still referred to today, dividing childhood into psychological phases, and showing how children proceed through or diverge from them.

She also continued to work with adults. The American psychoanalyst in training Arthur Couch (with a name like that, what else could he do?) wrote a vivid, touching portrait of Anna, as he encountered her in London in the 1960s, when he went into a training analysis with her. In a paper he titled "Anna Freud's Adult Psychoanalytic Technique: A Defense of Classical Analysis," he gives a rare description of receiving psychoanalytic training from her. "The most striking characteristic of Anna Freud as an analyst was her very natural manner during sessions. She was very relaxed and unconstrained in feeling free to talk to me as I came from the waiting room or as I was leaving," he wrote. "There were no constrictions on ordinary brief comments off the couch. Even on the couch, she was responsive to my realistic questions and answered them in an ordinary way."

Couch had arrived in London filled with assumptions about rigid Freudian orthodoxies. But he found that Anna was quite loose, more natural and conversational, more human, than his fantasy of what she would be like. Her father had been too—he had kept his famous dogs, Chows, in the consulting room during sessions and often strolled out with his patients into the waiting room after their session, chatting and telling jokes.

Again and again, Couch noted Anna Freud's simplicity, practicality, and calm. He spent several sessions preoccupied with a depressed young woman patient he himself was treating. The trouble was he couldn't hear this woman—she spoke barely above a whisper. He had been stuck on this lack of volume, not knowing how to understand it, or what to do about it.

"With the help of my supervisor, I had tried out a number of interpretations in an attempt to solve this symptomatic soft whispering with me. Some attempts were made to interpret it as resistance: such as the patient was afraid of my reproach about her thoughts; or she felt guilty about them herself; or that all material was like sexual secrets; or that she didn't want me to hear anything about her, and so forth," Couch writes. Finally, Anna Freud looked up from her knitting to deliver her verdict. "Tell her to speak up."

"I recall telling her once that she had helped me see the value of common sense about analytic things," Couch writes, in the same account. "She said: 'The trouble with common sense is that it is so uncommon.'"

When I was a student in London, studying Anna Freud's foundational ideas about child psychology, I was filled with admiration for her courage, stoicism, and decades of pioneering work, but I found that I wasn't ignited by her in the same way that I had been by her father. I wondered about that. "I'm sorry to say it—she was a woman; she was not a genius. When a genius writes, there is always so much. More, and it is open to the whole world," Kurt Eissler, the former director of the Sigmund Freud Archives, once told the journalist Janet Malcolm, as Malcolm records in her masterful book, *In the Freud Archives*. It was an absurd remark of course, especially delivered to the ingenious Janet Malcolm of all people; but, Eissler's chauvinism aside, it was true that Anna's writing did not have the poetry and grandeur of her father's. I was coming to realize that these were the qualities—literary ones—that had lured me to London.

Sometimes we were visited by guest lecturers from the Tavistock, which was the other psychoanalytic training institute in Hampstead. Housed in a large concrete, bunker-style structure just two blocks away, the Tavistock represented the legacy of Melanie Klein,

Anna Freud's contemporary, with whom she did serious battle over theoretical differences. Klein, who had also fled to London from Vienna, took issue with many of Anna Freud's ideas about child psychology and child psychoanalysis, including when and how the Oedipus conflict occurs. Anna Freud and Melanie Klein debated their differences in a heated series of arguments known as "The Controversial Discussions," which took place as bombs fell on London during the war. But their differences were never resolved. Even in 2006, as I walked down Fitzjohn's Avenue past the Tavistock, I would peer into the fluorescent-lit rooms of candidates in training with a strange, almost inexplicable, sense of spying on the enemy.

After a few months in London, I understood that what I really wanted to do was write about human nature—not treat it. I often thought of the parallel life in Los Angeles I could have been living, the boyfriend I had left, and wondered if I'd made a mistake. I didn't yet know that my time among the Freudians of North London would become the subject of my first book—and that I would always carry the Freuds around in my heart, no matter how old-fashioned their reputation would become, no matter how much emphasis was put instead, increasingly, on the field of neuroscience, of brain activity measured in modern fMRI labs.

I returned to London in the parched summer of 2022, after a long time away. In the July heat, the normally verdant parks were all the color of dried straw. Hampstead Heath, forever emerald green in my memory, now looked like an enormous field of wheat, pale yellow in every direction. The world had changed in the years I'd been away. And the Anna Freud Centre had packed up and left Maresfield Gardens, for the less rarefied environs of King's Cross. But the Freud house, which is now the Freud Museum, remained. I went to Hampstead to pay homage, as always.

Walking through the blooming rose garden into the sun-drenched back entrance of their home, Freud's last on earth, I reflected on Anna's legacy, for the first time finding for myself the full emotion in it, the deep love and care she had bestowed on her patients, and, in some sense, on every child, everywhere. At a time when it was still rare, even revolutionary, Anna Freud had recognized and honored the rich particularity of children's inner life. She had raised that recognition to an art and a science, one to which we are still in debt today.

But of course, I saw things differently now. I would turn forty in a few weeks, and back home in New York, I had a two-year-old son. In the Freud house, the usual crowds gathered on the first floor, to gape at his analytic couch, with its chic pile of oriental carpets, and his collections of ancient godheads and statuettes. But I climbed the steps to the second floor, much emptier, to see his daughter's plain analytic couch, with her father's portrait directly above it. In the empty room, I studied the shelves, and for the first time, my eye fell on a small frame. Inside, a piece of paper, with this single remark she had once made, somewhere: "The more I became interested in psychoanalysis, the more I saw it as the road to the same kind of broad and deep understanding of human nature that writers possess." Or strive to possess, I thought. I gave my silent thanks to her and left.

MY OEDIPUS COMPLEX

David Michaelis

> The Greek myth seized on a compulsion which everyone recognizes because he has felt traces of it himself.
>
> —SIGMUND FREUD, LETTER TO WILHELM FLIESS,
> OCTOBER 15, 1897

It must mean something that I've never learned to keep my mouth shut about Sigmund Freud. The oral phase of this trouble, if that's what it was, first presented in sixth grade, when, one day in class, I decided to show off my newfound interest in girls by making a general announcement to my classmates, all boys.

Our teacher, Mr. Green—short, roundheaded, balding—was at the board, his back turned. I can't tell you what he had chalked there in his neat Palmer cursive, but I can clearly remember informing my cohort, "We all have Sigmund Freud to thank for that!"

Mr. Green turned slowly and looked at me with interest. His gaze flickered uncertainly: Was this a ten-year-old trying to be cute, or a boy hacking off, as displays of individualism were called at the St. Albans School for Boys in 1968? His eyes narrowed: he meant to get to the bottom of it, whatever it was.

Walter Green came around to the front of his desk and with an ominous calm asked me to explain myself. I wanted to, badly. I liked Mr. Green. He was a serious and gracious man, a book lover. In addition to his teaching duties, he served as administrator of the

Lower School library, a hushed sanctorum of Mylar-bound volumes that he taught us how to handle. The books on those shelves spoke to me, and I wanted to please the man in charge of them.

But I had blurted all I knew about Freud. I would have liked nothing better than to go back to being a sixth grader with library privileges but was now stuck with my new Viennese maturity.

Mr. Green's inquiring gaze was just tolerant enough for me to take one more shot—man to man, as I imagined it, or patient to doctor, as I now see it.

"Well," I said, "if it weren't for Sigmund Freud, none of us would be here, right?"

Mr. Green directed me to stay after class. I expected at least four demerits, if not eight, or the maximum twelve—the metrics of a medieval disciplinary system that would bring me back to Detention Hall on Saturday morning to copy out the Constitution of the United States or clip the baseball diamond with toenail scissors for one, two, or three hours. But Walter Green had no such punishment in mind. He kept it short and sweet, dryly suggesting that when it came to certain subjects, I would do better to keep my thoughts to myself, until I was in the Upper School and could "do my research." I thought he meant "with girls" and must have betrayed myself with a grin.

"The *library*, Dave," said a firm Walter Green. "You'll start at the Subject Index in the card catalog: under 'F.'"

But I had already started. With my mother, of course. Two years earlier, I had painted a picture of my Oedipus complex in fourth-grade art class.

I wish I could show you this thing. We'd been assigned to choose a random image from *Life* magazine as the source for that day's painting. I had picked a full-page black-and-white photograph of a landscape—a wide western highway at whose vanishing point a perfectly halved ball of sun straddled the horizon. I sketched the image from an aerial point of view (perspective wasn't taught until the sixth grade) and, when it was time to paint, thought myself clever to imagine *Life*'s monochrome photo in full color: the sky blue, the desert green, the roadway flooded from end to end with pink sundown light.

When school let out for Christmas, I took home my portfolio of that term's artwork, and presented the images to my mother, one by one. At the watercolor landscape, her face fell.

"Dave," she began, and stopped, uncertain what to say, because what could she say? She was holding a picture of a big fat pink penis.

Now, I've looked at this painting recently. Any adult looking at this landscape, I promise you: you do not see a rendering of a highway at sunset. You see a penis, undeniably erect. Brushwork around the setting sun clearly delineates a throbbing tip; and the ascending line of penciled dashes, which are either pavement markings or a cross section of urethra scientifically glimpsed just prior to ejaculation, suggest to the viewer that this thing is about to blow.

In my mother's hand, it all but screamed: *What would Freud say?*

My older brother, joining our holiday art exhibit, said, "Gross."

My mother began again: "Gee, Dave . . ."

Odd to hear caution infuse her usually delighted response. My artwork had often drawn unguarded comparison to prodigies of the Italian Renaissance. Even my IQ score had been a matter of maternal pride, my mother having been led to believe by the revered head of my preschool, who had cruelly admitted me and not my older brother, that my higher score was predictive of future excellence—indeed, that great and rosy things were expected of me.

Now, three years later, my parents were divorced; and I was plainly trying to fill big shoes, though not those of my father. My brother had proclaimed himself man of the house, promptly taking over where Dad had left off in the basement, "fixing" the fuses, crossing hot wires with neutral, so that one night he caused a large amount of current to flow, which overloaded the circuit, sent sparks showering, fuses popping, and a billow of smoke upward, as every room in the house went dark during Mom's book party for the famed US ambassador to India John Kenneth Galbraith. But that's another story. What was fixed by my parents' divorce was my role as Mom's sensitive, artistic genius. Yet until this Yuletide exhibition, she had never shown any need to treat with concern my flair for pleasing her with art.

"Gee, Dave," she said, an octave higher than usual, "you painted a phallic symbol."

Painted a what?

It might have been interesting to ask Mom where she thought she was going with this. What is clear to me now was her ambivalence—on the one hand, her thrilled approval that I'd painted anything so primitively expressive; on the other, her instinct for protecting the very artlessness that empowered me to hand over to the object of my not-yet-conscious desire this innocent . . . *projection*?

No wonder Mom and I didn't say anything more about it.

"*Really* gross," insisted Mr. Hot Wire.

2

What responsibility do we have to the parts of ourselves we least understand and have most successfully kept hidden, from ourselves above all? Isn't *that* what we have Sigmund Freud to thank for? The discovery that, by regularly meeting with a psychotherapist in a consulting room, and bringing to light through the mechanism of transference feelings we've kept out of conscious awareness, we might attain relief from the hurtful influence of those long-buried feelings and behaviors?

"Anna O.," the subject of Freud and Josef Breuer's famous case study, was the first to call it "the talking cure." Freud meanwhile developed the concept of the Oedipus complex, named for the Theban king who accidentally kills his father and marries his mother, to explain his theory of the stages of psychosexual development: "At a very early age the little boy develops an object-cathexis for his mother, which originally related to the mother's breast and is the earliest instance of an object-choice; his father the boy deals with by identifying himself with him. For a time these two relationships exist side by side, until the sexual wishes in regard to his mother become more intense and his father is perceived as an obstacle to them; from this the Oedipus complex develops."[1]

The great essayist Kenneth Tynan called it "a secret you don't know you're keeping."[2]

Well, I knew my secret. I was attracted to my mother. I just didn't experience this as a sexual feeling until the age of twelve, when I happened upon my mother doing something she had done all my life—nude sunbathing. That one awkward glimpse on that one summer day became my Eden. From that time and place I went forth ashamed of my new and now fully conscious knowledge of desire. And—to echo a million modern Adams—*it wasn't just physical.* I was her confidant; she was my mind reader. We were soulmates, a matching pair. That's how it was.

Or so I thought. As a boy, I had no way of appreciating my mother's core feelings about her own life. She was clear about many things in the world, but of herself her knowledge was slender. I'm not sure she would recognize herself—or her fury and grief at being replaced in my father's heart—in one contemporaneous snapshot, which I came across not long ago, while looking up something in Alfred Kazin's newly published journals. I was surprised to discover her there on page 358, "looking very creamy, and au fond, sulky as the devil." This was in May 1966, at an "art crowd" party in a Fifth Avenue apartment. Kazin, the renowned postwar intellectual, spotted "the incipiently angry Diana Tead Michaelis" across the room, but seems to have avoided making contact, drawn instead to the "girls at [the] party," who "all looked like models grown a little old." Kazin then puts an "energetic" married woman on the spit; he sizes her up at six-foot-eight-inches ("enough for a whole battalion to feast on") yet records no insight about the "incipient" or early stages of my mother's wrath as a single woman, pausing in his sexist jottings only to brand—or bookmark—her as "just divorced."[3]

As a boy, I wanted to know everything about Diana Tead Michaelis. The mystery I only gradually came to understand was that though she seemed to want to give that knowledge to me, she was hardest to know the closer I got. For all her confiding and deep-voiced intimacy, my mother kept her distance, like the moon. Just as her nudity was the more powerful *because* she was my mother, the remoteness in her character was desirable exactly because it read to me as unattainability. Loving her was loving from afar an idealized radiance—a lunar longing.

Which was the problem with my Oedipus complex. I remember in 1972, when Mom sent me at age fifteen to see Louis Malle's *Murmur of the Heart*, a much-beloved coming-of-age comedy-drama in which a smart, sensitive fifteen-year-old French boy who feels an unusually romantic connection to his very romantic Italian-born mother (played by the magnificent and foxy Léa Massari) awakens to art, jazz, antiwar protests, sex, books, smoking, shop-lifting LPs—all my ruling passions. By the end of the film, Laurent Chevalier also just happens to become his mother's lover, one night only, after a Bastille Day celebration.

Which was also its saving grace: with *my* mother nothing happened. We remained entirely metaphorical. Mom stayed un-remarried, kept the stray boyfriend or three out of my sightlines; and right up through high school, the girls I liked all resembled her in one discreet way or another. In college, my first true love, a dead ringer for a certain member of the Smith College class of 1946, checked all the boxes. But no one seemed to notice except one psychologically astute friend, a returning alumnus who couldn't believe what I was up to. Every chance he got, he would deadpan, "Doesn't she look a *tiny bit* like your mother?"

After graduation and Mom's immemorial line ("Gee, Dave, I thought you'd win the English prize") retired my career as her sensitive artistic genius, I moved to New York City to become a writer. Then, just as life was beginning, Diana Tead Michaelis died of breast cancer. The date of this impossible-to-believe event was December 16, 1981. She was fifty-six, I twenty-four. My father and I drew briefly close during Mom's illness and death and, with my brother and a scrum of old friends, buried her on a chill sunny afternoon in Mount Auburn Cemetery, then returned to our corners, even less sure now how to belong to each other.

So long as she had been alive, so long as I had my mission, our secret was untouched. Writing was my calling, but what had charged it was my belief that if only I could fulfill the expectations of excellence that my mother herself had ceaselessly reached for and failed to grasp, in thrall to her overachieving mother—a college president, who herself was one big reach up from an Irish greengrocer's family—then I would defend us both against discovery as the second-raters we feared we were.

The first postmortem year, I got through the calendar moments of pathos (her birthday, my birthday, Thanksgiving, etc.) with controlled crying jags and kept up my shadowy end of our quest, freelancing for magazines and finishing a second book I had started before she got sick. When Mom was alive, I had had success enough at launching myself with a first book. But publication of the second fell short of expectations, and in the falling, I lost my confidence—a loss that seemed to contravene Freud's claim that a mother's favorite will automatically possess "that confidence of success which often induces real success."[4]

As my mother's son, I had known exactly what to do next and had done it. With her, the me I had been had seemed so me, I now had no idea who I was without her. And the more life rolled on as if nothing had happened, the more radically I rejected it. In the apartment I had been sharing with high school friends since we'd begun our lives in the city, I curated a shrine. Over my bureau went framed photos of my mother as a fair-haired child in Forest Hills, a schoolgirl bobbysoxer with a peaches-and-cream complexion, a lovely young UNESCO staffer in postwar Paris, a satin-doll bride, a bikini-clad pool party host in the swinging sixties . . . the Metropolitan Museum of Mom, one of my roommates dubbed it.

The apartment itself occupied the top of a townhouse on West Eighty-Fourth Street. Our block had been designated Edgar Allan Poe Street, and my third-floor bedroom became that winter a haunting that Roderick Usher himself could not have made more creepy. The walls, the shelves, the bedside tables were plastered with yet more sepia-tone images of my Annabelle Mom, scantily clad in her kingdom by the sea; and every relic, every dusty stick of furniture, save a new mattress from Sleepy's, had previously fitted out my mother's and grandmother's parlors, porches, and long-gone seaside cottages.

"Just hope you're fucking girls of this century," said my brother.

I *had* begun dating: a brainy, beautiful blonde (I'll call her Edie) who not only evoked you-know-who, in manner, dress, and physical type, but had the same first name as *her* mother, Edith, which made her seem even more an adult than she naturally was. We shared a past: a common hometown and high school; our single mothers (widowed and divorced) had been friends years earlier when we lived a few blocks apart. Edie had a radiant smile, all the more for its being slightly broken. She was urbane, scholarly, warm, gentle, and even—when she unpinned the chignon she wore her hair in—cuddly. One of her most magical attributes was the way, postcoitally, she'd let go of her grownup workplace dignity, becoming girlish and flirty as we smoked unfiltered cigarettes in bed. When I wasn't idolizing Edie, I was trying to seduce her from the long evenings of her job as executive assistant to one of publishing's most distinguished editors; and for a few winter weeks it seemed as if we might have something.

Then I did a strange thing. Before dawn one morning in my still-dark Poe chamber, I awakened to find Edie fully dressed and rushing to the hallway door—*fleeing*, it seemed. We had had what I thought was a watershed night, a real advance in our intimacy, for the first time completely relaxing, even going so far as to fall asleep in each other's arms. Clearly, though, some horror had happened. She looked as if she were being chased by a demon. When I called hoarsely over the sound of her bolting footsteps, she didn't return.

"I did *what*?" I said, finally getting through on her work phone.
She whispered: "You kicked me out of bed."

"What! Kicked you out—*with what*?"

"Your feet!"

I did not know what to say. I had never done anything like it
before, had no recall of the moment itself, nor of any dream state
that would explain it.

"Your icy feet," recounted Edie. "You turned away, pulled up
your knees, then—*Blammo*. Next thing, I was on the floor."

Idiotically, I said, "But why did you leave?"

After a moment, she said, "I think you wanted me to leave."

Edie, tragically fatherless since her teen years, had sympathized
sincerely and earnestly with the loss of my mother. She had com-
forted me in the more manic phases of grief. She was anything but
fragile: her affection was direct, caring, and tough. For her, there
was no ambiguity to being kicked out of a lover's bed.

I, meanwhile, felt—well, clearly, I didn't know how to feel, besides cornered. I neither apologized nor expressed understanding
nor renewed affection. All I managed was dazed dismay:

"Wow," I reflected. "I kicked you out of bed."

Edie gasped. Quickly she huffed out, "You should talk to someone," and hung up.

3

Into the woods. That's where I went. *Not* into talk therapy—not
yet. My circle of friends, especially those entering marriage and
the professions, had begun to embrace therapy as a redrawing of
the maps of childhood, a rite of passage to the grownups' table,
even as a kind of chemotherapy. Nodding, they would tell one
another, "If you had cancer, you'd get help, wouldn't you?"

Among the persuaders was one friend, a writer and painter, who
had lost her mother to a car accident. After holding the younger
members of her grieving family together for a year, and then driving
around the entire continental United States in a big circle, she had

had a nervous breakdown. Her situation dire, she moved into the Fifth Avenue apartment of a fashionable aunt who sent her to a prominent neuropsychiatrist known for curing blocked writers. The eminence's name was Daniel E. Schneider, such an ancient of the profession that he had once held the position of "assistant alienist" at Manhattan's Bellevue Psychiatric Hospital.

My friend blossomed under his care, began selling her stories to the *New Yorker*; and eventually, her reports of her own progress began to come accompanied by hints and intimations that my preoccupation with my mother amounted to more than grief—to the kind of obsession from which I might find some relief in psychoanalysis.

Doc Schneider, as my friend called him, had his consulting room on the garden floor of his East Nineties brownstone. The waiting room was serious and somber, as hushed as a museum. I took a seat—the very chair, I realized, where the celebrated journalist Tom Wolfe must have awaited entry. Here too had sat a giant of children's literature, Ruth Krauss, author of a favorite of mine, *The Carrot Seed*, who had come into the most productive period of her working life after sessions inside.

The door opened, a voice called from within, and the moment I set foot in the office—dank as a cave—I knew I was in over my head. It was like Spelunking Day at summer camp. Terrified, I asked if I could smoke.

No answer.

I fidgeted like a boy in a barber shop.

I began to speak. My Oedipus complex seemed like the right place to start, so I dove right in. At the end of what seemed like fifty seconds exactly, the ancient alienist abruptly interrupted. He declared that I was afraid of the vagina, afraid of success, afraid of living. (I later discovered that some of his patients called him "The Sledgehammer.") He said he had no free hours until the fall, but in the meantime recommended that I take better care of the women I took to bed; take a more realistic view of my successes and failures; and, while I was at it, take better care of myself.

"When was the last time you went to a gymnasium?"
Before I could remember, he said we had to stop.
As I stood to go, Doc Schneider offered a parting prescription.
"Relax this summer. Relax and make love."

Boy, thanks, Doc. What a feeling. I spent that *Flashdance* summer
of '83 pretending I was nineteen, and when that didn't work, I tried
seventeen and sixteen. And when regression became just another
excuse for unbridled lust, I unplugged the phone and existed as a
ghost, a revenant. There came a day in August when my cocaine
abuse was so extreme, I found myself in the tiny bathroom of a
commuter airplane going through its landing procedures over a
fog-swirled airport that so far as I knew was Providence, Rhode
Island, but turned out, when they shut off the engines, to be Bangor,
Maine.

That fall, things got worse. In September, my sophomore-year
college roommate was shot down by the Soviets aboard the
doomed Korean Airlines Flight 007. My current roommate (I had
moved from E. A. Poe Street) reached the end stages of chemical
addiction in October. I would return to our apartment to find him
passed out in the oak-floored hallway, needles and strange bowls
of blood-clotted water on the hexagonal bathroom tiles; or, still
awake at sunrise, crawling on all fours across the Persian rugs, his
nose snurdling like a truffle pig's as he searched the rug weave for
the most infinitesimal granule. That November, my brother's job
at ABC News moved him to Atlanta, and my father announced he
was marrying a third time. If all that were not enough to redraw a
few maps, I decided on my twenty-sixth birthday to sell my childhood home. It was time to put away childish things.

Two days later, on October 5, 1983, I went to 63 East Ninety-
Third Street to begin psychoanalysis.

Somewhere back that September, I had returned to Doc Schneider's office to follow up after my summer of love. My journal has
no record of this session, and what I recall of it is sketchy. I do
know that I was dismayed by Doc Schneider's analytic fee, which,

if memory serves, was something like $300 per (fifty-minute) hour. I had felt the same queasiness that summer when I'd had to come up with the exact same amount for three grams of cocaine; coincidentally, a pair of black lizard-skin cowboy boots I needed for a wedding I was in had also cost that much; and after paying and wearing them out onto East Fifty-Ninth Street, I threw up on the sidewalk, literally sickened by the excess. So, I shouldn't have been surprised to break out in a full sweat in Doc Schneider's consulting room.

I had no health insurance, I told him, and was struggling to come up with my $400 share of the monthly rent for the below-market Upper West Side sublet I was sharing with my dear bingeing roommate.

When Doc Schneider strongly suggested that my treatment would require four and possibly five sessions per week, I asked again if I could smoke.

Briefly, we argued about where I was going to get $6,000 a month on freelance earnings that barely yielded $1,000 in a good month. Then, sensing I was wasting his time, I said I was sorry but I wasn't selling my childhood home to spend $66,000 per year on psychoanalysis.

He was kind. He said once more that I was an intelligent and ambitious young man whose fear of success and intimacy was costing me more than psychoanalysis ever would, and he offered a referral for a doctor who had some free hours and a lower fee. Scribbling down the name and address, he wished me luck with my writing career.

"And please," said Doc Schneider, "get yourself to a gymnasium."

Out on the sidewalk, I looked at the referral: *63 East 93rd Street*. I looked up at the two brownstones I was standing in front of: number 61 was Doc Schneider's; number 63 was right next door.

Wait, I was already here!

I looked down at the name of the doctor with the free hours and the lower fee: *Laurie Schneider Adams, PhD.*

His wife? *Next door?* His first wife? *Now remarried?*

His married daughter. Laurie Schneider Adams, then in her early forties, was a psychoanalyst and professor, a scholar in Italian Renaissance art who specialized in the application of psychoanalytic theory to art history. Better still, she was a writer, the author, eventually, of more than two dozen books, including several widely used art-history textbooks. Best of all—her fee: $40.

There was no waiting room, as there had been next door. A Caribbean-accented housekeeper answered the door on the parlor floor, and a slightly irritated woman's voice from the third floor called down to come up.

Laurie was already seated in an armchair when I entered her consulting room. She smiled, eyes downcast—a stringent but friendly smile, as if we both knew the rules. Something about this complicity allowed me to enter the room and, without a word between us, to lie down on the couch that ran perpendicular to Laurie's chair. It felt like the most natural thing, as if I were already in treatment.

"How can I help?" she said.

All my life I'd heard about the Couch. Finally lying down on one, going full horizontal, felt like a trip to Disneyland, a ride on Space Mountain: off I went! Ranting, raving, huffing, puffing, squalling. Back behind me and over to the right, Laurie floated along, Cheshire-cat-like, her attention a steadying force as my flurry of memories gusted onward.

I knew we were getting somewhere when she started to sniff, even to snort, in response to the positive or negative beats of my story line. These noisy exhalations would increase in tempo and affect, quickening to an outright sigh or slowing to a disapproving groan when I dug out some valuable fossil from the family tar pit and preciously held it up to the light. If I was completely deluded about present-life behavior, Laurie would call me on it with a single word:

"Piffle!"

Daniel Schneider may have been a strict Freudian, but Laurie Schneider Adams turned out to be post-Freudian, by way of Lewis

Carroll and the Royal House of Windsor. It was absolute *piffle* to suggest, for example, that getting to a midday session on time was any more challenging for a freelance writer using the crosstown bus than for a Wall Street stockbroker with a car and driver.

Laurie freely mingled her own opinions and practical solutions with my long-winded complaints; and I don't think I stopped complaining for a moment that first session.

"Elated at the end of the hour," I wrote in my journal.

That weekend, my brother was back in town.

I told him I'd started psychotherapy.

"You are a psycho," he said. "You and Mom." He leered. "How much?"

"Forty bucks."

He whistled. "To *talk* to this person?" Then, sounding hurt: "You have me to talk to."

"Right," I said. "The blind leading the blind"—a formulation, I realized, that Laurie Adams was going to like when I brought it up next session: Oedipus and his sibling rival Schmedipus . . .

"You can talk to me," insisted Peter. "I'm your brother."

"Oh, right," I redirected, offering proof of our common blindness: "How about *Charlotta*? Still want to talk?"

Not a flicker, his face a blank. Charlotta, one of the unexamined traumatic figures of our common boyhood, was off-limits for Peter, the way Mom was for me.

At the second session, Laurie became even more interactive.

I was telling her how our move back to Cambridge in 1969—my father remained in Washington with his new family—had forced me to confront my sexual feelings about my mother.

"You haven't mentioned your father," she said. "Did you see him regularly after the move?"

"Once every other month."

It had been a long time since I had thought of the enforced jollity of those meals in Harvard Square after the tense pickups at my mother's house, our old family home on Berkeley Street. It was a big enough place; Dad could easily have stayed over on a separate floor. So went Mom's side of the argument. But my stepmother's feelings had prohibited such arrangements. Dad would get a room at the Sheraton Commander a block away, and after fighting bitterly with Mom over another of my orthodontist bills, he would take my brother and me into the Square to an eatery called the Wursthaus.

"It served sauerbraten and schnitzel and imported beers from around the world. My father loved it. We loved it."

"I thought you said he wasn't fond of German things."

"I was going to say, he wasn't, but he was fond of us."

The memory of my father's bravery those evenings, taking his lumps at the house, bearing Mom's pleading entreaties and my sullen foot-dragging all the way to the restaurant, brought me up short. But Laurie was not one to stop and push a box of Kleenex at you.

"Ah," she said, "now we're getting somewhere: your stepmother forced your father to take you to the *Worst* House."

She loved puns. They might not embody wishes, as slips of the tongue so famously did in Freud world, but often concealed a truth, in this case the concealment my father made of his early life. Michael Michaelis, a Berlin-born-and-bar-mitzvahed scientist and engineer, did not want to know himself, and therefore how could the world—how could I? He was an essentially tolerant and loving man, perfectly well entertained by the whole folly of being human. He just had no use for looking back on any of the actual people, places, or things that had made him who he was, neither his parents nor their religious traditions nor his country of origin nor any memory, record, archive, or remnant of any year before 1934, which was odd for a man who by training and profession put everything to use.

"You said you played tennis with him?"

Nineteen-thirty-four, by the way, was the year his name changed from Wolfgang—he, too, was intended to be a genius. That year, his mother got Wolfie out of Nazi Germany, onto a ship at Hamburg, and over to England, where he became an English schoolboy known as "Michael." Across the next two earth-shattering decades Michael Michaelis's brains got him from developing radar with the RAF during the war to a job in atomic energy in midcentury America, where he met my mother, herself a study in contrasts.

"Tennis—oh, God." The tennis games with my twice-exiled, émigré father when he visited us in Cambridge were torture. "Even though I was the better player," I explained, "I couldn't bring myself to beat him and would deliberately throw games by speeding up my serve and double-faulting."

"So, you arranged for your own failure?"

"Well not exactly *failure*."

"You're afraid of your own success," she said, echoing *her* father. "As a teenager you unconsciously associated success with transgressing the Oedipal taboo, and so you arranged your own failure as a way out of destroying your father. If you had beat him and won your tennis match you would have surpassed—you would have 'killed'—him."

Our third session felt slow and painful. Laurie kept bringing the narrative back to the present.

"But nothing's happening in the present. I've given up drugs and alcohol, taken a job to pay for therapy. I go the gym. Who am I kidding? I don't have a life in the present. I don't *want* a life in the present!"

"What do you want to happen?"

"I want everything the way it was."

"How was it?"

"You mean back when I was my mother's favorite, and she was my mind mender?"

A silence opened up, during which Laurie snuffled—her I'm-interested-now snuffle.

"Mind—*what*?" she said.

"Reader. My mother could read my mind, she really could."

"You said 'mender.'"

So I had.

"Congratulations," said Laurie, delighted. "You've replaced your mind-reading mother with a mender of minds. Very nice!"

And with that—*who knew?* Had the transference begun?

From then on, I rarely if ever rescheduled an appointment, never "forgot" that my hour at 63 East Ninety-Third Street started at 12 noon. It would be ten years and another therapist in another town before I had progressed enough to completely space out an appointment. With Laurie, our next session was always the actually biggest part of my day. No chance I was a no-show, though I was often late ringing her bell, and would complain bitterly about the unreliability of the crosstown bus, just as I did about the maddening regularity of her bills, which she handed to me at the end of the first session of each month.

"Four hundred and eighty dollars!" I would bleat.

"Piffle!" Laurie would say. "Your neurosis is costing you more than therapy."

It took me a while, but once I realized that my psychotherapist's plain-sense practicality was its own form of liberation, it helped free me.

"What's your first thought?" she said one day, after a more-stuck-than-usual silence.

"I was thinking," I said, "about how my brother once walked in on Mom and a congressman—in her bedroom. She was completely naked, but the congressman had all his clothes on, his suit, his shoes, even his necktie."

"Go on."

"The clothing part bothered him," I said.

"I should say so," tutted Laurie. "Had this brother of yours been taught to knock?"

She was a strategic thinker, decisive about problem-solving. Want to have an affair with a congressman while you have small children at home? Put a lock on the door.

From time management to productivity to financial planning and legal consulting, Laurie was big on getting all the necessary information first. Her belief in searching out knowledge and wielding it as a tool had an endearing, down-to-earth quality—an everyday extension of her analytic power. I trusted and learned from her tire-iron approach to fixing things in the here and now. She was, after all, the daughter of "the Sledgehammer."

After the first few months of three-times-a-week sessions, the subject of my mother was beginning to feel like a car stuck in a ditch. I had thought that if I only owned up to my early sexual feelings, I'd eventually be cured. At the same time, I wanted to honor my mother, her life and memory. Yet no matter what spin I loyally put on the Working Mom narrative—producer for Eleanor Roosevelt's public-television series! First director of the Office of Economic Opportunity's film-television office! Supervisor of an Academy Award–winning documentary about VISTA, the volunteer arm of the President's Task Force on the War against Poverty! Television producer who specialized in international and domestic issues of human rights, racial equality, food and hunger, and what was then called "third-world development"—invariably some family story would once again touch on Diana's seductiveness, which on the couch could play either as carefree or careless.

Whether it was Mom conversing from her bathtub covered only by a washcloth; or inviting me to mix her evening cocktail, à la Auntie Mame's golden bugle boy, Patrick; or illustrating one of our onset-of-puberty sex talks with recollections of my father's skill in the sack, Laurie would snort and groan and fume with such disdain, I couldn't help but dig up still more: Mom's frank discussion with preteen me of the issues involved with an unwanted extramarital pregnancy; or how Diana had reminisced romantically about her postwar adventures in Paris, including a screening of Luis Buñuel's groundbreaking surrealist film *Un Chien Andalou*, during the most famous scene of which—a man slicing open a woman's eyeball with a razor—she had had a sexual response.

I could protest all I wanted that my childhood fantasies had never developed to the point of real incest. Laurie would insist that at my house reality itself had been stimulating enough. Case in point, our most inappropriate of taboos: Mom's Haitian voodoo doll.

She kept it on her bureau the year after the divorce. It was a horror, that unclean human effigy, staring with its red peppercorn eyes, teetering on its stick legs, holding up an armless body made of bits of dung, stone, bird-claw, tar, and goat hair.

"You'd have to check with a lawyer," interposed Laurie, "but I think they're illegal."

Fortunately, the thing had no name. Its intent, I thought, was merely as a totem of Mom's endurance of my father's new marriage, which she secretly believed she would outlast. For the doll to work an actual evil spell, Mom would have had to steal a strand of my stepmother's hair or nail clippings to add to the anthropomorphic clay. And for that bit of sorcery, she would have to have enlisted me or my brother as her accomplice.

Then came a day when I noticed that a scattering of corroded pins and needles now pierced the doll's thighs, if not its privates, I couldn't bring myself to lift its witchy skirt and look. I didn't want to touch that thing. But that's when it came to me, like a crossing of electrical wires and popping of fuses: the doll wore a leather skirt with a fringe, not unlike the miniskirt that my mother had been so interested to learn from my brother and me had been worn by my stepmother to some Washington occasion.

4

"What's your first thought?"

"Charlotta." Standing by the bedroom door, one hip slightly outthrust, the light of the autumn afternoon silhouetting her head, a sharp high cheekbone, long thin arm, and the oval hairbrush in her hand. She points to the bed with her chin. "Down with the pants. Underpants on. I will take care of those."

"Who was Charlotta?"

Not her real name, by the way. She's possibly still alive, and when she disappeared from our lives it was not because of the abuse. No surprise: she was not our first sadistic caregiver. As small boys my brother and I had been held more than once in a lightless closet by another torturer.

"Funnily enough," I told Laurie, after opening our file on Charlotta, Abusive Caregiver Number Two, "Mom ended up firing her because she and her husband, Reggie, got a case of pubic lice. They were living in our attic apartment, and spread the parasites to the laundry, and Mom got them."

"What about you and your brother?"

"Crabs? No!"

Laurie sniffed. "Because when they're found on children, pubic lice can be a sign of sexual abuse."

That the abuse was sexual was news to me in 1984. As an eight-year-old, I took it as just another bad day that began after my mother went off to work in the morning. Charlotta, resting her feet, would charge us with some minor infraction. She would warn us that we were going to get a beating when we got home from school and send us off to our buses to spend the day riven with anxiety whenever we paused in class to recall what was going to happen when we got home to an empty house where Charlotta was in charge.

Each episode repeated the one before it. The instructions that detailed the taking down of pants and leaving on of underpants. This last was then used in a final negotiation: if the apology was sufficient, the underpants were left on for the spanking. If insincere or mumbled, off came the tighty whities. Next, the close positioning on the bed, Charlotta taking full control of the bared ass. Then the announcement of the number of strokes. Ten, usually. Then the first blazing sting of the cold hard plastic brush accompanied by the counting of the strokes. Afterward, the red-faced mumbling of a second coerced apology during which it seemed important to cover the genitals with the tail of the shirt.

Once, after getting off the school bus on the day of a beating, I hesitated in the front hallway. From upstairs, I could hear my brother. He was going first; but he was protesting. Charlotta, evidently unmoved, replied in her aloof, impassive voice. I then heard my brother cry out, "No!" followed by a struggle of some kind, and then a pleading howl, which was no longer just distress. This was now the sound of animal misery, and I opened my mouth to yell out to Charlotta to stop, but my heart was racing so fast, nothing came out of my mouth, and I sat down on the bottom step of the stairway, chest heaving, in a complete panic.

"Your first panic attack, no doubt."

I could feel it still.

"Your mother," said Laurie, flatly, "was where exactly? And how would she have explained why all this was going on?"

That was the strange part. From the first day of Charlotta's arrival as housekeeper, my working mother had completely abrogated her domestic authority and given weirdly reckless instructions: "If they're obstreperous," said Mom, "give them a good, hard, old-fashioned spanking."

Though I protested this edict at the time, I also recognized it as the new sound of my mother's professed helplessness, now that the divorce was final, and a curious new lawlessness had misted our fatherless house as Mom learned to tolerate Dad's new marriage and second family in Cleveland Park.

Recalling all this, I suggested to Laurie that, therefore, maybe it could be argued that Charlotta was "just doing her job."

Laurie didn't even piffle with that one. "About how many months did Charlotta go on doing this 'job' without reporting any of these 'old-fashioned spankings' to her employer?"

Then an even tougher question:

"Did you ever report the molestation to your mother or father? Did your brother?"

I objected to the term; Charlotta had never touched my private parts.

"You'll have to check with a lawyer," said Laurie in the business-like tone I now knew well. "It varies from state to state, but the legal definition of the crime of sexual acts with children includes exposure of genitalia and the forcing of physical contact, both of which are present here."

"My first thought? *Lincoln*."

"Abraham Lincoln?"

The same year of Charlotta—1966—the year my parents divorced. Fourth grade. I couldn't fall asleep at night because Abraham Lincoln began appearing in the corner of my bedroom.

"You saw Lincoln?"

"Night after night."

There he would be—the forehead, the cheekbones, the haunted gray eyes. I could see his pores, the whiskers of his beard. I was scared the first time, but I knew Lincoln. I had *been Lincoln*—the year before, in a third-grade pageant, draped in black cape, bearded by black construction paper, cradling the stovepipe hat. My parents had attended as a couple. I wore white socks because on the morning of the pageant we hadn't been able to find the black ones. Nonetheless, without a hitch, I took the stage and from memory recited the Gettysburg Address. It was a proud family moment. Every word had mattered—now, nothing did.

Ken Burns once described the Civil War as "the traumatic event in our childhood."[5] He could have been describing the distance between that school pageant in 1965, in Washington, DC, and the John Brown Wax Museum in Harpers Ferry, West Virginia, the following year.

One weekend in 1966, my brother and I were brought to meet my father's—"our"—new family. Here was our stepmother, for whom my feelings did not at first go beyond confusion (she was pretty!); and her two children, who had moved from their home in Boulder, Colorado, and matched Peter and me in age. The day trip out of Washington to the West Virginia countryside was by way of a normal family outing, but I remember that I made trouble, giving my father lip, trying to shake him out of the weird cheerful veneer he was putting on for *his* new family.

Dad's usual manner was stiff, formal, sometimes gruff. My friends would ask if he were—*British?* The slightest trace of a German accent was detectable beneath his smooth disguise as an American technology consultant. Scotch played its part in keeping the wolf in the forest, but one of Dad's unmistakable Mittel Europa tells was the way that roadside diners softened him up. Free wooden toothpicks! Free mints! Free full-color tourist brochures! Michael Michaelis could never get over the money Americans poured into freebies, as if giving away smooth, splinter-free, pointed sticks was freedom itself. His euphoria—his *gemütlichkeit*—and the approval it found in my stepmother must have been the reason we made our freshly minted Brady Bunch way into Harpers Ferry after eating in a highway diner.

The John Brown Wax Museum had opened in 1961 in a narrow brick row house. Visitors clomped up and down dark, windowless hallways, at the end of which stood brightly lighted, life-size dioramas that told the story of the firebrand abolitionist's doomed attempt to raise a slave rebellion at Harpers Ferry in 1859. Each tableau, more violent than the last, was populated by cheesy wax figures, all of them with real hair and wax eyes—the very latest in "wax science." Even the shoes were made of wax.

Dad paid our admission and led us into the self-guided hallways. My stepmother was game. She was a Livingston from Philadelphia, by way of the Great West, and whispered that John Brown was a respected sheep rancher who had had twenty kids. But of course, me being me, I saw no livestock in the dioramas, no dutiful farmhand children. I was so petrified of the blood luridly splashed all over everywhere, all I could do was stand behind my father's legs and focus my attention on the other tourist families, which only made it worse, since I immediately sensed that, compared to those madras-shirted nuclear groupings, our cobbled-together, wax-science "family" was just as frightening and freakish as the figures in the almost-real tableaux.

From the first childhood scene, where young John Brown looked on to see one of his enslaved playmates being whipped, to the death of Shepherd Hayward, the first person killed in the Harpers Ferry attack, a "free Negro" whose chest ballooned and emptied as he gasped his dying breaths, I was a wreck of terror. It didn't help that Dad pointed out that we could hear the hydraulic pump wheezing under ol' Shep's red shirt.

By far the biggest jolt came in the final diorama staged in the basement—John Brown's execution by hanging. There on the gallows stood the martyr, "waiting," intoned an unseen narrator, "with majestic serenity for the drop into eternity." And as John Brown lingered with the noose around his leathery neck, his huge white-haired wax head with its bottomless blue eyes pivoted up to stare at us.

Lincoln had not been present at the Harpers Ferry bloodbath. But in my room, he had the same uncanny near-actuality. Mercifully, he did not speak. He just stood there, benign, homely, and monumental, his dark head slowly pivoting until he found me in the gloom. I dreaded that moment. Lincoln's kindly eyes would find me and wait me out until I was brave enough to look him back in the eye. And so, each night, I *had* to stay up. I could not shut my eyes until I had met the Great Emancipator's gaze.[6]

"Hold that thought about the Great Emancipator," said Laurie. "Let's get back to Carlotta."

"*Char*-lotta."

"These 'old-fashioned spankings' your mother ordered up," said Laurie. "During them, did you talk? Did Charlotta?"

"Only the instructions and the counting and the coerced apologies."

"You said she would watch you undress."

"Yup."

"Lincoln," said Laurie. "Did *he* talk?"

"Neither of us did. He watched, I waited."

"So you could say he was *on watch*?"

"You could say that."

"Keeping a lookout. For disruptions of his authority."

At first, I didn't see where she was going.

"Look here," said Laurie. "Lincoln's first appearance in your bedroom occurred after you met this uncanny new family of yours from out west. And with them, you saw John Brown hang as punishment for heading the first revolt of enslaved peoples that led to the Civil War. John Brown witnessed the misery of his childhood comrade's whipping, just as you heard your brother's beating. You panicked, gasped for breath, your chest going up and down like a hydraulic pump . . ."

I was silent.

"What's happening here," said Laurie, "is that you needed a father. You were a frightened child in a house divided. And so, you brought Lincoln—Father Abraham—into your bedroom to heal the house, to end slavery and its whippings, and, wishfully, to save your parents' Union."

She paused to let it all sink in, then in a rueful voice recited, "A house divided against itself cannot stand."

5

This account is long yet feels incomplete. Psychoanalysis felt the same way. At least once a month I vowed to terminate what came to seem pointlessly interminable. But for as long as I believed in it, therapy gave me relief—a kind of moratorium on time itself, with a useful tilt toward the future.

Real self-knowledge requires humor and optimism. Lucky for me, Laurie Adams had both. Talk therapy may not have cured me, but in our many doctor-patient tableaux over the next eight years Laurie played her shapeshifting role impeccably. It was another decade before I knew for real that she had cared about me.

In the decades after therapy ended, she became a friend to the book-length efforts of my adult life. She put her editorial suggestions into the margins of my two artists' biographies and thereby taught me the art of writing about works of art. I was about to send her a new book when I learned that she had died at seventy-three. Her absence—at first, its appalling suddenness—remains a hole in my heart: an *Alice*-like rabbit hole down which I can easily imagine falling, only to land on her couch to hear, *Piffle! You're angry with me for dying.*

Well I may be—but I'm sorrier for the loss and pain to her beloved husband of forty-five years; her grown daughters and their families; her patients, students, and readers.

As for my Oedipus complex, well—in the rotation of the generations, it seems to have ended with me. The other day, I got to spend some time with one of my grown sons and his longtime girlfriend; and, looking at her, I had to smile.

"Nope," I said to myself. "Doesn't look even a *tiny bit* like his mom."

FROM FREUD'S ORDINARY UNHAPPINESS TO WINNICOTT'S GOOD ENOUGH

Susie Orbach

Does each psychoanalyst and each psychoanalytic theorist have to make their own sense of the wisdom the field has accrued?

Psychoanalysis, the study of the human subject in the process of change, finds its clinical and theoretical strength in the refashioning of received knowledge through the personal idioms of its practitioners. Freud's monumental contributions continued throughout his working life as he developed and rescripted his understandings. He gave us a model for reappraising what we believe we know—a model that is paradigmatic for psychoanalysis. We take his model, and we refresh it for our day, for our time, and for the circumstances of the analysands who seek our help. We enunciate his understandings in our vernacular, with recourse to our practices and the times we inhabit. We bring our shadings and those of our active collaborators—our analysands—to our work. The practice and understandings we develop are the outcome of an internal dialogue between Freud and subsequent analyst theorists, between the impact of analysands on ourselves and the times we live in.

The terrain of late capitalism in which we work is soaked with notions of personal success. Display and self-presentation dominate.

It starts early with children who have already learned to pose for cameras by age three. Desire is expressed in terms of being great, clever, beautiful—and, if you ask children—rich and famous. Many individuals from a range of class and ethnic background now strive to "have it all," to be a brand, to garner recognition and commercial success (often through social media). Thirst, greed, and narcissism are cultivated in late capitalism, which fosters a culture of consumption and material success as desirable while it buries the costs of planetary exploitation. This shaping of desire and thus of subjectivity, which is penetrating more and more of the world as it enters modernity, puts psychoanalysis's aims of "ordinary unhappiness" in a subversive, revolutionary, and potentially liberatory mode. People seek out psychoanalytic therapies as they look for relationships that can help them to know themselves, to find meaning rather than performance.

When I think about the achievements of a therapy in our current circumstances, I feel the depth of Freud theorizing about hysteria and the pediatrician D. W. Winnicott's work on infancy and early childhood. They are not the only influences, of course, but their work dovetails for me in textured manner when I think of the dilemmas of analysands today. How I use their work is undoubtedly idiosyncratic. Perhaps it parallels the interpretive aspect of psychoanalysis's ability to land on an individual and become sense making. We work to find particular words that will have meaning for the individual. Far from a paint-by-number practice or the often ridiculed psychobabble we are told therapy is, the particular moods, words, smells, and feel infuse the therapeutic relationship on both the analyst's and analysand's side, making it unique to each therapeutic couple.

———

An individual or couple or family enters therapy with hope. There is a desire for change. A desire to be happy. A desire to understand and be understood. There is often, as well, a fear of change, a fear of being happy, a fear of what it means to understand and, equally significantly, to be understood.

When I meet a person or a couple for therapy, I'm interested in their narrative and how they tell it. Does it emerge coherently? Do they pause? Do they hesitate? Can they self-correct as they catch themselves in a story that may no longer ring true for them? How much does hyperbole or a coherent story dominate? Are they able to notice their feelings as they share what so troubles them?

Further, am I able to sketch from what they convey an ever-so-preliminary sense of the interplay between their inner world and their self-presentation and knowledge? Can I discern the impediments—let's call them defenses—that are operating? Can I sense the shape of their inner world? As they tell me more of their family history in a first session, do I get a hint of how they might translate—from their sedimented history—aspects of their current relationships so that they (disconcertingly) conform to what may have been hurtful in their families? Do they have a capacity to experience and feel what is novel in the new?

These are big questions for a beginning therapy.

To freight the matter further, I observe how they come into the room, how they are within their body, how their face and their tone expresses or is at odds with what they are telling; how they act with me. Finally, of course, and this is not meant as step one, then two and three (for these processes cascade in ways unique to this individual or couple), there ensues the impact of the person or people on me.

I notice whether I am drawn to them and what they evoke in me. I notice the feelings that are aroused in me by being with them. In the best of worlds, I am curious and interested. It is my job to be so. In our strange profession, one can find oneself curious and interested in people who are not overtly charming or especially desperate or compelling. Where we fail to be drawn, where we find ourselves "knowing it all" or detached or turned off or just plain uninterested, that too becomes interesting and "diagnostic," alerting us to—not just our personal proclivities, but what might need addressing—what is wrong and why the individual or couple have chosen therapy.

So much for a first session. There is more to say, of course, such as how I engage and question and what I make of our explicit interactions, but what I am holding in my mind is how Freud and his collaborator Breuer aimed to help a person with hysterical symptoms to come to accept ordinary unhappiness.

Freud and Breuer addressed physical symptoms that they believed had no organic basis but were rooted in the psyche. They encouraged the patient to say whatever came into his or her or their mind as the way of getting at the core of the symptoms. This method was called free association. Where the individual suffered with a paralyzed arm, or with an imagined pregnancy and labor pains, the emotional conflicts that produced the "hysterical" symptom could surface through being spoken of and in time be faced rather than foisted onto the body. This shift to language, emotions, and conflict would open up the way for the individual to understand the causes of their symptoms and the psychological suffering that had generated them. As they worked through their conflicts—how they could accept them and try to understand why they felt the way they did—the hope was that they could move out of a "hysterical" state, to states of acceptance, of mourning, to what Freud and Breuer termed "ordinary unhappiness."[1] It is a profound idea, and it doesn't in any sense mean that a person lives in unhappiness. I take it to mean that we contest the illusion or delusion of happiness so as to be able to live *inside and from oneself with all its conflicts and longings and the connections it is possible to make with others.* This is what I can envision and hope for in my clinical endeavors.

———

To an outsider, this might not seem much of a dividend from spending time in therapy. It is perhaps one of those statements that feel too thin and depriving to make much sense of until it is lived. But psychoanalysts have aims and desires for their analysands and the work they do with them. For me, "ordinary unhappiness" links to Winnicott, who gave us the notion of "good enough."[2] He was challenging the idea that if mothers are perceived to be less than perfect, they are considered failures. He very much wanted women to have confidence in their parenting. He understood the idealization—and its opposite, denigration—that could lodge in a child's developing mind when her or his needs went unrecognized. His concept of "good enough" was to extend to our understanding that mental health is partly constituted by an individual coming to a sense of being "good enough" too.

This is what strikes me as the satisfying outcome of a therapy: not just for me as an analyst, but more importantly for the analysand. It is a bulwark against the excessive and psychologically damaging claims of happiness as *the* goal. The transformation that occurs from hysteria to ordinary unhappiness enables living from oneself with the boldness as well as the quieter range of emotional reactions. The acknowledgment of good enough is the gateway to understanding the limitations of self, of others, of parents who were only as adequate as they could be. "Good enough" is a sense of understanding. It is not a giving up but a challenge to the manic grandiosity we are all offered in consumer culture. It poses personal reconciliation and connection to others through analytic-emotional work that is profoundly affecting and transformative.

The process of finding oneself living in and from oneself in which a range of difficult emotional states can be tolerated doesn't remove conflict. It doesn't take away desire. What it does challenge is a world of ersatz "having great days," of synthetic happiness, of the relentless treadmill of being "amazing."[3] Ordinary unhappiness can be uncomfortable and perplexing, yet curiosity in one's emotional states when lived with another in the session can be a prelude to growth and emotional understanding.

Mark Solms's 2021 book *The Hidden Spring: A Journey to the Source of Consciousness* privileges the role of feelings. Emotions allow us to know we exist and to be self-reflexive. This key role of emotions guides me in my understanding of individuals and couples in the consulting room. I don't mean this in a superficial manner, as in "you are what you feel," but more in the sense that "I am, because I am able to feel." Dread, confusion, despair, bleakness, loss, repetitive behaviors that are devoid of pleasure, and so on, can propel people to seek therapy. Whereas in many encounters such feelings are hidden, our job in therapy is to meet them and the complexity of emotional and cognitive states of mind they can occlude.

The emotional spaces that we have come to inhabit can be constrained by the emotional states that have been conveyed as acceptable in our families of origin, which are situated by class or racial or ethnic background, within geographic locations and within our gender. Despite the prevalence of worldwide social media, anthropologists can still point to the variations in acceptable emotions depending on how our personal locations are culturally saturated. It is within family structures that large cultural and local—to that family—norms are imbibed. It is not so much that we are implicitly policed as infants and children. It is more that ways of being, feeling, and acting are enacted by family members, thus forming the sense of what and how it is to be.

Each family conveys what is acceptable and expected, and in our journeys to adulthood, the management of these prescriptions and proscriptions can wrong-foot us with the emergence of "unacceptable" emotions and the ensuing ideas they produce. If we have experienced a limit on "acceptable" emotions, then our feeling canvas is devoid of the receptors to receive other emotions. Such constraints can veer off into the creation of hysterical symptoms misshaping subjective experience.

Rami came to therapy feeling empty. He worked hard, was a dutiful firstborn son of Indian parents who met in the United Kingdom before he was born. They had prospered here and had ambitions for him.

Rami absorbed the idea that he was to get on with things, do well, not bother his parents too much, and be a guide to his four younger siblings. Intermittently bullied in school, he learned to become athletic and apparently uncaring about grades, while getting up early to do his homework and get his siblings ready. He did do well, but now, at thirty-nine, with a partner and two kids, he felt driven and frazzled and realized how central those states of being had been from childhood. From early on, to be OK, he felt he needed to be great.

The pleasure he experienced in his work life was in being essential to the legal consultancy he worked for. His knowledge base and competence were relied on by his colleagues. There were endless reports and presentations to give, always on a deadline. His emotional life narrowed into managing the next challenge, which he met by overcoming extreme tiredness and sacrificing time with his partner. Although he looked sociable, was collegial at work, and engaged with his family at home, he was anxious and psychologically isolated. He relished problem solving because it gave him a sense of adventure and competence. The rush of deadlines impinged but simultaneously gave him a sense of value because he knew he would meet them. His self-image rested on being a miracle worker who would never let the organization down.

In therapy, we came to understand how this identity reassured him: adrenalized, he would deliver. He was trustworthy. He could rev himself up to produce. As soon as the children were in bed, he would get back to work. He thought he wanted to slow down, but it became achingly apparent that he was compelled to uphold his Superman identity in which he was needed and seen as superreliable.

Rami shared psychological characteristics with people who were less productive than him but who had chaotic work, friend, and family patterns that meant they were always busy, always apparently responsive. In a sense his "hysteria" helped. Up to a point. Always being on drowned him in obligations. These obligations and a self-image of service and provision had largely kept Rami away from emptiness and not knowing until a year before he started therapy. He had been realizing that unless he was delivering, he did not know how to relate to himself or others. He didn't know much about what he felt—besides empty and driven. His fortress of obligation denied other people's capabilities while a grandiose structure kept him aloof and invulnerable.

To get to know others and connect with them, he had to acquaint himself with who he was. Initially, this idea was humiliating. But gradually, the notion that he could be curious about himself *as a project* won him over intellectually, and in time, he began to loosen the constraints and recognize that he could indeed team up with his colleagues rather than be a one-man producer. He also saw that in the family he could become aware of what he didn't know. Of course, he had shown his vulnerability to his wife in the early days of their relationship, but that had receded as he had geared up intensively to support the family when babies arrived.

His gradual move in therapy from being a supremo to being a man who could begin to collaborate allowed him to countenance disappointment and not getting everything right. His limited emotional palette now felt inadequate. He was learning a new emotional language while unlearning his existing one. That was no easy feat. In daring to show me his needs, he opened up a channel to receive acknowledgment for what had been sequestered. He liked the therapy and the sense of mattering to me and to himself.

Freud and Winnicott are masterful in their understanding of what it means to live inside drives, to live from a self who can express personal desires while recognizing that others will not always be responsive to one's wishes. Their work and theories implicitly rein in grandiosity. In its place, psychoanalysis looks to address the underlying insecurities so that the analysand can find what is nourishing and work on what stops them being able to do so. I don't mean this "reining in of grandiosity" in any kind of depriving or do-gooding manner. Psychoanalysts are not moralists. Psychoanalysis is not per se a moral practice. Psychoanalysis is interested in the discoveries of human subjectivity and intersubjectivity, in how significant relationships help to shape an inner world that copes with conflict, disappointment, abandonment, misunderstanding, hope, longing, desire, and so on.

The world of Freud is a world of the intrapsychic; what goes on inside of us unbeknownst to ourselves is fashioned in early childhood and shapes us. Freud's world is also an interpersonal one. It explains how what we have experienced affects what we can hope for and feel in other relationships. We can misread what is being offered by another, and we can be open or reluctant to experience closeness in relationships of all kinds.

Psychoanalysis is concerned with inner and outer worlds: it investigates and theorizes about the devilish mental structures that are created and then solidified when things in early childhood are repeatedly askew. Analysts—and our analysands—find ourselves acting in ways that are not in our interests. We can hystericize relationships so that the love and connections that might be being offered to an individual, appear out of reach, implausible: 'Can he/she/they really love and want me?'

Rami had discovered early that he was to be his own source of solace, and that his success would provide solace for his parents. Inadvertently, he turned away from relationships and brutishly tempered his need for ordinary soothing and compassion.

Freud's understanding of hysteria's best outcome, "transforming misery into ordinary unhappiness," shows the power of the therapeutic relationship. Therapy works to interrogate and deconstruct the symptom, to transform it by replacing confusion, conflict, and despair with meaning. That is not to say that this is in any way simplistic, as in "you suffered, you developed this hysterical symptom to protect you, and now you can be free." Rather, the therapist observes how her analysand approaches relationships, both from the account she receives and from the personal experience she has of her analysand in the room. She feels his longings, his hesitancies, his fears, his reluctances as they are brought to her. She discusses these and the way in which they can play out in the therapy relationship between the patient and the therapist. Does a Rami expect a version of the need to provide solace to the therapist as he felt he needed to provide for his parents? Does Rami feel the need to take charge of the therapy, or can he let his therapist help him, thus breaking patterns built up until then? As an exploration of these kinds of dynamics between the analysand and his therapist, the therapy enriches understandings while offering a stage, an in vivo experience in the now to understand and risk new possibilities. It enlivens the individual or couple or family to see things from multiple perspectives.

Freud is a theorist of relationship. He investigates how mind and body are made in relationship; how the rhythms and structures of parental relationships form the substrate of a child's psychic structure and how psychic structure solidifies to incline the person into confirming through behaviors and thoughts what has been known and relied on. This known, which can be thought of as a structure on top of a void, is held together and reinforced through reiteration.

Fifty years after *Studies in Hysteria*, when the study of infancy began to enter psychoanalysis, Winnicott showed that when a baby's gestures are repeatedly missed, ignored, or rejected by the person(s) on whom they are utterly dependent, the baby has to make sense of the refusal by adjusting their gestures to bring forward what they hope will be accepted. In finding acceptable gestures, they separate from parts of self (what Winnicott terms the true self) through the mechanisms of splitting and repression, while developing imitative or acceptable gestures (the false self) that will engage and hold the parent.

The parent who is unable to respect or value a child's expression of quietude, for example, may chide the child into a kind of false sociability and performing in order to feel reassured in their own parenting. The parent may not know what alarms them about their child's quietude. They may inadvertently nudge their child to fit in with the family culture, and as the child complies, the parent might feel better, but the child might develop a sense of inauthenticity, of losing something nameless and unacceptable while paradoxically feeling bolstered by pleasing their caregiver.

Or let's imagine the child who is frowned on or scolded for crying and fussing. They, too, might learn to perform by damping down their upset quickly. They substitute approval for distress.

The adapted false self that wins acceptance through self-denial, however, is unstable. It is bolstered through repeating the approved-of behaviors. This further alienates the self.

In Rami's case, with his childhood needs unrecognized, he found a self—a false self—that appeared need-free, which gained him approval from his parents. In adult life he soothed himself by deploying this false self and becoming the person who was needed and valued by others.

As Rami's adaptations ran out of steam for him, the struggle to be less extraordinary morphed into something more sustainable. His acceptance of the dilemmas and position of his immigrant parents allowed him to understand and accept their limitations and begin to live more fully from within himself.

———

We expect ourselves to be exemplary, but our strengths often arise out of our perceived deficits and our facing up to the disappointments in what we have received. Out of failure and disappointment we develop agency. We endeavor to come to terms with what we lost or didn't have or were not given, and then what we in turn were unable to receive.

In therapy we work to marry up what we developed with a need to settle. Our false self can drive us to prove things, perhaps to harness that energy to create or to contest what we did not receive or were offered. In therapy we don't simply cast off these adapted selves. We introduce them to the less well known and rather undeveloped "true selves" that are underexposed, may feel more vulnerable, and will need more light and experimentation in order to grow and flourish.

Rami's gradual expansion of self was scaffolded by an understanding of how his self-reliance had developed out of feelings of helplessness and bewilderment. As he now met those feelings in himself, he realized how driven he was by fear. New words, new emotional states grew within him. His compassion for himself, although not easy at first, expanded, and with it, his capacity to feel for and be authentic with others.

Winnicott's idea of "good enough" thus shows us the process by which the mind can work through and achieve Freud's idea of "ordinary unhappiness." Both ideas demonstrate the struggle to move away from perfection and idolization of what should have been, to enable us to acknowledge what we *did* experience, what we did with it (at a psychic, structural level), and how that then could become a template for misreading in the present—skewing behavior and understanding. Their ideas guide us toward receiving the good enough, on the one hand, and accepting good enough in ourselves, on the other, so that we can live with the range of experience offered by ordinary unhappiness. These two ideas, separated by fifty-eight years and two world wars, have lived alongside the Western move to modernism through the democratic moment, to today's world in which extremism, dictatorship, and fundamentalism of different stripes flourish. Freud and Winnicott's formulations, their idioms and wisdom—their sanity—speak to this moment again and afresh. They give us something substantial to think and act on against the prevailing winds of the superficial and the scary.

GROWING UP FREUDIAN

Peter D. Kramer

From my earliest years, I had an image of Freud. I saw him as stern, incisive, and irascible, a rigid older man like my father's father. My Opa Kramer had been a German military officer in the First World War and a demanding schoolteacher after. He and, by analogy, Freud could size up your character straight away and find you lacking. I can't say where this impression or association came from. I don't remember having been without it.

I suppose that I learned about Freud at home. I was born in the late 1940s and grew up in and around New York City in the 1950s. My mother was an occupational therapist who had worked with psychiatric patients in a Veterans Administration hospital in World War II. We had many volumes by Freud on our bookshelves.

We were Jewish. Doubtless Freud's Jewishness helped me adopt him as a near relation—like Einstein, another one-named scientist who also felt familiar. Opa Kramer wanted me to grow up to be Freud or Einstein—to take advantage in that way of the opportunity that America offered. *Freud* was something between a bogeyman and an aspiration.

Not only in our family but everywhere, Freud was a presence. If you misspoke and corrected yourself, someone would ask whether the error did not express deep feelings—your unconscious wishes. Freud's technical concepts, like parapraxis, were part of everyday life.

We all took Freud to be a scientist, and a great one. Implicitly, he had likened himself to Copernicus and Darwin, genius innovators whose work faced initial resistance and later gained general acceptance.[1] We adopted the comparison.

In my public school, the fifth-grade curriculum included the assignment of a research paper. My teacher knew that I enjoyed reading about the lives of famous scientists. He suggested that I choose one of their discoveries as a topic.

I had been plowing through books by Paul de Kruif, the microbiologist, starting with *Microbe Hunters*, celebrating researchers like those who had helped explicate the causes of malaria. What my teacher did not know was that I had also picked up *The Story of Psychoanalysis* by the *New York Times* journalist Lucy Freeman.[2] As in de Kruif's books, each chapter described an innovator: Anton Mesmer, Phillipe Pinel, and so on. But Freeman had a central hero, Sigmund Freud. The other figures were treated as precursors or followers, presaging or validating Freud's insights.

According to Freeman, Freud had made a monumental discovery: the human unconscious. From it, he elaborated a science, "the science of understanding the mind." The book describes controversies, seemingly similar to the controversies over priority in research about mosquitoes as the vector for malaria. But there is no ambiguity on the key point. Psychoanalysis was a breakthrough on the order of vaccination and pasteurization.

To my schoolteacher, I proposed an essay on Freud's discovery of the unconscious. I liked the idea of science grounded in a knowledge of myths and folktales, which I read in bulk, and in self-examination.

My teacher gave the project a hard no. He suggested that instead I research the discovery of ether anesthesia. My parents explained that my idea had been fine, but that a teacher might not want to be seen as inviting a ten-year-old to write about sex. Now for me, Freud had extra cachet. He was both icon and outlaw.

I am not pointing to my family life, not in particular. My father had no special interest in psychology. My mother was an admirer of Harry Stack Sullivan. She was a pragmatist, aware of social circumstance and suspicious of Freud's more extreme claims.

People write memoirs of their lives as red-diaper babies, aware of Karl Marx from an early age. My childhood was nothing like that. If I had been introduced to Freud at home, still the exposure was more general. Freud was everywhere.

In my preteen years, I gained entrée to the forbidden territory where sex and psychology overlap. Finding me anxious, my pediatrician sent me to a child psychoanalyst. This sort of referral was routine. Effectively, psychotherapy was the only treatment for emotional problems, and insurance plans covered it.

I know that the therapy took place as I was turning twelve because after the sessions, waiting for my mother to fetch me, I volunteered stuffing envelopes at the local Kennedy-for-President headquarters.

The analyst I'd been referred to struck me as intrusive and socially awkward. I disliked sharing private thoughts with him. He let me know that I was manifesting resistance.

One idea I resisted concerned my unconscious attitude toward my father. The analyst made me out as competitive, wanting to surpass or kill my father in response to hostility from the other direction. I experienced my father as loving and lovable, a mild and humble man—and I would not bend.

Worse, when I confessed that I felt uneasy around certain girls, the analyst explained that I needed to acknowledge sexual feelings toward my mother. I found the notion creepy.

Pursuing his clumsy version of orthodox Freudianism, the analyst steered the conversation toward sex at every opportunity. For reasons not entirely congruent with analytic theory, I found this approach helpful.

I gathered from what the analyst said that it was okay for me to think about sex a lot. I learned that I did not need to like a girl to desire her. That possibility was new to me. If I slow-danced with a girl who had a developed figure, I would find myself idolizing her, even if I had previously considered her dull or unkind. Being able to separate out desire from love spared me confusion.

I also learned that masturbation was normal and expectable and that it need not be a source of shame. Altogether, the centrality of sex to psychoanalysis proved liberating for me. I took a leap forward in the social hierarchy at school.

Although I hated going to analytic sessions, they did seem to help moderate my anxiety. I was more confident. I made out with girls. In time, I got a girlfriend. I might reject certain interpretations, but because the therapy worked, I did not doubt the method. And of course, the analyst was validated by other adults, like the pediatrician.

Freud had helped in my daily life. The therapy had given me an angle on other kids. I knew better how to listen to them and how to confront them. I remained uneasy about sex and dating, but less so. A little loosening up on that front goes a long way.

Because of the analysis, because Freud's work was forbidden fruit, in high school, I read Freud. There was another motivation as well. Freud was on a par with Dickens or Shakespeare. Reading Freud rounded out your education.

Freud's writings were disseminated in mass-market paperbacks. We had some around the house, mostly the late, peripheral work. I read *Totem and Taboo* and took it to be anthropology. I gathered that the structure of human society arises from guilt over father murder. Yes, I had rejected that assertion as regards my own makeup, but at a distance, attributed to cavemen, it sounded plausible enough.

What's odd is that I was studying science, and seriously. In high school, each Saturday I attended the Columbia Science Honors Program. I focused on mathematics, but I took courses like physical anthropology, too. I knew what research looked like.

I knew and did not want to know. I loved fiction. For Freud, a literary sensibility, a talent for storytelling, and a general knowledge of human nature seemed to suffice to remake anthropology. I suppose that I wanted my future career, whatever it might be, to look like that. The notion that you need not be a scholar to advance scholarly work appealed to me.

My exposure to Freud continued in college, at Harvard. He was everywhere. Girlfriends would call me repressed or defensive, and I would respect the criticism. They had been in therapy for years and were adept. They had me sized up.

My classmates' take—theirs and mine—on our situation and our surroundings was straight out of *Civilization and Its Discontents*, which everyone had read or knew about. The gist was that society, built to protect us from unhappiness, inevitably leaves us unhappy.

The iconic poster for the campus's turmoil in 1969 was a call to action: "Strike to seize control of your life . . . Strike to become more human . . . Strike to make yourself free . . . Strike because they are trying to squeeze the life out of you." Herbert Marcuse, another icon, had integrated Freud with Marx, and the amalgam provided a framework through which my classmates and I viewed institutions and our private lives.

It's not that college provided no alternatives to Freud. Erik Erikson and Jerome Bruner were in residence. They had their own theories—psychology had moved on—but both also saw Freud as a seminal figure.

I took Jerome Kagan's basic course on child development. He emphasized experimental observations meant to probe the infant mind. The research provided narrow insights about humans' emotional lives and cognition. It might take decades before researchers demonstrated the basis for symbolic thought that underpinned Oedipal anxieties. In the meanwhile, couldn't Freud and empiricism coexist?

Years later, Kagan would explain that his approach was meant to challenge Freud and put the study of the mind on a new basis.[3]

He confessed that in the 1950s he had been a starry-eyed Freud follower. But Kagan's independent work began as Freud's intellectual dominance waned. Kagan wrote: "No one has offered a satisfactory explanation of why so many educated Americans and Europeans during the period 1910–1960 were convinced of the essential truth of Freud's assertions."

Kagan's own guess involved sex. Instead of attributing anxiety to the diverse uncertainties of daily life, Freud pinned the problems on sexual repression. This, during a half century when Americans spoke more openly of sex but remained restrained in their practice of it. Freud flattered his public further by valuing confession and introspection.

For Kagan, the sexual freedom and self-involvement of the young in the 1960s and 1970s disproved Freud. Kagan asked why my generation wasn't either less neurotic (because we were sexually liberated) or more aware of the shortcomings of Freud's framework.

This line of thought played no part in Kagan's child development class. Perhaps he had not yet formulated it. I doubt that the argument would have swayed me. Sex remained hard to come by. My encounters, when they occurred, were hedged by guilt and self-doubt. Neuroticism, desire, and lack of emotional and creative fulfillment all seemed entwined.

I was more influenced by Lionel Trilling. I did a concentration in British history and literature and wrote a senior thesis about Dickens. When Trilling came to Harvard for a year, he reviewed a draft of my essay and advised me on it.

I had read Trilling in bulk. He did not approach Freud uncritically, but it was Trilling who wrote, "The Freudian psychology is the only systematic account of the human mind which, in point of subtlety and complexity, of interest and tragic power, deserves to stand beside the chaotic mass of psychological insights which literature has accumulated through the centuries."[4] If I wanted to be a writer, and I did, there was no doubt about whose work I should master.

I present this brief personal history as a sort of answer-through-example to a question that must arise for anyone who did not live through the years of Freud's peak influence: However did he maintain his standing?

Freud's core notions, the ones that compose the theory of psychosexual development, the ones that he considered foundational, sound utterly implausible. The claim that obsessions arise from overstrict toilet training and that, in contrast, paranoia stems from difficulties in the oral—breast-feeding—stage of development? The theory that panic attacks arise from undischarged sex drive or (in a later version) repressed violent or sexual impulses? Today, I doubt that a single psychiatric residency instructs trainees that the goal of therapy is to free patients from constraints of the Oedipus complex.

Freud turned out to be unlike Copernicus, Darwin, or Einstein. Historians of science still debate Freud's contributions, but I think it's fair to say that most of what was original in Freud came to be understood as fantasy.[5]

Still, for the first half of the twentieth century and longer, those same theories were science, passed down as all science was through instruction, memorization, and testing. They were sustained in other ways as well, in the humanities and in medicine. Studying Freud remained a requirement for a liberal education. Meanwhile, psychiatry had become Freudian, and the profession proved especially prone to inertia.

Jerome Kagan must be right about the decades of Freud's dominance in scholarly circles. Anthropologists never took his writings seriously. By the 1960s, psychology rejected core Freudian constructions like penis envy and castration anxiety. New psychiatric medications cast more doubt on Freud's theories. If one neurotic symptom responded, others should have arisen in its place. Mostly, they did not.

In psychiatric practice, Freud's theories outlived their tenure in academia. Analysts occupied the major academic chairs. Clinicians had worked for years to master the fine points of psychoanalysis;

they tended to protect that investment. For most of the last century, for almost any mental illness or psychological ailment, the optimal treatment, if the patient could tolerate it, was psychoanalysis, often with attention to theories that researchers had long since discarded.

I underwent one of those treatments.

Toward the end of college, I found that although I was succeeding in my studies, I was not finding the pleasure that was meant to accompany success. Many kids—my writer friends—were getting psychotherapy through the university clinic with a psychiatrist (he was later defrocked for sexual misconduct) who specialized in creative types. When I made an appointment, he asked why I had not come sooner. Seeking therapy in the second half of senior year was a form of resistance. Just as my child analyst had, years prior, the health services doctor framed the problem in Freudian terms. I had shown myself reluctant to examine my unconscious impulses. Or for Oedipal reasons, I was out to frustrate the doctor, to make the method fail.

After graduation, I would be studying in London. Instead of treating me, the psychiatrist referred me to a colleague there at the Hampstead Clinic, the home of classical psychoanalysis. London had more innovative centers, but the message was that quality resided in tradition. Harvard men got Freudian analyses.

Nothing cemented my attachment to Freud more strongly than the therapy that followed. My analyst, Max Goldblatt, was a master.[6] Max, as I called him privately, was an attentive listener and a caring doctor. I thought of him as an especially wise and imperturbable friend.

In the manner of midcentury psychoanalysts, Max said little. When he made interpretations, they hewed to the party line. Preparing for a summer visit home after my first year in London, I wondered aloud whether my parents would notice the improvements in my tennis game. Max told me what I meant: implicitly,

I hoped that they would understand how much sexual competence I had acquired. (We're speaking relatively. My tennis game
was never that strong either.)

On the question of resistance, Max was a bear. One day I arrived
late to a session because London transport workers had called a
wildcat strike. Midjourney I had to leave the Underground and jog
miles to the consulting room. Max wondered what in the prior session had made me reluctant to continue our discussions.

What he meant was Freudian. In arriving late, I was avoiding
exploration that would lead to disturbing feelings related ultimately to repressed violent or sexual impulses. There were also
transference considerations. Was I wary of opening up to Max
because I had made him out to resemble one of my parents?

I respected this line of inquiry. I could hardly have anticipated
the work stoppage, but I understood that treatment would proceed best if we operated on the invariable conviction that anything
that interferes with the analysis must be interpreted as the
resistance. Illness, emergencies, transportation issues—all could
have a psychological basis. The motive for missing part of a session
would need to be explored.

I was in London on a scholarship that allowed me to study literature and philosophy, but before I had left the States, I had been
accepted to law school and then delayed admission. In the therapy,
Max and I concluded that I now wanted instead to go to medical
school and become a psychiatrist. My father was a pharmacist. My
mother had recently become a school psychologist. Previously,
because of my ambivalence about my parents—reluctance to
compete with them or please them—I had suppressed awareness
of my calling.

What was at issue was not a decision but a realization. The
analysis had unearthed a wish that had existed, fully formed, in my
unconscious. I arranged to take chemistry and biology courses
back at Harvard in the summer between scholarship years in
London.

In London, researching the thesis I was struggling to write, I spent long hours in the library of the British Museum. Taking occasional breaks—I was trying to read Heidegger in German—I tackled Freud in English translation, working my way through the *Standard Edition* in preparation for my new career.

By now, I had encountered competing schools of thought. My girlfriend was in treatment with a Kleinian analyst. Richard Wollheim, who taught a philosophy seminar I attended, had undergone a Kleinian analysis, and spent time with Melanie Klein. At one point, I had a landlady who practiced Kleinian analysis. London was a hotbed of psychoanalysis.

I was aware of ego psychology, too. It grew out of the writings of Anna Freud, the doyenne of the Hampstead Clinic.

But both Melanie Klein and Anna Freud styled themselves (Sigmund) Freudians, and Wollheim was a respectful interpreter of Freud. I saw the alternative theories as variants of the core discipline. Freud was bedrock, the ultimate basis for understanding the mind. Best to start there.

When I entered med school, I did not know where the kidneys were located and could not have said with confidence whether measles was an infectious disease, but I had read through half of the Freud corpus—all his early writing on psychoanalysis.

I went directly from London to Harvard Medical School, whose psychiatry department was among the most Freudian in the nation. Introducing psychotherapy, our first-year instructor in psychiatry asked a homey question: Why are boy toddlers so squirmy in shoe stores? The answer, which we were expected to accept unquestioningly, was that as the clerk slips on the shoe, the foot vanishes in a manner that arouses castration anxiety. Who knows whether the toes will reappear?

Most of that first term was devoted to subjects like anatomy and physiology. To assure myself that the memorization of metabolic pathways would lead somewhere, I spent my free time working at an outpatient psychiatry clinic at Beth Israel Hospital.

I was meant to treat only carefully selected cases, but the intake process must not have been thorough. My first patient was a young woman who had slept with her prior therapist. Alarmed at my initial report, my supervisor said that my job was to sit with the patient for the remainder of the prescribed ten sessions and not have sex with her. Meanwhile, I was to listen as a Freudian, paying special attention to early childhood traumas that had left the patient vulnerable.

I modeled myself on Max; minimal intervention, a caring and kindly attitude, and a steady oscillation of attention between past and present. Fortuitously, Max's focus on resistance proved useful. When the patient turned impulsive or self-destructive, I asked whether the therapy had aroused uncomfortable feelings. If the patient idealized me, I wondered what past relationships were being replicated in treatment.

The Freud-friendly clinic reinforced my identity as a therapist. Other settings at Harvard Med were similar. A group therapy instructor taught me to sit quietly with five or six gravely ill patients and direct such conversation as there was toward classic analytic topics, like early disappointments in the family.

In the middle of medical school, the tide turned. The 1970s and 1980s saw a flowering of psychotherapies based on varied dynamics—social, familial, marital—and diverse theories of mind.[7] Mentors were intent on broadening my scope.

I worked in community settings—court clinics and a rural mental health center—where supervisors had me focus on behavioral issues and social support.[8] Often, I found that alternative therapies allowed me to reach patients better than Freud's methods did.

Existential psychotherapy had a special appeal for me. I seemed suited to it, philosophically and operationally. I liked coming to patients without preconceptions, liked trying (metaphorically) to sit beside them and look out on the world as they did. I treated very ill patients. They seemed damaged more than conflicted. I came to appreciate the therapeutic power of empathy, a tool that Freud barely mentioned.[9]

Soon, too, I met some of the pioneers in psychopharmacology. I began combining medication and psychotherapy and saw patients progress at a pace that psychoanalysis did not anticipate.

A story for another essay: how I became less Freudian. The major influence was work with patients.

But change in perspective came gradually. I continued to study psychoanalysis, and Freud's work in particular. Years into my practice, in a tense clinical moment, I might find myself thinking *Oedipal* and *resistance*.

In his famous eulogy, W. H. Auden writes of Freud as being "wrong, and at times absurd" but as having been transformed into "a whole climate of opinion. / Under whom we conduct our differing lives."[10] Writing in 1939, Auden was referring to Freud as a liberator on two levels, political and psychological. He made us look at our darker impulses.

Later in the century, Freud was a climate of opinion still, but in different fashion—routinized, codified, part of a standard curriculum. His work could still be inspiring, as it was for me, but Freudianism had also become an inescapable part of daily life, a pervasive and largely unexamined ideology.

Did it do harm? My life would have been poorer without it— poorer or very different.

A thought experiment: I imagine myself traveling to London and undergoing treatment with an early form of cognitive behavioral therapy. If I had improved, I would have thanked the therapist as I would thank a dermatologist for handling my acne and gone on to study the law.

Exposing complexes, interpreting dreams, applying close reading to patients' free associations—those aspects of Freud's method led me to believe that I could offer help from the perspective of the literary arts. It was only because psychiatry was Freudian that

I considered medicine as a profession. Absent Freud, I would not have been a doctor.

As a psychiatrist, I wanted to follow in Freud's footsteps. I told my residency director that I would not pursue an academic research career. I would treat patients, explore the mind through psychotherapy, and write about what I found. The director told me that those days were long past—there was no such career.

There was, for me. I did not make grand discoveries, did not pursue the great existential questions as Freud had, but in outpatient private practice, I saw enough that was new to sustain a career as a writer.[11] Explaining psychiatry to a general audience, I made constant reference to sociology, anthropology, and the fine arts.

Did my Freudian bent, what remained of it in the early years of that practice, cause patients harm? I worry that it may have. When a young man floundered in his career, I might see him as competitive with his father and self-destructive or self-undermining in the resulting efforts—when I should have attended more to the patient's learning differences and attention deficits. When a patient criticized me, I was prone to absorbing the content as material, as an amalgam of transference and response to my own countertransference. It was only with experience that I became more down-to-earth.

In a more general sense, my Freudian leanings served patients well. I listened intently. I sought layers of meaning. Even as I pulled away from the posture of psychoanalysis—as I aimed to have psychotherapy better resemble ordinary, by-the-way conversation—I remained quieter and more restrained than most modern therapists.[12]

In time, I came to accept many of the scholarly criticisms of Freud and his methods. He was a highly imperfect clinician, his case reports were often unreliable, and much of what we still value in his work was borrowed from other colleagues. Yes, his ambition, his preeminence, his adoption by the culture in midcentury America—all that exaggeration had its value, opening the door to psychotherapy in general and to discussions of feelings that are unstated or even denied in intimate relationships. Still, the widespread acceptance should give us pause. How extraordinary that such implausible theories should predominate in the scientific community, in medical practice, and in popular culture, for decades.

As for my own absorption in Freud—I do not want to deny personal responsibility. There were always those around me who had doubts. I was a willing student, a willing Freudian. I wanted for the mind to work as he said it did—for it to be highly plastic in the face of self-examination. Most especially, I wanted for psychiatry to be a humane discipline, wanted for it to be a literary art.

PSYCHOANALYSIS IN THE COLD WAR AMERICAN RACE MOVIE

Gerald Early

For we found, to our great surprise at first, that each individual hysterical symptom immediately and permanently disappeared when we had succeeded in bringing clearly to light the memory of the event by which it was provoked and in arousing its accompanying affect, and when the patient had described that event in the greatest possible detail and had put the affect into words. Recollection without affect almost invariably produces no result. The psychical process which originally took place must be repeated as vividly as possible; it must be brought back to its status nascendi and then given verbal utterance.

—SIGMUND FREUD AND JOSEPH BREUER, *STUDIES ON HYSTERIA*, 1895

One [a Black Harlemite] wanders dazed in a ghetto maze, *a "displaced person" of American democracy.*

—RALPH ELLISON, "HARLEM IS NOWHERE," IN *SHADOW AND ACT*, 1964

[My father and I] did agree that the Jews and blacks were in something of the same boat together, and there seemed to be ample reason for us to support each other. Both groups were outside the American mainstream. Both groups were discriminated against. There was an affinity between us.

—BLACK PSYCHIATRIST PRICE M. COBBS, *MY AMERICAN LIFE: FROM RAGE TO ENTITLEMENT*, 2005

Before the producer Stanley Kramer made his 1949 World War II film *Home of the Brave*, Black characters in Hollywood films were generally seen in simplified ways, most often as humorous stereotypes—that is, humorous for a White audience. Kramer characterized it in this way: "Until 1949 the only roles for black actors were in the Step'nfetchit [*sic*] category. 'Yowsah, boss. Right away.'"[1] Blacks could also evoke grand pathos or a sort of ethnic authenticity or ethnic simplicity, as in the two big all-Black Hollywood musicals of the 1950s, *Carmen Jones* and *Porgy and Bess*, or even an earlier film like King Vidor's *Hallelujah* (1929).[2] The abiding stigma of minstrelsy reduced Blacks to surfaces without depths; there was nothing behind their servile or folk-like faces. They were knowable to Whites in the audience—happy dancers, comics, natural salt of the earth—as they were knowable to themselves. In Hollywood films, Blacks were, in a word, obvious, transparent.

In breaking with this "tradition," *Home of the Brave* seemed to make a statement about how Blacks had been portrayed in Hollywood films as much as it was making a broader statement about, as White liberals of the time would put it, the then-current dilemma of race in the United States. From the first, Kramer told his cast and crew that they "had to expect opposition from almost every corner."[3]

James Edwards's character, Peter Moss, has returned from an island reconnaissance mission against the Japanese unable to walk and with partial memory loss, although he has no physical injuries. He was the sole Black man on the mission, accompanied by four White men, one his childhood friend, Finch, played by Lloyd Bridges, who is killed. Another is T.J., a racist, played by Steve Brodie. Mingo, played by Frank Lovejoy, is a hard-nosed type who takes people as they come, and the untested Major, played by Douglas Dick, simply wants to get the job done.

The death of Finch in the jungle amid the pressures their friendship endured while on the mission induced Moss's neurotic paralysis: a combination of guilt about his friend's death, for which

Moss feels partly responsible; relief that while his friend died, he survived; and a sense of betrayal because, in a fit of anger, Finch was about to call Moss "a nigger." (Audiences were likely jarred by how much "nigger" was uttered in the film, including four times by Moss himself in a fit of frustration, despair, and shame.)

Here was something new under the American sun: a Black person as a neurotic. As the White psychiatrist who is treating Moss says, "There's something inside him, deep inside him that caused all this." Moss is just the kind of patient Sigmund Freud encountered in Paris when he studied with Jean-Martin Charcot in 1885–86: someone then called a hysteric, suffering from a psychosomatic illness that we would now call post-traumatic stress disorder, causing paralysis from the waist down. A Black man suffering from trauma, partly induced by the stress of combat and partly by racism, was now the subject of a film. Sigmund Freud had entered the intersection between popular culture and race.

Moss is treated with narcosynthesis, a common treatment for psychologically battered soldiers during World War II, which is not unlike the hypnosis that Charcot and Josef Breuer, Freud's mentor, used in treating neurotics. It included administering drugs to the patient in order to facilitate an interview; or what Freud's famous patient Anna O. would fittingly call "the talking cure," without drugs or hypnosis. *Home of the Brave* is told in flashbacks, but these represent or symbolize Moss *talking*, even though he rarely narrates in voiceover. In this sense, no Black person had ever talked so much in a Hollywood film before. And no White person—in this case, Moss's psychiatrist—had ever been so interested in what a Black person in a Hollywood film had to say about himself, about his feelings, about his life. This film posed the question: What is wrong with the Negro? Further, it made it the responsibility of Whites to cure him.

At the end of the movie, Moss tells the bigoted T.J. and the maimed Mingo, "Toward the end the Doc and I just talked. . . . It was part of the treatment." But he and the doctor had been talking all along.

The talk is about getting Moss to remember, so that the doctor and Moss can locate the source of his neurosis. One is reminded of the famous line from Freud and Breuer's book *Studies on Hysteria* (1895): "Hysterics suffer mainly from reminiscences." The film suggests that Blacks suffer mainly from reminiscences, or the inability *to read* their reminiscences properly and make something constructive from their memories. In this sense, the film suggests that being Black is an act of repression that Moss's experience, not simply with war, but with racial integration in the military, provokes and intensifies.

The film is built around a Black person being psychoanalyzed, literally on the couch. (Moss is lying down when he tells the doctor his story.) Psychoanalysis in this instance, however, is more than talk. Freud, inspired by his time with Charcot, insisted that hysteria, the manifestation of the neurosis, was not the result of an injury to the body or the nervous system. As novelist Irving Stone describes Freud's thinking in his monumental work about Freud, *The Passions of the Mind*:

> Where [Freud] had departed from Charcot, though he had not said so in his letter, was that Charcot believed hysterical paralysis resulted from a lesion, a wound, in the nervous system, if only a slight one; and that recoveries took place, as in the cases of Porcz and Lyons, when an arising emotion was so strong that it overcame or cured the lesion. Sigmund Freud had come to doubt this, since no one had ever found a cerebral lesion in a hysterical paralytic alive or dead. *The lesion was in the ideas of the mind.*[4]

Stone poses the issue more vividly earlier in the novel, depicting a conversation between Freud and the American neurologist Bernard Sachs, both of whom are studying under the German-Austrian neuropathologist and psychiatrist Theodor Meynert in 1883:

> The only argument Sigmund had with Sachs was over the use of the word "mind." Sachs kept talking about "diseases of the mind." Sigmund said:

"Barney, that specimen you are looking at through your microscope is not a thin slice of a human mind. It's a slice of brain."

"How can you separate the mind from the brain," Sachs insisted.

"The brain is a vessel, a physical structure built to contain. The mind is the content: words, ideas, images, beliefs. . . ."

"Indistinguishable, my dear friend."[5]

The idea of seeing himself as just another person is what the White psychiatrist tries to get Moss to accept in order to cure him. Black viewers of the film might have wondered, however, if that idea was impossible at the time and have thought that the psychic aspiration merely made Moss sicker. On the other hand, because Blacks suffer from such intense racial self-consciousness that it sometimes is hard for them to distinguish between the misfortune that befalls them because of their race and the misfortune that befalls them because misfortune befalls all people, finding out as a Black what you share as a human with others may indeed cure some Black neuroses, or so goes the reasoning of the doctor in this film. If you can successfully undergo psychoanalysis, then you must be like the White people for whom it was invented.

The film is a drama not of segregation, but of integration. Moss is suffering because he is living an integrated life, but he is the only Black person in the film. From the scenes of his high school days to the dramatization of the military mission, he is surrounded by Whites, and never shown with any other Black people. Indeed, he volunteers for the mission knowing that he will be sent with a company of Whites. The viewer assumes that he wants integration, but also fears it. He is the modern *aspiring* Negro. The film demonstrates that racial integration has made, to borrow Ralph Ellison's phrase, "a displaced person in American democracy."

Home of the Brave is based on a play of the same name by Arthur Laurents that briefly played on Broadway in late 1945 and early 1946. In the play, however, the Moss character (named Coen) is a Jew. The dramatic arc of the play is otherwise the same as the film's. The reason for the change, according to Kramer, is that, "Jews have been done."[6] As Kramer writes in his autobiography, "anti-Semitism had already been treated in American film. I always felt that the drama and difficulty of *Home of the Brave* could be made more powerful by shifting its focus to antiblack prejudice."[7] In Kramer's view, presenting a Black character in this way was a radical departure. In fact, Laurents, who had originally written the play with a Black lead character, changed it to a Jew so that Broadway producers would feel more comfortable mounting a production of it: "To stage it about a black man would be so dangerous as to make it unfeasible. The possibility of riots in the streets was very real."[8] Kramer shot the film in secret, under the working title "High Noon."[9]

—

Blacks had been depicted as heroes in Hollywood war films before *Home of the Brave*. In 1943, a watershed year of American racial violence, three movies were released showing heroic Black soldiers: *Bataan*, featuring Kenneth Spencer as a brave Black soldier among a company of Whites making its last stand in the Philippines; *Sahara*, featuring Rex Ingram as a fearless Sudanese soldier; and *Crash Dive*, a submarine film featuring Ben Carter as a Black messman who goes on a commando raid with his White crewmates.[10] In *Home of the Brave*, Moss and the others who return from the mission are cited as heroes, but is Moss really a war hero in our conventional understanding of that term?

If segregation isolated Blacks *as a community*, *Home of the Brave* dramatizes how integration isolates the Negro *as an individual*. Moss's anxiety is heightened by his uncertainty—not simply about whether he will survive the rigors of the mission, but how much his White colleagues will support him and trust that he will support them in their mission. As the film shows, even a friend like Finch can turn racist when annoyed or angered or tense. If Moss cannot trust his friend, how can he possibly trust the other Whites who profess either hostility or indifference to him? Moss's great concern is that he fulfill his function on this team despite expectations among his team that he will let them down. The film dramatizes the challenge of defying racist stereotypes, one of the great psychological problems that Blacks face with integration. This is a completely Freudian presentation of racism: Black neuroses result from internalizing and then trying to exorcise bad ideas. Indeed, the entire film can be seen as a Freudian exorcism, not of racism itself but of a Black person's debilitating reaction to it.

When I watched *Home of the Brave* as a boy, I did not think Moss was a hero. In fact, I felt ashamed because the White soldiers had to save him. A captured, tortured Finch dies in Moss's arms, and the Japanese come after the men. Moss is stricken with hysterical paralysis and cannot walk. The racist T.J. winds up carrying Moss back to the ship that is waiting to pick the men up.

To me, Moss simply seemed weak. Despite T.J.'s racism, he saved Moss's life. This made me feel uneasy about the film's message: T.J. saved Moss, but his racism did not mellow. Was he simply performing his duty as a solider by aiding a stricken comrade? After all, the Whites could have simply left Moss on the island to be killed by the Japanese and told whatever story they wanted to their superiors. Who would have known otherwise? Why did the White soldiers not feel some resentment toward Moss because his paralysis nearly got them all killed? The film almost seemed to suggest that integration will not work because Blacks are not psychologically ready for it. They have been too maimed by segregation.

At the end of the film, Mingo, who lost his arm on the mission, and Moss wind up owning a tavern together, something Moss and Finch had talked about earlier. While forced and false, this ending suggests that integration is the future of the country. But if Mingo is maimed by the loss of his arm, Moss is equally maimed by his skin color and his doubts.

The thesis of the film is that the Negro is psychologically damaged by racism and discrimination and needs to be cured: the same argument that the Supreme Court would use in the 1954 *Brown* decision that declared government-sponsored segregation unconstitutional. This is virtually the same argument that Ralph Ellison makes in his 1948 essay "Harlem Is Nowhere," about the establishment of the Lafargue Psychiatric Clinic in Harlem. Ellison's point is that Blacks need psychotherapy because of the trauma of their experience in America, their harsh transformation from rural to urban, their cruel isolation from American social institutions. Freud is needed in Harlem, Ellison writes:

> For [Harlem] is a world in which the major energy of the imagination goes not into creating works of art, but to overcome the frustrations of social discrimination. Not quite citizens and yet Americans, full of the tensions of modern man but regarded as primitives, Negro Americans are in desperate search for an identity. Rejecting the second-class status assigned them, they feel alienated and their whole lives have become a search for answers to the questions: Who am I, What am I, Why am I, and Where?[11]

Of course, Moss does not quite know who he is (and what he knows he does not like) when the psychiatrist begins to treat him. In part, the talking treatment enables him to reconstruct his identity by reconstructing his past. The failure of the film is that even in reconstructing his past, Moss still has no identity. What the film tells us is that Moss knows he is not White, and nothing will make him White, but the film does not tell us what being Black is or what that has to offer Moss. To want to be like everyone else, as the psychiatrist tells Moss, is not an identity but the absence of one. Moss is isolated at the beginning of the film and remains isolated at the end. His Freudian treatment has merely disguised the isolation by defining it as a form of debilitating racial self-consciousness that he must overcome. That is his mental lesion, as it were.

But what if, instead of the Black person receiving the Freudian treatment to cure him of his inferiority complex caused by racism, a Black person were to administer psychiatric care to a racist White person? Hollywood has dramatized that. too.

———

I believe [my father] felt that surgery was the finest expression of the medical art, and he wanted me to pursue that area of study. I myself, though, wanted to spend my life in the mind and the soul, probing in my patients for an understanding of the emotions and, most particularly, emotional dysfunction. I wanted to understand such dysfunction and to help my patients understand it as well, so that they could do something about it.

—BLACK PSYCHIATRIST PRICE M. COBBS,
MY AMERICAN LIFE: FROM RAGE TO ENTITLEMENT, 2005

"Whoever heard of a Negro psychiatrist, anyway? Don't you people have enough troubles?"

—PATIENT SPEAKING TO HIS BLACK
PSYCHIATRIST IN *PRESSURE POINT,* 1962

Producer Stanley Kramer thought of *Pressure Point,* his 1962 film about a Black psychiatrist treating an American Bundist, or Nazi sympathizer, during World War II, as "a failure." He blamed himself "for undertaking the project before I knew enough about it to think it through completely."[12] Kramer did think it through enough to change the Jewish psychiatrist on whose case the story is based to an African American. (The story is from Jewish psychiatrist Robert Lindner's *The Fifty-Minute Hour: A Collection of True Psychoanalytic Tales,* published in 1955. Lindner is most famous for the 1944 volume *Rebel without a Cause: The Hypnoanalysis of a Criminal Psychopath.*) It was a studied decision, for in the early drafts of the scripts the doctor remained Jewish.[13] In fact, a version with a Jewish doctor, titled *Destiny's Tot,* aired as a television adaptation in 1960, and Lindner used this same title for the case in his book.

Kramer said he made the change because "in the contemporary scene it seems more pointed, valid and dramatic. Also, I was anxious to show the Negro in a different position to that of the subservient, non-educated one."[14] The reason for the change is nearly identical to that for the change in *Home of the Brave*: uplifting the image of Blacks by uplifting the Black character on the screen. Sidney Poitier, who played the psychiatrist in *Pressure Point*, praised Kramer: "What particularly impressed me was his willingness to have a key role rewritten so that it could be played by a Negro actor."[15] Kramer again: "There should be no reason why any number of properties could not be changed to reflect the improving position of the Negro in our society."[16] *Pressure Point* was the only film of 1962 that featured a Black actor in a lead role. Whether it inspired more Black youth to become psychiatrists, as Poitier hoped, is unknown.[17]

The singer Bobby Darin was chosen for role of the Nazi, after Paul Newman and Warren Beatty turned it down, even though Darin was a relatively inexperienced actor and did not look remotely like the stereotypical Aryan type that Hubert Cornfield, the scriptwriter and director, and Kramer, the producer, had in mind. Darin was a big star at the time, and Kramer felt another star was necessary as, Cornfield noted, "Sidney at that point couldn't carry a picture by himself."[18]

Darin, in keeping with his brash, temperamental persona, wrote a piece for *Ebony* magazine explaining to Black readers why he accepted the part, and emphasizing that he was nothing like the character he was playing: "I could not do this picture if I were a fascist. I could not do this picture if the final message was against my beliefs."[19] He continues, with Darin-esque bravado, by criticizing the actors who turned down the role, saying "they didn't have enough courage to do anything any more intrepid than 'let's run down the road and pick daisies, fellows!'"[20]

In short, Darin argued that playing a racist was a creative exercise. Certainly his role was better than Poitier's doctor character, who is nothing more than "a social symbol," a cardboard figure not simply of the knowledgeable, forbearing physician but also of the liberal, modern, dignified but indignant Negro or the White liberal's version of the liberal Negro.[21] It should be noted that Darin had to play the role in such a way that he was not utterly unsympathetic to the audience. That was the key to the film's psychoanalytic and racial bent. If racism is a mental disorder or illness that can be cured, the patient must impress the audience at times as someone worth saving. So, Darin's character is more interesting and, in some respects, in the end, more convincing than Poitier's.

Pressure Point takes place almost exclusively in a prison during World War II, 1942. (The characters have no names, emphasizing the institutional nature of their identities.) In fact, in the opening interview with Poitier's character, Darin's character denigrates Poitier by telling him that as a Black psychiatrist he could not possibly have a private practice because he could not get the patients to support it. Whites would not consult him, and Blacks could not afford to. He could work only in a prison. In this way, it might be said that both characters are in prison, creatures of a repressive, confining institution. It is not the only perceptive remark that Darin's racist character makes in the film, at least perceptive for Blacks who saw the film who would have agreed with it.

The film follows the outline of Lindner's account of the case fairly closely, even using snatches of dialogue from its source. The racist patient is at first resistant to the psychiatrist but then submits to being treated for insomnia and blackouts. He reminisces about his childhood—his brutal, womanizing, hard-drinking father who is a butcher and grocer; his weak mother who lies in bed and constantly complains about her illnesses, while slobbering attention on her son that is semi-incestuous. As a boy, he is smart. Lindner describes him as having "an alert and eager mind, more than an ordinary amount of curiosity."[22] But he is disruptive in school. He is picked on by the older boys and is unpopular but, in turns, bullies younger boys. The film makes only the most oblique reference to his being forced to perform fellatio on bigger boys and his, in turn, forcing younger boys to do this on him. He shows signs of being a leader; becomes a petty criminal, a thug; is sent to prison and released; is attracted to an ideology that worships power, eventually Nazism. He gets into trouble of one sort or another because of his crude political activism and is eventually sentenced to prison for three years for sedition. The film has a brief interlude where he grows fond of a Jewish girl but is ultimately rejected by her father, which apparently made him an anti-Semite. This is contrived Hollywood melodrama that is not in the source material. In *The Fifty-Minute Hour*, Lindner diagnoses him as "bisexual," his sexual encounters with men and women having little emotional significance for him, only satisfying a physical need.[23] The film version, naturally, could not touch that.

The difference between *Pressure Point* and *Home of the Brave* is not simply the racial reversal of doctor and patient. What is clinically more important is that the racist in *Pressure Point* is a psychopath, not a neurotic. He is less helpless about his condition, as he is driven more by action than by developing hysteria-based behavioral tics, and less likely to be helped. Lindner calls considerable attention to the fact that the subject could not be hypnotized, a feature more common to psychopaths than neurotics. As Lindner writes:

> Psychiatrists deplore [psychopaths'] inaccessibility to therapy; psychologists regret their utilization of a special variety of intelligence that defeats clinical tests; psychoanalysts are chagrined by their usual impenetrability and disinclination to remain long enough in therapy for a working relationship between analyst and patient to be established. So, the psychopath is a kind of therapeutic orphan who, even if he has enough insight (and few have) to realize the fact of his personality distortion, ordinarily finds it almost impossible to get the treatment he requires.[24]

Freud did not treat psychopaths or psychotics. In fact, the clinical and social range of people he treated was very narrow. He generalized greatly from small samples, the fact of which led to the calling into question of a lot of his theories in relation to their relevance to people who were not educated, middle-class Europeans or people who did not want to or could not talk.

The drama of *Pressure Point* turns on why the doctor decides to treat this patient, not only because he finds him abhorrent, but because there is not a great chance of success, as the patient does not have to see him, and psychoanalysis requires a great time commitment. (This is true in the source material.) It also turns on why the racist patient chooses to see this particular doctor. After all, as Kramer has changed the dynamics by making the doctor Black, the racist patient must overcome both his dislike of the doctor and his lack of confidence in his ability because he is Black. The patient might have been more willing to believe that a Jew would be a competent doctor. In the age of integration, a major barrier that had to fall was White (and even Black) doubt about the ability of the Black professional.

One way of looking at the situation presented in *Pressure Point* is as a perverse kind of anti–buddy movie, the opposite of Kramer's *The Defiant Ones* (1958), which starred Tony Curtis and Sidney Poitier as two escaped Southern convicts chained together who wind up caring for each other (a simplistic endorsement of the contact theory is one unfavorable way of interpreting this film).

Changing the race of the psychiatrist in *Pressure Point* results in the most significant departures from the source material. Poitier's character's relationship with the prison hospital board is entirely different from that of Lindner's. The prison officials are White. They pressure Poitier to take a case he does not want. After Poitier's initial success with the patient, the officials want to release him on parole, which Poitier adamantly refuses on the grounds that the patient is not cured. In a tense confrontation with the board, with Darin's character in the room, Poitier tells them that Darin has been lying to them about the nature of their relationship. Poitier bolts from the room when he sees that his White colleagues do not support him. They believe Darin's false interpretation that Poitier holds a grudge against him because he had been a Nazi and said racist things to him but that he now has forsworn those beliefs. (In actuality, the character has not.) The board disregards Poitier's recommendation and grants parole. Poitier quits his job. (The viewer cannot hold the board entirely to blame as Poitier initially informs his superiors that he did not want to treat Darin because he did not feel he could be objective, that he felt his race would get in the way.) Darin needles him on the day of his release, saying that the prison officials, being White, were naturally going to believe him over his Black doctor. Poitier, in a rage, confronts Darin:

> This is my country. This is where I've done what I've done. And if there were a million cruds like you, all sick like you are sick, all shouting, "down, destroy, degrade"; and there were twenty million more sick enough to listen to them, you're still gonna lose. You're gonna lose, mister, because there is something in this country, something so big, so strong that you don't even know. Something big enough to take it from people like you and come back and nail you into the ground. You're walking out here? You are going nowhere. Now, get out!

For Kramer, Poitier's speech was one of the big emotional payoffs of the film: "The film is concerned with ideas and ends in a ringing affirmation—by the Negro—of American democracy and its ability to improve and survive extremists."[25] Whether Black audiences found the speech quite as rousing—or simply naive or unconvincing—is difficult to say. Some Blacks might think, Why should a Black professional have such faith in a country whose institutions so persistently undermine him? Whatever the case, the speech was clearly meant to have a Black person affirm that Blacks are not displaced people in American democracy. In this regard, the film achieves something more than *Home of the Brave* does. Poitier's character may be professionally restrained and institutionally constrained, but the character shows greater strength than Moss does in *Home of the Brave*. Perhaps that is the difference between the Black person being the doctor and the Black person being the patient.

None of this matches the source material, where Lindner and his patient agreed to discontinue treatment. The patient's symptoms had disappeared, and his personality was sufficiently altered so that Lindner no longer thought he was a psychopath. There was no institutional wrangling or disagreement about releasing the patient. In the film, we are told that the patient was hanged ten years later for senselessly killing an old man in the street, a stranger. In the source material, the patient was killed in combat in the Philippines. The film's ending is meant to justify Poitier's character's assessment of the patient.

The triumphant liberalism of both *Home of the Brave* and *Pressure Point*—the universality of Freudian psychoanalysis, and that Blacks need to be understood through psychoanalysis—would, for many Blacks today, be the films' weakness. Consider how *Pressure Point* is framed with Poitier's character, twenty years later, a senior supervisor, insisting that a White psychiatrist, played by Peter Falk, stay on the case with a belligerent young Black patient who hates Whites and will not respond to treatment. Falk's character thinks that a Black psychiatrist should take the case. Poitier tells his story about treating Darin's Nazi character as a lesson in cross-racial treatment, difficult but worth the perseverance.[26] In the end, Falk's character leaves Poitier's character's office rejuvenated, inspired, ready to continue treating his recalcitrant patient. Cold War liberalism's insistence on the virtues of color-blindness as the solution to the race dilemma is suspect or, for some, even offensive now, and was probably a source of uneasiness for many Blacks at the time the films were made. Black Americans realize they are Americans but that they cannot be made into being just like any other Americans. Nonetheless, the films' message of America as a multiracial society committed to integration and to respecting the complexity of the Black American psyche were profoundly pathbreaking.

Whatever Stanley Kramer's feelings of producing a failure, *Pressure Point* reflects a moment in popular culture in which racism was denounced as a serious illness that needed psychiatric treatment, rather than indulged as a regional or cultural quirk or custom or simply bad manners, as it generally was before World War II. Freud's entry into the popular debate about the nature of racism was, in this regard, a considerable change for the better.

ONCE A NEUROLOGIST

Richard Panek

During the second week of October 1895, Sigmund Freud discovered the answer to an eternal question: How does the brain work?

How do thoughts happen? How do figments of the mind—wishes, words, fantasies, urges, memories—come into existence? Freud knew how, courtesy of a blinding moment of revelation, and he committed that knowledge to 102 handwritten pages that he mailed to a friend, along with an account of his epiphany: "The barriers suddenly lifted, the veils dropped, and everything became transparent."[1]

For at least a century now, Freud's primary public identity has been as the founder of psychoanalysis. Which he was. But this emphasis on his later career does a disservice to his earlier career, one that dominated the first twenty-plus years of his professional life, one that wound up influencing the next forty-plus years, and, in retrospect, one that might put his work on the unconscious into a fresh perspective. He was a neurologist.

—

Freud's investigations of the brain date to his admission to the University of Vienna's medical school in 1873. For the next eight years, first as a student and then as a researcher, he devoted himself to the study of the nervous system. In choosing to specialize in neuroanatomy, Freud was entering a field of research that, for the first time since the invention of the microscope two centuries earlier, promised imminent progress.

Just as the invention and refinements of the telescope in the early seventeenth century rendered accessible the workings of the outer universe, so the invention and refinements of the microscope over the next several decades rendered accessible the workings of the inner universe. Both lens-dependent devices allowed observers to see previously unimaginable phenomena. In telescopy, those phenomena included innumerable stars otherwise invisible, mountains on our moon, moons orbiting Jupiter, and the . . . *somethings* around Saturn. Handles, maybe? Galileo couldn't be sure. Not until the understanding of lenses had sufficiently advanced could the Dutch astronomer Christiaan Huygens, in 1655, twelve years after Galileo's death, solve the mystery of Saturn's "handles": a "thin, flat ring, nowhere touching."[2]

In microscopy, similar struggles with how lenses work fostered similar struggles with interpreting what observers were observing. In the 1670s Antonius van Leeuwenhoek, a Dutchman as curious about what he might see by pointing a microscope down as Galileo had been by pointing a telescope up, put a drop of water under a microscope and observed "upwards of one million living creatures."[3] In the plaque from the mouth of an old man who had never cleaned his teeth van Leeuwenhoek reported "an unbelievably great number of animalcules, a-swimming more nimbly than I had ever seen up to this time." Upon close inspection of the finest components of animal tissue, van Leeuwenhoek identified objects he called "globules," a description that, owing to the limitations of lenses, persisted for the next century and a half—microscopy's equivalent of "handles."

In 1826, the British physicist Joseph Jackson Lister revolutionized the microscope by making improvements to the objective lens—the one nearer the specimen—that mostly eliminated distortions and color aberrations. This advance allowed him to settle the question of what globules are: They aren't. The illusion of their existence had been merely a trick of the light that Lister's new lens system could now correct. "Instead of globules," Lister wrote, his achromatic microscope reveals "a multitude of very small particles, which are most irregular in shape and size."[4] Anatomists named these particles "cells."

A major discovery soon followed: Cells always seem to be in the immediate vicinity of long strands of some sort—fibers, microscopists called them. Were these fibers independent entities, or did they in some fashion "belong" to the cells? The technology was still unequal to the task, and so the answer would have to remain a matter of speculation until the next breakthrough.

It came in 1858, two years after Freud was born, when a German professor of anatomy, Joseph von Gerlach, invented microscopic staining: the method of dyeing a sample so that the specimen under observation—in this case, the cells—would bloom into a rich color easily distinguishable from the background.

Two more major discoveries followed in quick succession.

First: Fibers do not float free. They extend from the central nerve cells.

Second: The cells *do* float free. They always exist in isolation from other cells.

But if the cells don't connect to one another, then how do they communicate? How does one cell "know" what the others are doing and therefore act in concert, registering a sensation, creating a thought or emotion, committing the nervous system to an action? The answer, neuroanatomists reasoned, must be through the fibers, though validating that hypothesis would have to wait for another technological breakthrough.

It seemed to arrive in 1873, the same year that Freud entered medical school, when the Italian physician Camillo Golgi developed a staining method that did for fibers what von Gerlach's method had done for cells: bathed them in vivid color, thereby isolating them from the background. Even this level of clarity, however, proved unequal to the task: the mesh of fiber networks was still too dense for anyone to pinpoint where a fiber from one cell connected to a fiber from another.

So the hypothesis continued to hang in limbo, if only nominally. Maybe neuroanatomists didn't have *proof* that fibers connect with fibers, but what else could the answer be? For the most part, they simply turned their attention to other frontiers in the still-new field of neurology.

Sixteen years later, a description of Golgi's staining method reached the Spanish neuroanatomist Santiago Ramón y Cajal. He was incredulous. Science doesn't proceed on assumptions. What if the assumption that fibers connect is wrong? And why had nobody tried to improve on Golgi's method?

So Ramón y Cajal did just that—he improved on Golgi's method, and there, under his microscope, he discovered the answer to where the fibers connect: Nowhere. Fibers don't connect. Instead, they *contact*. A fiber, under the excitation of an impulse, reaches out to touch a neighboring cell's fiber, and then, when the excitation has relaxed, it retracts to its previous state of isolation.

"A connection with a fiber network," the German anatomist Wilhelm Waldeyer wrote two years later, "or an origin from such a network, does not take place."[5] Here, then, was the brain's basic unit, a discrete entity that Waldeyer named the neuron: one cell and its accompanying fibers, a whole that exists in isolation, until it doesn't. And here, too, was a hint, perhaps, of how the physical components within the brain can lead to an abstract psychological manifestation within the mind.

———

Freud would have had every reason to think that if anyone were in a position to unite the physical with the psychological, the brain with the mind, it was he. He'd dwelled in both realms, immersing himself in the intricacies of each.

In the physical realm, Freud had excelled at neuroanatomy. Twice he had developed valuable new methods of microscopic staining: first in 1877, as a student at the university's Institute of Physiology, "for the purpose of preparing in a guaranteed and easy way the central and peripheral nervous system of the higher vertebrate"; then again in 1883, as a diagnostician and researcher at the General Hospital of Vienna, "for the study of nerve tracts in the brain and spinal cord."[6] That same year, Freud also demonstrated his mastery of the achromatic microscope by conducting an examination that drew praise in a contemporary medical journal for its "very valuable contribution" to a field "heretofore lacking in detailed microscopic examination."[7] He also made significant breakthroughs in the study of the medulla oblongata, the patch of matter connecting the spinal cord and the cerebrum. He discovered that cocaine can serve as an anesthetic during surgery. (To his horror and enduring professional regret, he inadvertently made a gift of this insight to a colleague, and with it the priority for the discovery.)

As someone fluent in microscopy and staining, Freud had naturally tried to see for himself a connection between the fibers of one central nerve cell and the fibers of another. He hadn't succeeded, but that defeat had led him to speculate in a way that anticipated Waldeyer's neuron doctrine. Speaking to the Vienna Psychiatric Society in the early 1880s, Freud said that because he himself had been unable to locate the point of connection, he had begun to wonder if cells might *not* connect through their fibers. But Freud wasn't making a prediction. He was merely speculating.

Freud, however, wasn't just trying to determine whether a connection existed. He was also trying to determine if such a connection or its absence might explain the workings of the mind. His assumption was the same as the assumption that had been guiding other neurologists. Effects, in this case psychological ones, have physical causes and only physical causes.

Isaac Newton's 1687 *Principia* had laid down the laws of the universe—the laws of motion; the law of gravity. Causes lead to effects, which in turn cause new effects, which cause more effects that cause more effects: on and on and on, the gears of the universe grinding, in the reigning metaphor of the age, like clockwork. Planets work that way; the elements in Mendeleev's periodic table work that way. Why would the human brain be any different? The director of the university's Institute of Physiology when Freud studied there in the late 1870s and early 1880s had been, in his youth, part of a group of physiologists in Berlin that had vowed to uphold this specific doctrine: in the words of a fellow member, "that in the organism no other forces are in effect than the common physical and chemical ones."[8]

The cause: a physical process in the brain. The effect: a psychological phenomenon in the mind.

Freud had spent the decade before Waldeyer's formulation of the neuron doctrine educating himself about the curious workings of human psychology. In 1880 he met Josef Breuer, a researcher at the institute. Over the following two years, Breuer told Freud about a patient he was treating in private practice, one Bertha Pappenheim. Breuer, seventeen years Freud's senior, related to his mentee a most remarkable development. He was able to alleviate some of the symptoms of her hysteria and paralysis not through standard medical means via physical contact but partly through hypnosis and partly through her reflections on the source of her trauma. A "talking cure," she called it.

Freud next encountered the powers of hypnotic suggestion in 1885, when he received a grant to travel to Paris and continue his studies in neurology at the Salpêtrière, the legendary Left Bank medical complex. The first weeks were unsatisfying; Freud found the laboratory facilities chaotic and unwelcoming. Even Paris disappointed, as he wrote his fiancée less than two months into his stay: it was expensive; he was poor; the shopkeepers cheated customers with "a cool, smiling shamelessness"; "all you hear is *charmé* (which is not true)."[9] He was thinking of returning home.

He did, however, enjoy one aspect of his stay: the two sets of weekly lectures on hysteria by Jean-Martin Charcot, the diminutive yet dominating hospital director. The word *lectures* actually doesn't begin to do justice to what Freud found himself witnessing. Charcot paraded specimens of human misery whom he culled from the hospital or who had traveled from great distances in the hope that Charcot could cure them. Through hypnosis Charcot could induce symptoms and remove them. After volunteering to be Charcot's German translator, Freud entered the great man's inner circle, even regularly attending dinners at Charcot's palatial home on the Boulevard St.-Germain. Three weeks after writing his fiancée that he wanted to come home, Freud was sighing like a born boulevardier: "What a magic city this Paris is!"[10]

How to account for the phenomena on display in Charcot's subjects? What could possibly be their physiological cause? Charcot professed not to care. In the laboratory, neuroanatomists were trying to locate the lesions corresponding to the behavior—to no avail. Charcot, adhering to the Newtonian matter-and-motion, cause-and-effect model, had no doubt the lesions were there. Instead, he committed himself to examining what he *could* examine: the symptoms.

Freud agreed. If neuroanatomists couldn't locate the lesions, then, like Charcot, Freud would concentrate on the symptoms themselves. Freud realized it wasn't Paris he needed to leave. It was the lab.

—

Upon his return to Vienna he accepted a position as the director of the new neurological division at the Institute for Children's Diseases and opened a private practice in which he applied his knowledge of neurology to patients' symptoms. Like Breuer, he tried to ease their suffering through hypnosis, but he proved to be inept. Instead, also like Breuer, he encouraged his patients to try to trace their current circumstances to the source of the trauma.

In this respect he and Breuer were following the standard Newtonian model. A symptom of hysteria, for instance, can't simply emerge out of nowhere, can it? It has to have had an initial cause, which led to an effect, which caused another effect, and so on. Trace the current trauma to its initial cause, he reported in a talk before the Vienna Medical Society, and the symptoms will disappear.

"*Cessante causa cessat effectus*": When the cause ceases, the effect ceases.[11]

The news of the neuron doctrine, however, revived in Freud the old dream of matching the machinations of the brain with the mysteries of the mind. Although by this point he hadn't been working in a laboratory for five or six years, the neuroanatomist who had anticipated the nonconnection (though not the contact) of fibers was still residing inside him.

The mind, he'd discovered, was more complex than just about anyone had anticipated. Which made sense: The brain was more complex than just about anyone had anticipated prior to the dawn of neurology as a science. The challenge now was to disentangle the mind by disentangling the brain.

Freud began writing tentative outlines of some ideas bridging the two realms. Some of these outlines he included in letters to his closest friend and constant correspondent Wilhelm Fliess, an ear, nose, and throat doctor in Berlin. In the summer of 1895 Freud and Fliess convened for one of their days-long congresses, as Freud called these occasional periods of intense and inspirational discussions. This one proved to be especially productive. Within the next two months, Freud saw the project whole, and it was nothing less than the unification of brain and mind, neurology and psychology.

"The intention of this project is to furnish us with a psychology which shall be a natural science," he opened the manuscript. "The project involves two principal ideas." The first: the workings of the brain are "subject to the general laws of [matter in] motion"— the Newtonian principle of cause-and-effect. What contributed to Freud's sense of urgency, however, was that he now knew what the "matter" was: "2. That it is to be assumed that the material particles in question are the neurons."[12]

In the letter to Fliess accompanying a draft of the manuscript, Freud described his postcongress epiphany: "I had a clear vision from the details of the neuroses to the conditions that make consciousness possible. Everything seemed to connect up, the whole worked well together, and one had the impression that the Thing was now really a machine and would soon go by itself." By the "Thing"/"machine," Freud's biographer Ernest Jones wrote some six decades later, Freud meant "the mind."[13]

Almost immediately Freud realized that he'd overreached. On November 8, less than three weeks later, he wrote to Fliess that not only did he now know the paper "required a lot of revision" but that he had "flung it all aside."[14] The following month he wrote to Fliess: "I no longer understand the state of mind in which I hatched [the project]; cannot conceive how I could have inflicted it on you." He concluded: "To me it appears to have been a kind of madness."[15] He put the pages, he reported to Fliess, in a drawer— not a proverbial drawer but a literal one. The closing of that drawer marked the end of his career as a neurologist.

No longer would he occupy himself with attempts to bridge the brain-versus-mind divide. Instead, from that moment on-ward, his focus would be exclusively on a different dichotomy: mind versus mind.

Even as he was working on the psychological/neurological project, a book he'd written with Breuer was coming out. He had convinced Breuer to collaborate on their separate experiences in the clinic—*Studies in Hysteria*, they titled their collaboration— beginning with that of Bertha Pappenheim (on whom Breuer bestowed the pseudonym Anna O.). In another case study, Freud explained the technique he had developed for eliciting memories from patients—a method he would name, in two papers he sent out only two months after abandoning his project, "psycho-analysis." It was a method that he could deploy in an attempt to relieve his patients' suffering, but it was also one he could use as an exploratory tool—an instrument of sorts, one that would allow him to study the mind in much the same way that he had dissected the brain, one that he could use just as he and his predecessors had used *their* instrument, the achromatic microscope.

What was the human mind? Freud would lay it open on the examining table, so to speak, and see for himself. He would hover gently behind the patient and, by listening, look. A chair, a couch, and more than meets the ear: Sigmund Freud had found his way back to the lab, after all.

———

Freud never abandoned the possibility that the inner processes of the mind follow a Newtonian determinism originating in physiological phenomena, even if current knowledge couldn't articulate the precise sequence of cause and effect. In his 1924 *Beyond the Pleasure Principle*, he echoed the doctrine that Brücke had transposed from his youthful advocacy into the halls of the University of Vienna's Institute for Physiology: "The deficiencies in our description would probably vanish if we were already in a position to replace the psychological terms with physiological or chemical ones."[16] In *An Outline of Psycho-Analysis*, which he completed the year he died, 1939, Freud wrote, "The phenomena with which we were dealing do not belong to psychology alone; they have an organic and biological side as well."[17]

Today's neurologists have access to technologies that Freud couldn't have imagined, machines that light up the neuronal pathways in vivid colors reminiscent of von Gerlach's and Golgi's microscopic staining. Yet well more than a century after Ramon y Cajál resolved the identity of the inner universe's equivalent of the handles of Saturn, we still await—and perhaps always will await—a claimant to the title that Freud sought for himself: the Newton of neurology.

TANGLING WITH FREUD IN A POST-FREUDIAN WORLD

Sherry Turkle

Professionally, I challenged the psychoanalytic institution but remained a fervent champion of central tenets of Freudian psychology. Now I think technology demands a return to Freud in our post-Freudian world.

—

I became a Freud critic in the 1970s through my work on the French psychoanalytic movement.[1] By studying a group of institutional rebels around the dissident analyst Jacques Lacan, I saw how the cloistered walls of officially sanctioned psychoanalytic institutes reflected a tension between the idea of psychoanalysis as a living, scientific enterprise and psychoanalysis as an esoteric knowledge passed from fathers and mothers to symbolic (and sometimes, actual) children.

Freud chose to pass on his teaching through a church-like institution. Within sanctioned institutes, only those anointed as "training analysts" could create the next generation of analysts. But being in a "training analysis" meant that analysts in training were often judged on their professional progress by the same person listening to their free associations. So, it became commonplace for analytic candidates to tell their analysts life stories that matched standard theory to be accepted for full training at their institute. Then, after they had secured their professional lives, new graduates would go back to do second and even third analyses, in which they could just be themselves. That was the world Freud set up when he demanded theoretical loyalty and gave out rings to the compliant.

My focus on contradictions within the psychoanalytic institution contributed to the "Freud Wars" of the late 1970s and early 1980s. Other writers in this movement took on Freud more personally. Most devastating was to insist that Freud knew that the women he treated were not fantasizing about the sexual advances of the men in their lives. The abuse was real.[2] And critics retold the story of Freud's life to demonstrate how Freud broke his own rules. In particular, he analyzed his daughter Anna. A daughter would have Oedipal love for her father. When love manifested in treatment with her *actual* father, it could hardly be interpreted as analytic transference. The Anna Freud analysis was a fundamental transgression, common knowledge, and a well-known secret.

In 1977, I included this bit of information in the submitted draft of my book on Jacques Lacan and French psychoanalysis.[3] My publisher's legal department advised me that since this wasn't central to my main argument, I should delete it. I was a young scholar publishing my dissertation. I gave in to the pressure. That's how a well-known secret remains well kept.

But my critique of the Freudian establishment left me a Freudian. I was always interested in separating the contradictions of the psychoanalytic institution from what seemed to me most useful in Freud's ideas. I had a troubled childhood. I thought that one day, when I could afford it, psychoanalytic treatment could help me. But there were other considerations central to the researcher I wanted to be. As I worked on my recent memoir, I found intellectual connections made very early that inspired my lifelong fidelity to Freud.[4]

Erikson: Identity and Interiority

As I worked on my memoir, I read through college notebooks and found one from my 1965–67 introduction to Freud as a Harvard freshman and sophomore. In one class, the psychoanalyst Erik Erikson argued that Freud should be recast as a theorist not of the libido but of self and society. Freud was relevant to thinking about Martin Luther and Gandhi in their historical moments and to my generation's consideration of civil rights and the struggle against the war in Vietnam. In other writing, Erikson reimagined Freud's psychosexual stages (oral, anal, phallic) as metaphors for social tasks: to trust, have control, and exercise autonomy.[5] No handle ever cranks, or gear turns to graduate you from one stage of development to another. So, for example, the issue of basic trust comes up in infancy, and identity is most pertinent in adolescence. But you work on both of these your whole life, always bringing different skills to bear, always using the new materials you have on hand at the time.

When I was forced to drop out of college in my junior year after my mother died, I was bereft. My family had been torn apart. I left Cambridge for Paris and did housecleaning in exchange for a room. Alone in Paris, I was too fragile to truly mourn my mother. I couldn't bear to think of her as she had been. I tried to reclaim only what I admired, starting with her relentless optimism, which was what I most needed at the time. Erikson's reading of Freud (You work on every life task over the long haul) helped me make peace with my limitations. I could think, "You are here to mourn your mother, but you'll be doing that for a long time. What you are doing now is your best possible first step. Or rather, it's the only step possible for you now."

When I took my first job—as a professor in the newly formed science, technology, and society program at MIT—Erikson came to talk to us about education in America. Now, he was older and retired from formal teaching. I remember his prepared remarks as unremarkable. But people were simply happy to have him there. It was an imprimatur for our efforts. After his talk, I told Erikson that his work had been vital to me. He passed over the compliment and asked me what I was doing now. "I study scientists and engineers and how they relate to their computers." He said just this: "Scientists and engineers, well, that's not the same thing at all. Engineers, they're not convinced we have an interior. It's not necessary for their purposes."

Fifty years later, the center of my work is how digital technology hollows us out. The engineering dream of the metaverse, the cadences of TikTok, and the push to have robots substitute for companions undermine the long-term possibilities for human empathy by saying, "It doesn't matter. We have something more efficient." I often think of that moment with Erikson when what came to him was to point to something essential in Freud: Humans are more than their behavior. We have an inner life.

Sophomore Tutorial: Social Theory Needs Clinical Sensibilities

But how does the outside world come inside us?

That question was at the center of my next encounter with Freud during my sophomore tutorial in social studies, led by a political scientist, Martin Peretz, and an intellectual historian, Paul Robinson. What interested them was putting Freud in dialogue with Marxist questions: How do people who grew up in one social circumstance come to demand another? How do people bring lived inequality inside them and come to see it as either unnatural or simply the order of things?

I took this note in the spring of 1967: "Robinson: Distinguish between Freud's clinical and social/theoretical work. After Freud's death, the clinical and theoretical work have been isolated from each other. We should open up this much-needed conversation."

I was thrilled to find the note. When I wrote it, I was already a fan of Erikson, who used clinical insights as background for writing about broad historical moments. Robinson was certainly encouraging that kind of work. But Erikson was a glorious exception. Robinson was saying that social scientists, social theorists, and historians should as a matter of course look to what was most robust in Freud's *clinical* insights to energize their work. We were living in times that promised radical change. We had to understand how bourgeois society makes revolutionary change hard to accomplish.

This imperative was not new: After World War I, when bourgeois Europe survived moments of what should have been a revolutionary crisis, Marxists acknowledged that "objective" forces alone could not "force" revolution. Bourgeois society shapes individuals in ways that inhibit them politically. Theodor Adorno asked for a social psychology that could "reveal in the innermost mechanisms of the individual the decisive social forces."[6]

Psychoanalytic Culture

Writing a memoir put me in contact with touchstone moments that kept me grounded in the belief that beyond helping me personally, psychoanalysis could deepen my practice as a social researcher. Robinson had the Frankfurt School theorists in mind when he suggested that his social studies students should pay attention to the clinical Freud. I was sustained by more concrete experiences. My first sociological fieldwork included a study of French students who had participated in the May 1968 events. This movement began as a university protest but ended in a general strike that almost brought the government down. Families had been torn apart in May 1968. My subjects answered my questions, but sometimes there were tears and evasions. Some wrote notes saying that, on reflection, they were trying to get back to everyday family life and put the May experience behind them.

In real life, thought and feeling are joined. I felt that people steeped in psychoanalysis respected this. I thought it was their comparative advantage in academic life. Professional sociologists too often hid behind questionnaires that kept things cut-and-dried. And there were concrete ways that a psychoanalytic sensibility could contribute to ethnographic work. Patients' and analysts' feelings for each other become critical elements of analytic treatment. They reveal a special kind of projection, transference, and countertransference, where the shadow of past experiences falls on this new relationship. Projection shows up in field research as well. In any interview, researchers should ask themselves: To whom is this subject speaking? For whom is this subject potentially performing? If this subject is belligerent, what might be frightening them?

And further questions for researchers: Who does this subject remind you of? What feelings does this interview arouse in you? If ethnographers better understood their pasts, they could see the objects of their work with greater clarity. Ethnographic empathy had some of the effects of a psychoanalytic interpretation. It may uncover elements of a social puzzle that are perhaps unknown to one's informants.

Psychoanalysis encourages patience. A research interview isn't a therapy session. But it should allow space for people to discover something about themselves. Psychoanalysis teaches that people tell small, unconscious lies. In this spirit, ethnographers should continually reflect on the truth of what they hear and respect its emotional reality even if it is not the literal truth. For example, some participants in the May events told me they were now in analysis, but subsequent conversations revealed these declarations to be aspirational. The literal truth was often that they had gone to a few preliminary sessions with therapists they might like to see someday. But their aspirations told their own stories.

Over time, I found my own way to what Paul Robinson had suggested during the sophomore tutorial. I got a joint doctorate in sociology and psychology. Then, as a licensed psychologist, I applied for psychoanalytic training. I had a name for the kind of work I wanted to pursue: the intimate ethnography of contemporary life. I loved my life as a clinician, but I had another passion: Freud offered models for how things in the outside world come to inhabit our inner lives. I needed to think about this when I turned my attention to how our digital lives change not only what we do but who we are.[7] I argued that the computer was an evocative object that affects how we experience the self itself.

Return to Freud

Now, I argue for a return to Freud.

Digital culture threatens our capacity for spontaneous talk, and perhaps even more important, it undermines our ability to understand the value of talk. These days, we're tempted to stay in the safety of our screens when we communicate. One young man I interviewed put it this way: "Conversation? I'll tell you what's wrong with conversation. It takes place in real time, and you can't control what you're going to say."

While technology seduces with its offer of control, in-person talk offers the chance to directly experience imperfection, empathy, and vulnerability. But we find ourselves in a cultural moment where talk therapy is marginalized for not being scientific enough and not providing the outcome studies that would prove it cost-effective. The world turns to cognitive-behavioral models. Yet, a psychoanalytic sensibility is needed more than ever in a larger culture that has, in many ways, gone silent. Otherwise put, Freudians are experts at the kind of talk that digital culture needs most, the kind of talk in which we give each other full attention, that's relational rather than transactional.

It's hard to get to relational talk if you grow up texting or if most of your conversation takes place on screens where eye contact is at best an illusion. In this world, it's not surprising that young people suffer from a loss of empathy.[8] And social media has left depression, suicidal thoughts, and loss of self-esteem in its wake, especially among adolescents. Again, none of this is surprising since social media encourages us to present ourselves as "better"— certainly thinner, better looking, and better dressed—than we are in the physical real. We can never really compete with our avatars.

The movement to self-curation is culture-wide; adolescents are just the most vulnerable. Instead of avatar-to-avatar talk, they need relationships with caring humans—family, friends, and mentors.

Not everyone can be in psychoanalysis or should be. But everyone can cultivate a psychoanalytic sensibility. That sensibility aims to increase our capacity to sit quietly with others, give them our full attention, and create a space to pay attention to our own thoughts as well. It teaches that we are not likely to share the most important things about ourselves in perfectly crafted bits but in stumbles and retakes and afterthoughts. It teaches that vulnerability is the best friend of empathy.

To make the point that these things are important is a point that life today too rarely makes. On the contrary, conditioned by screens, people expect the world to come to them in a steady, curated stream. A quiet moment is painful. A continual and edited feed challenges our capacity for reflective solitude.

But a capacity for solitude is a cornerstone of our capacity for relationships. Only when we can gather ourselves can we turn to others and hear what they have to say and who they are, rather than projecting onto them what we need them to be saying to support our fragile sense of self. Right now, digital culture closes down the questions that psychoanalytic culture knows how to open.

The mores of psychoanalytic culture—the value it places on authenticity, forming an empathic bond, and the quiet attention necessary to do this—have become increasingly necessary as a cultural corrective. If psychoanalysts once allowed patients to develop the capacity to talk about sexuality in a way prohibited outside the consulting room, now there are new imperatives. For me, the two most important are the experience of being "alone with" accompaniment, the first step to trying solitude without a screen. And the experience of empathic connection with the experience of vulnerability.

So it's troubling that so many analysts are tempted to turn away from the complexities of in-person treatment for the convenience of doing online therapy and even psychoanalysis. The community that brought us some of the most moving writing about presence and the body seems quick to overlook the body's importance in treatment.[9] The Freudian tradition taught that we're with each other, body and mind, words and bodies, all tied together. Freudians have elaborated on how, when we deeply listen to each other, we also have a direct bodily experience of each other's words that demonstrates our connection and complexity. Yet, in my meetings with analysts, I find that when remote treatment is up for discussion, the body is sometimes presented as close to irrelevant. And I often see a progression in thinking. At first, treating a patient or client remotely is presented as "better than nothing." Gradually, what you can do remotely begins to be presented as equivalent to or better than what you can do with the patient or client in the room.[10]

In an exchange with one analyst, at an analytic meeting, she tells me that in a treatment she's doing via Skype, she feels "a quickening," and sessions "feel more intense" than when the client is in her office. I feel sad when I point out that there's literature on how the online experience puts us into a state of hypervigilance, in which it's natural to feel a quickening. Our online experiences with each other may be exhilarating. Still, they don't necessarily encourage the relaxed, free-floating attention that the analytic tradition has long argued is a privileged way to access the unconscious and deeper levels of awareness.

Why are analysts so quick to abandon the body and what it brings to our understanding? Or have we always wanted to run from our bodies, from the anxieties of being together in this messy way, and now we're given a chance? At the same time, we're being challenged to affirm the values at the core of what it means to be human and to stand up for a kind of therapeutic work designed to speak most directly to our full capacity for meaning, empathy, and relationship—and for the untidiness that all of these bring.

The analytic community isn't alone in the desire to run away from the messy toward something that feels more tidied up. Their potential clients dream of it as well. One mother of a nine-year-old describes why she would feel comfortable putting her child in the care of an artificial-intelligence therapist. It would be nonjudgmental in a way she doesn't trust any human could be. As an example, she tells me her daughter enjoys "venting" to Siri on Apple's iPhone. With people, says her mother, she's more likely to play the "good girl." Isn't this self-expression a good thing? Perhaps, but one of the most important lessons for children is that the fantasy that one can kill a parent with angry thoughts is only that, a fantasy. This lesson that words don't destroy frees up children's capacities to experience and express emotion. But opportunity to learn this lesson is lost if children turn to a machine when they want to say the "hard things." That's exactly what this mother should *not* want to teach her daughter. And yet, to her and many others, it seems an increasingly acceptable solution.

Freud, for Now

Several years ago I met Sara Konrath, the lead author of a study that established that since the introduction of mobile technology, college students had become less empathic. She told me that she'd become despondent after she'd surveyed the findings. Konrath's first response: she began to design what she called "empathy apps" for the iPhone. She thought it a sensible move: if people practiced on these apps, they might develop empathy.

In this, Konrath followed a common impulse: if technology got us into a problem, technology will get us out of it. We're all tempted by this idea. But I believe it's a myth that takes us away from the obvious—*we are the empathy app! And we're not apps at all!* This simple truth should place the practitioners of empathic listening at the center of today's most important cultural conversations. But many psychodynamic therapists are held back by a crisis of confidence. They've too often been pushed aside for those who rely on psychopharmacology and cognitive-behavioral protocols. These have their place. But Freudian sensibilities help us remember that people are messy and complex. Freudian sensibilities support us in the multilayered and nontransactional conversations that are essential for our moment. And all the more essential because they are often portrayed as old-fashioned, superseded by something faster, cheaper, and more precise. A Freudian sensibility helps us value human relationships over the cold instrumentality of treating each other as apps.

I think of Konrath during a recent conversation with a computer science student, I'll call him Jed, who tells me that if he received the same amount of useful information, he wouldn't mind if he learned that I was a robot. "It might be better because I wouldn't be intimidated by what you know." I have had warm conversations with Jed, so I feel comfortable asking him what he thinks might be better with the Turkle robot. "We've talked about Covid, the stresses of living abroad, and navigating relationships with an adviser. You know I've grappled with these things in my own life. What could you count on when you talked to the robot?"

Intellectually, Jed appreciates my question. But, as actors say, it doesn't "land." I hear silence and then he can only explain that if the robot said the right things, it wouldn't matter to him. I formulate an unspoken, unreasonable ambition: To make Jed a member of the psychoanalytic culture. I have an odd science-fiction fantasy of a "Freudian chip." But that wouldn't work. The culture I'm interested in is transmitted by talk. If I want to do cultural recruitment, what's ahead is a relationship with Jed.

Across fifty years of studying and teaching engineers, I think of Erik Erikson and his comment at the very beginning of my career: "Engineers, they're not convinced we have an interior. It's not necessary for their purposes." As we teach and work and socialize on Zoom, as we spend more and more time on social media and are aggressively pitched a new life in the metaverse, I ask myself if we are all engineers now.

In his own day, Freud was subversive because he opened up a conversation about sexuality. These days, talking about authenticity, meaning, and interiority are the imperatives for a return to Freud.

PERSONAL HISTORY

FREUD'S FIRST SCIENTIFIC PUBLICATION

Mark Solms

In this short chapter, I describe Freud's first piece of scientific research, which I have recently translated into English for a forthcoming four-volume set: *The Complete Neuroscientific Works of Sigmund Freud*. The paper was entitled "Beobachtungen über Gestaltung und feineren Bau der als Hoden beschriebenen Lappenorgane des Aals" ("Observations on the Configuration and Finer Structure of the Lobulated Organs of the Eel described as Testicles"). It was published in April 1877, in the Viennese journal *Sitzungsberichte der kaiserlichen Akademie der Wissenschaften.*[1]

As it happens, the paper had nothing to do with the nervous system. It did, however, deal with the topic of sexuality, or reproduction, the driving force of biology. As Ernest Jones mischievously remarked, it even hinted at the later discovery of castration anxiety, since the task of the young Freud's first research project was to find the missing testicles of the eel.[2]

This project was assigned to Freud when he was a third-year medical student by the head of the Institute of Comparative Anatomy at the University of Vienna, Carl Claus, an early supporter of Darwin. Funds were placed at Claus's disposal to send a few students for several weeks of study to the Zoological Station at Trieste (then still part of the Austro-Hungarian Empire), which he had just established. Freud's grant was one of the first to be made, in

March 1876. His task was to determine through microscopic examination whether a lobulated organ that a Polish zoologist, Szymon de Syrski, had identified in 1874—on macroscopic grounds—as being the long-sought testicle of the eel, was indeed so.

Claus was clearly satisfied with his student's performance, as he renewed the grant for a second visit in September. Later, some time before October 1876, he supplied Freud with additional (and more mature) specimens to study at the Institute in Vienna. He presented Freud's findings to the Academy of Sciences on March 15, 1877. Despite a somewhat inconclusive outcome, this study is remembered today as being the first in a series that eventually confirmed Syrski's hypothesis.

Freud's research question had a venerable history. It was generally recognized, from ancient times, that animals reproduce by means of some sort of sexual exchange between the males and females of each species. However, nobody had ever witnessed such an exchange in eels, not least because it had not been possible to identify sexual organs in them. On this basis, Aristotle had speculated in *De generatione animalium* that eels reproduce spontaneously, through interaction with decomposing organic material in the mud beneath the water. Later, Pliny the Elder suggested that when eels rub themselves against rocks, the particles of skin that fall from their bodies come to life spontaneously. Later still, Oppian observed that eels had a habit of coiling around each other, producing a foamy secretion which, he believed, burst into life upon falling into the mud.

With the translation of Aristotle's works into Latin in the mid-thirteenth century, his "spontaneous generation" hypothesis gained renewed status. It was only during the Renaissance that a more critical attitude began to emerge. Thereafter, in 1707, Vallisneri claimed to have proved the existence of sex organs in the European eel by identifying ovaries in a particularly large female. In 1777 Mondini reported that the structure described by Vallisneri was a diseased air bladder, and he himself described the true ovary. Mondini's findings were not confirmed until 1824, though, when Rathke independently described the ovary of the eel, and later, in 1850, when he described a female with eggs 0.1 mm in diameter.

However, biology's ongoing failure to locate corresponding male testicles and spermatozoa in eels frustrated efforts to free the species from Aristotle's shadow. Even the Comte de Buffon, the leading naturalist of the eighteenth century, admitted to being stumped. As long as eel reproductive organs remained unknown, he confessed, the very foundations of reproductive biology would be unsteady. When the great German microscopic anatomist Max Schultze died in January 1874, he is said to have expressed the consolation that all the important questions except the eel question had now been settled. This is why Syrski's claim to have found the testicle—later that same year—was so significant.

Freud was less satisfied with the outcome of his research than his professor was, as is perhaps reflected in the fact that the written report was hastily prepared for publication just a few weeks after Claus's presentation. Jones says that Freud considered the project to be a fool's errand. It had long been known that eels disappear from European waters for extended periods, at around four years of age; and it had recently been suggested by Philipp Franz von Siebold that *the males develop their sexual organs only after embarking on their journey to the Sargasso Sea*—which is where European eels spawn.[3] That no one had found their testicles was therefore unsurprising: unless they were caught in the Sargasso Sea (rather than somewhere like Trieste), there would be no testicles to find.

At first, Freud had nevertheless hoped to identify spermatozoa in Syrski's organ, using the microscope, and thereby to settle the matter, but that was impossible to achieve in the immature specimens at his disposal. Accordingly, his abstract of the work,[4] written twenty years later, gives a dismissive impression and, shortly before his death, he described it as "feeble."[5]

The following tongue-in-cheek letter, which Freud wrote from Trieste on April 5, 1876, to his childhood friend Eduard Silberstein, sets the scene for what would become Freud's first professional publication:

> I obtain sharks, rays, eels and other creatures daily, which I investigate first from the general anatomical viewpoint and then in relation to one specific point. That point is the following. You know the eel. For a long time, only the female of this creature has been recognized; even Aristotle did not know where they found their males and thus conjectured that eels spring from the mud. Throughout the Middle Ages and in modern times, too, a veritable hunt has been on for male eels. In Zoology, where there are no birth certificates and where the beasts behave in accordance with Paneth's ideal[6]—without training—we do not know which is male and which is female if the animals do not possess external sexual differences. That certain distinguishing features are indeed sexual differences must also first be demonstrated, and that is up to the anatomist (since eels do not keep diaries from the orthography of which one can deduce gender); he dissects them and discovers either testicles or ovaries. The difference between the two organs is this: under the microscope, the testicles display spermatozoa and the ovaries—even to the naked eye—reveal eggs. Not long ago, a Trieste zoologist [Syrski] discovered, he says, the testicles, and with that the male eel; but since he apparently does not know what a microscope is, he failed to provide a detailed description of them. Now I am tormenting myself and the eels to rediscover his male eel; but in vain, all the eels that I cut open are of the fairer sex.[7]

SEARCHING FOR MARTHA FREUD

Daphne Merkin

September 29, 1939, 20 Maresfeld Gardens, Hampstead, London: The first Friday after Sigmund Freud's death, having accepted more than half a century's imposed impiety at her husband's insistence, seventy-eight-year-old Martha Freud started lighting Sabbath candles again.[1] *Licht-benching*, as the ceremony is called. You light a pair of candles just as the sun goes down; circle your hands in a sweeping motion three times as if to gather the light and savor the candles' warmth, the spirit of restfulness they are meant to convey; then you cover your eyes with your hands while reciting the blessing: *Baruch ata adonai, elohenu melech ha'olam, asher kidshanu be-mitzvotov ve-tzivoni, le'hadlik ner shel Shabbat.*

Enter Shabbat Ha'Malkah, Shabbat the Queen, a presiding feminine presence in a patriarchal environment where most of the active, time-specific *mitzvot*, or injunctions—such as the putting on of *tefillin*, or phylacteries (a pair of small black leather cubes, containing pieces of parchment inscribed with Biblical verses, one of which is strapped around the left arm, hand, and fingers and the other of which is strapped above the forehead) for the morning prayers—fall on men, since women are presumed to be busy with other priorities, such as housekeeping and childcare. And now here was the widow of one of the most formidable enemies of religion fulfilling one of the few obligations incumbent upon women under Judaism. It was, surely, a form of poetic justice—or perhaps a testament to the hold of the past, however abjured it may be.

She was born Martha Bernays on July 26, 1861, in Hamburg, into a highly regarded and intellectually advanced family to whom such recurrent observances meant a great deal. With her performance of the act of lighting candles at a prefigured moment on the Jewish calendar, one might argue that Martha Freud was being more than assertive; she was being defiant. In doing so, she was taking a step backward toward the lively, book-loving girl she had been and the traditionalism of her origins before she became the more compliant, devoted caretaker that Freud desired her to be: the "adored sweetheart in youth" who became "the beloved wife in maturity."

She was also taking a step forward, toward the postspousal woman she would become (she outlived her husband by twelve years), reclaiming a small part of the ancient, ritual-laden religious tradition that had been instilled in her while she was growing up. It was a tradition that her avidly secular husband (whom she always referred to as "Professor," as though she were his eternal student) ridiculed, forbidding her to light Friday night candles when they set up their own home.

According to Freud's Women, by Lisa Appignanesi and John Forrester, a cousin of Martha recalled "how not being allowed to light the Sabbath lights on the first Friday night after her marriage was one of the most upsetting experiences of her life." And one visitor to their house, the philosopher Isaiah Berlin, observed that husband and wife were still arguing the issue of lighting candles, however playfully, as late as 1938: "Martha joked at Freud's monstrous stubbornness which prevented her from performing the ritual, while he firmly maintained the practice was foolish and superstitious."

All the same, the Freud marriage was reputed to have been exceptionally harmonious—one of their few disputes over fifty-three years was said to have been about the correct way to cook mushrooms. While her husband worked up to sixteen and occasionally even eighteen hours a day, Martha (also known as Frau Professor) carried around an enormous bunch of keys, the better to oversee a household that included a cook, a governess, and a nanny, and keep it running like a well-oiled machine. Lunch was served promptly at one every day, a formal meal often featuring *tafelspitz* (boiled beef and vegetables, with a horseradish sauce), a favorite of Freud's. The Freuds' six children were well behaved, having had instilled in them the importance of their father's work. As one of Freud's sons, Martin, noted in his reminiscences: "There was never any waiting for meals: at the stroke of one everybody in the household was seated at the long dining-room table and the same moment one door opened to let the maid enter with the soup while another door opened to allow my father to walk from his study to take his place at the head of the table at the other end."

The critic Jenny Diski suggested in a 2006 review of a translated biography of Martha Freud by Katja Behling in the *London Review of Books* that the exemplary bourgeois surface Martha helped provide—"the rigid table manners, ordered nursery and bustling regularity"—enabled her husband to organize his "deeper, hardly thinkable thoughts" into "something that looked like a scientific theory. By polishing that surface and keeping clocks ticking in unison," Diski concludes, "Martha was as essential to the development of Freudian thought as Dora or the Rat Man."

Still, the couple's divergent attitudes toward Judaism remained a source of underground conflict. On the face of it, they were wholesale de-Judaized Jews, celebrating Christmas and Easter; their son Martin recalled that none of the six children had entered a synagogue, and it is commonly assumed that neither Martin nor either of his two brothers was circumcised. Freud, a confirmed atheist with little tolerance for religious belief in any form, would delight in ribbing Martha about her religious attachment, pretending not to know the Hebrew name for "candelabrum" in a note he wrote her in 1907 after visiting the Roman catacombs: "In the Jewish [catacombs] the inscriptions are Greek, the candelabrum—I think it's called Menorah—can be seen on many tablets." As if he didn't know that it was called a menorah!

Although Freud never denied his Jewishness and went so far as to credit his religion with a lack of prejudice and an uncowed single-mindedness, he also went to great lengths to separate the theories and practice of psychoanalysis from both the religious and the Jewish, especially given how anti-Semitic thinkers attributed a Jewish character to his work, which in turn led to a resistance to their views. But, Freud wrote in a letter to Ferenczi, "there should not be a thing as Aryan or Jewish science. Results in science must be identical, though the presentation of them may vary."

To better understand the Freuds' respective positions on the issue of Jewishness, one need go no further than their immediate backgrounds. Whereas Sigmund Freud came from an Enlightenment-influenced assimilated Viennese family, Martha's background was one where traditional observances were scrupulously maintained. Her mother, Emmeline, wore a *sheitel*, or wig, and was a tenacious and domineering personality though outwardly coming across as mild and soft. (These traits would antagonize her future son-law; he described her as "alien" and wrote his fiancée that "I seek for similarities with you, but find hardly any.")

Martha's family was renowned in the Jewish community for their scholarship and leaderly qualities. Isaac Bernays, her grandfather, was the chief rabbi of Hamburg; upon his death, he was acknowledged by no less a figure than Heinrich Heine to have been an extraordinary personality. (Despite Bernays's strict commitment to Orthodoxy, he was considered to be something of a religious modernizer, known for his innovative sermons and for his willingness to incorporate German into the synagogue service. In an odd coincidence, my great-grandfather, Samson Raphael Hirsch, was a student of Bernays and followed in his tradition of bringing together Jewish and secular realms.) Two of Martha's paternal uncles were university professors: one, Jacob, was a classicist whose adherence to religious convictions prevented him from becoming a full professor at Bonn University; the other, Michael, was a Goethe and Shakespeare specialist who converted to Christianity and was baptized, which estranged him from his family at the same time as it furthered his career. Martha's father, Berman Bernays, was a merchant, as were the parents of his wife; her father later became the secretary to a well-known economist and constitutional law expert named Lorenz von Stein, and when Martha married in 1886 his profession was given as "journalist." Martha grew up in fairly modest circumstances, and when she was six her father served a stint in prison for criminal fraud; she is said never to have talked of this incident. (Freud's uncle was imprisoned for trading in counterfeit rubles, and rumor had it that his father was implicated in the scandal. Diski argues in her *London Review* essay that the couple was united by the legacy of public shame.)

The family moved to Vienna when she was eight, and one of two elder brothers, Isaac, died at the age of sixteen, when she was eleven—a kind of loss she shared with Freud, who also lost a brother early on. Despite being portrayed in later years as culturally indifferent (in particular to her husband's profession), Martha developed an interest in art and literature during her years at school. She had a keen appreciation of music and was an avid reader who knew the German classics and some world literature; during their courtship, Freud shared his thoughts on John Stuart Mill with Martha, and his first present to her was a copy of *David Copperfield*, although he warned her off the rude parts in *Don Quixote*. By the time he met Martha in April 1882, her sharp mind, attractive appearance, and coquettish charms had attracted many suitors, and she had already turned down one proposal of marriage.

—

The first time Sigmund Freud spotted Martha Bernays, just shy of twenty-one, she was at his family's home, visiting his sisters together with her own sister Minna, around the dining-room table. She was peeling an apple: a decorous, quintessentially feminine activity, suggestive of industry and nurturing. One wonders whether things might have gone differently if the twenty-six-year-old Freud, an anxious, somewhat self-important medical student with little experience of women despite being the brother of five sisters, had glimpsed Martha in a different guise—less the privatized woman in a Vermeer painting and more an engaged woman like her sister Minna, eager to compete intellectually, inclined to take up more air.

The simple truth, however, is that Freud never had any plans for Martha to be an intellectual partner. He was happy for her to put the toothpaste on his toothbrush to save him the effort and to be viewed by her as the genius of his age, equal to a Newton or a Darwin. At the start of their engagement correspondence, he referred patronizingly to "the charming confusion in your dear sentences," and in his memoir Martin Freud recalls that when his parents had distinguished visitors over for dinner and one learned guest began to recite from the *Iliad*, Martha had departed the premises. "My mother," Martin writes, "who knew no Greek and, in consequence, was without any admiration for Homer's immortal epic, had quietly withdrawn earlier." Then, too, there was the slight puzzlement she expressed at her husband's choice of profession, as though such high-flying doings were beyond her ken. "I must admit," she said, "that if I did not realize how seriously my husband takes his treatments, I should think that psychoanalysis is a form of pornography."

In any case, the young Martha presented a winsome picture, with her center-parted hair pulled back in a chignon, and dressed in modest garb, a high-necked dress with a lace collar. Sigmund would later tell Martha that theirs was an instance of "leibe am ersten blick," love at first sight, although it is unclear whether this was mutual. He would also go on to observe to her in one of the 940 letters that he would write her during the four and a half years of their courtship and engagement that she was not "in the strict painterly sense" a beauty but that she had qualities he considered more important, such as generosity, wisdom, and tenderness. (Freud's own mother had been considered a great beauty in her day.) Freud had good features, a thick beard, and a penetrating gaze, but it seems that Martha initially found him too short and a bit intimidating.

Though rather awkward and shy to begin with, Freud was sure of his feelings for Martha and began sending her a red rose every day accompanied by a poem in Latin or another language. By the middle of June 1882, a mere two months after they met, the couple was secretly engaged despite Emmeline's opposition to the match— she considered Freud's prospects to be dim—and Freud was writing his "darling girl" and "darling Marty" long, rhapsodic letters. In his first letter to her, he wrote, "Dear Martha, how you have changed my life," but he was also an incorrigibly jealous suitor, expressing patriarchal horror that his fiancée had traveled on holiday with only her younger sister for company: "Fancy, Lubeck! Should that be allowed? Two single girls travelling alone in North Germany! This is a revolt against the male prerogative!"

Somewhere along the course of their epic engagement, un-doubtedly helped along by Freud's sneering at her efforts to put her foot down and his dislike of what he called her "tartness," Martha lost some of her moxie—her independent and even assertive spirit. One can still see that spirit peeking through late in their engage-ment, when she wrote Freud with irritation: "You now always only write once about each thing, and then nothing more however much I ask. I'm not used to this my good man, it is certainly high time I brought you to heel, otherwise I'm quite sure to go com-pletely thin and green for sheer annoyance and exasperation."

On the other hand, Martha could not have been left in any doubt as to precisely what it was her husband-to-be expected of their partnership, which was that each would have a clear and separate sphere of influence. "I will let you rule [the household] as much as you wish," he decreed, "and you will reward me with your intimate love and by rising above all those weaknesses that make for a contemptuous judgment of women." Almost from the first, Freud tried to remake Martha in a more subservient image than was naturally hers. Some of her letters show her in a poseur-like position of an innocent in need of Freud's assistance: "I finally have read your postcard with Max's help," she wrote, "because it was difficult to read. Yes, that's how stupid your dear girl is."

One doesn't need to be a raging, disenchanted Freudian like Frederick Crews to agree with certain of his opinions. "When he wasn't complaining about his present aliments and future neglect,"

Crews writes in *Freud: The Making of an Illusion*, "the unhappy fiancé was instructing his beloved in how to become a properly deferential mate. He made it clear that she would have to change some of her ways, and the sooner the better. It was precisely Martha's most admirable qualities—unselfconscious candor and spontaneity, a trusting nature, freedom from class prejudice, loyalty to her family and its values—that struck him as in need of revision. Thus he rebuked her for having pulled up a stocking in public; forbade her to go ice skating if another man were along; demanded that she sever relations with a good friend who had gotten pregnant before marriage; and vowed to crush every vestige of her Orthodox faith and to turn her into a fellow infidel."

—

One of the more intriguing questions about the Freuds' marriage, especially given Freud's own interest in the age-old problem of how to maintain both passion and durability in a connubial relationship, was the conspicuously deromanticized and possibly desexualized nature of his own marriage after its romantically impassioned beginning. (The analyst Martin Bergmann quipped: "We have wonderful courting letters before marriage. After marriage we only get laundry letters. It's all practical. We don't have a single love letter after marriage.")

The union produced six children in nine years, after which the couple decided to practice abstinence as a means of contraception. (Freud believed that birth control led to neurosis.) Freud made a reference in a letter on October 31, 1897, when he was forty-one, to his colleague Wilhelm Fliess, about ceasing connubial relations: "Sexual excitation is of no more use to a person like me," although he hinted at some incidences of sexual intercourse with Martha later on, recording in his diary at age sixty that he had "successful coitus Wednesday morning." He also wrote to Fliess that he often suffered from impotence. One paper I have read argues that Freud's decision to abstain from sex, although ostensibly to avoid having more children, may have stemmed in part from a desire to get back at Martha for her sexual retreatism during their prolonged engagement.

Freud characterized his married life with a degree of restraint when he spoke to Princess Marie Bonaparte, one of the many female friends with whom he shared his thoughts and ideas (including Lou Andreas-Salomé, Hilda Doolittle, and Helene Deutsch) in 1936: "It was really not a bad solution of the marriage problem, and she is still today tender, healthy and active." And to his son-in-law Max Halberstadt he conveyed his relief that his children had turned out well and that Martha "has neither been very abnormal nor often ill." A far cry from the sentiments he felt during their engagement when he clashed with Martha's mother over who had the greater claim to her daughter: "Marty, you cannot fight against it; no matter how much they love you I will not leave you to anyone, and no one deserves you; no one else's love compares with mine."

———

This is as good a moment as any to mention the speculation, originally started by Carl Jung and fanned over the decades by Peter Swales, also known as "the guerilla historian of psychoanalysis," that after ceasing to sleep with his wife Freud had an affair with his sister-in-law Minna Bernays, Martha's smart, witty, and acerbic younger sister. The two had corresponded while Freud was pursuing Martha, and they had a companionable relationship, not least because they lived together in the same household for forty years—first on Berggasse 19 in Vienna, where Minna moved in in 1896, and then at 20 Maresfeld Gardens in Hampstead, London. Indeed, the sleeping arrangements in Vienna were weirdly intimate: Minna's small sleeping quarters were right next to Freud and Martha's bedroom, separated only by a flimsy partition rather than by a wall and door. The only way Minna could get to her room was to go through the bedroom that the Freuds shared.

The two also took trips together, and the rumors of their illicit liaison were fueled in 2006 when a German sociologist found a yellowing hotel ledger entry written in Freud's distinctive scrawl at the inn in the Swiss Alps that the psychoanalyst, then forty-two, and Minna, then thirty-three, stayed in for two weeks in 1898. The couple had registered at the inn as "Dr Sigm Freud u frau"—husband and wife. They took the largest room in the hotel, but one that had the equivalent of a double bed. This last detail has persuaded some Freud loyalists, like Peter Gay in *The Freud Reader*, of the veracity of the rumors, although I myself remain unpersuaded. For one thing, they might have checked into a single room because of Freud's parsimonious attitude toward money; they were used to being in close quarters, and it is unlikely that, given the ethos of the Victorian era, they would have been able to rent the room if their actual unmarried relationship had been made clear. For another, despite his heretical approach to religious mores and his advocacy of greater sexual freedom, Freud strikes me as fairly inhibited when push came to shove, as well as fairly Jewish in his guilt complex. There was also the fact that Minna was not particularly attractive, and female appearance was important to Freud. In one of his early courtship letters he told Martha that her nose and mouth were shaped "more characteristically than beautifully, with an almost masculine expression, so unmaidenly in its decisiveness." Such a microscopic analysis of his future bride's less-than-perfect features suggests that he was a critical observer of female appeal. Last, he himself had once noted to his future wife that "similar people like Minna and myself don't suit each other specially."

—

Who was Martha Freud, and why is she so hard to find? Was she really just a contented *Hausfrau*, an efficient manager of a household staff, a firm but affectionate mother (although she and Anna, Freud's youngest daughter and his torchbearer, were not particularly sympatico), and most of all, a devoted wife who "tried as much as possible," as she wrote in a condolence letter after her husband's death, "to remove the *misere* of everyday life from his path"? Assuming that Freud's theories on everything from domesticity to sexuality to pathological conflict were drawn even partly from his own experience, what influence did Martha's personality and the couple's interaction have on psychoanalytic theory? It's hard to imagine her living with him for fifty-three years and not having had some impact on him beyond making sure his lunch of boiled beef was served on time. Why, then, does she appear to be of so little interest or consequence to the many biographers of her husband? (There has been one biography of her, written in German, as well as a novel called *Mrs. Freud* translated from the French; both books were published in 2005. There is also a short memoir by the Freuds' longtime housekeeper, Paula Fichtl, that I had translated from the German but that didn't add much except for a spirit of adulation for Herr Doktor and admiration for Martha's capable handling of the household and the vicissitudes of their life together).

Is Martha's featureless, sphinxlike presence an odd gap in the story—a patriarchal glitch in and among the hermetic, all-consuming narrative of male genius—or does it point to some deeper absence, some way in which Martha willingly went along with being sidelined from her husband's larger concerns the better to ensure a peaceful home life from which Freud could venture out with his unconventional, often alarming theories? One might argue that in a certain fashion she was her husband's muse, albeit not a particularly glamorous one, but more the consistent, enabling figure who helped him freely roam about in his head. It was perhaps Martha's very ordinariness—her "fully developed and well integrated" personality, as Ernest Jones put it—that offset the damage and abnormality that Freud found everywhere he looked.

Still, Freud's attitude toward Martha, which verged on the fondly dismissive, is not irrelevant to the sense one has that psychoanalysis missed out on some of the big questions, particularly about women, and fell short of its liberating aspirations. But it seems too easy to dismiss her as a martyr, unless one adds that she was a willing and seemingly contented one. Not every wife, no matter how intelligent, wishes to compete with her husband's aura. One might even see Martha's suspension of self as an example of "altruistic surrender," which was the term her daughter Anna Freud coined for children who abjure the primacy of self in the service of another. In any case, Martha seems to have gone through something of a change after her husband's death at the age of eighty-three in September 1939 after several years of excruciating jaw cancer. Aside from lighting Shabbos candles, she took to reading again and even developed a curiosity about Anna's patients, marveling at how expensive child analysis was. Although she said life had "lost its sense and meaning" without her husband, she appears to have relished being at the center of the crowd of doting visitors who came to pay homage and to have continued on with her orderly, energetic existence. She outlived her husband by twelve years, dying at the age of ninety, taking the mystery of who she was with her.

FREUD'S DOGS

Rivka Galchen

The first one to join the family was Wolf. He was brought in as a four-footed bodyguard. This was Vienna, in 1927. To walk the streets alone, as a Jewish woman, wasn't considered wise. Anna especially liked to take walks in the evenings. Wolf, a German shepherd, accompanied Anna to the Prater most days. He had dark fur, pointy ears, and great devotion. He bit Ernest Jones, the founder of the British Psychoanalytical Association, and Freud's seminal biographer; Jones, also, is said to have been making advances on Anna. Of Wolf, Freud said, "I had to punish him for that, but did so very reluctantly, for he—Jones—deserved it."[1]

On one walk, Anna and Wolf came across soldiers firing blanks; Wolf, startled, dashed away. Anna searched and searched for him. Eventually she returned home. Wolf was already there! He had taken a taxi. As the driver told it to her father, Wolf had entered the taxi and, despite polite pleadings, would not exit. He seemed to be holding his head distinctly high, as if to draw attention to his collar, which bore his name and address. Sigmund Freud, seventy-one at the time, asked the driver how much he owed him, but the taxi driver said he had failed to set the meter for this passenger.

Freud had not grown up with dogs. Nor had he been noted to have shown any particular fondness or interest. It was only in the last decades of his life that they became, arguably, central. Wolf was Anna's dog, but they lived in the house all together. Later came a series of Chow dogs that were Freud's own. He brought dogs into his consulting room with him. He claimed one of his Chows wagged its tail when a patient had an insight; this Chow also rose at the end of a consulting hour, sparing Freud the need to look at a watch or clock. Freud also wrote movingly in letters of the comfort his dogs gave him again and again: through mourning, through excruciating physical pain. With his dogs, he even celebrated his birthdays, though he otherwise hated celebrating his birthday. He allowed a ritual in which he and the dogs—and no one else—wore conic birthday hats. Several of his dogs composed (maybe with an assist from his children) birthday poems for Freud. In 1939, the last year of his life, Freud devoted much of his time to working with Anna on a translation, from French to German, of *Topsy*, the biography his friend Marie Bonaparte had written of her Chow Chow.

—

In 1923, Freud's four-year-old grandson Heinerle went into a coma. He died soon after of tuberculosis. That same year Freud himself was diagnosed with the cancer of the jaw that, thirty-three surgeries and thirteen years later, would end his life. Of Heinerle's illness, Freud wrote to a friend: "I don't think I have ever experienced such grief; perhaps my own sickness contributes to the shock. I work out of sheer necessity; fundamentally everything has lost its meaning for me."[2] It was at that time that Freud began to become very close to Wolf. Later, in writing about children, he interwove their special quality with that of animals, at times with the animals coming out more brightly. In a letter to the Dutch psychoanalyst Jeanne Lampl-de Groot, who had trained under him and was also a friend of Anna's, he wrote, "How is it that these little beings are so delightful? For we have learnt all sorts of things about them that do not correspond to our idea and must regard them as little animals, but of course animals too seem delightful to us and far more attractive than the complicated, multistoried adults." The ambivalence that Freud detailed, and made room to accept, was precisely what he didn't see in dogs, of whom he said he admired that they loved their masters, and bit their enemies. "I am experiencing this now with our Wolf, who has almost replaced the lost Heinerle."[3]

On the occasion of Sigmund Freud's seventy-first birthday, Wolf wrote him a poem that—in marking time, a wolf at the door—also offered an alternative sense of time. Wolf presented the poem by wearing it on a string round his neck:

> On a Wolf's or Dog's day
> all the hours, you might say
> are equal in their sight
> for following a trail
> or for wagging your tail
> any time is right.
> But whoever too long
> among human wrong
> habits has his habitation
> will strive with all his heart
> to imitate their art
> of congratulation.
> So the one crowned for your feast
> is a tail-bearing beast.[4]

Time is marked by the purported poet, but almost as by a nonbeliever. To take the passing of days seriously is to imitate a human art. But the crown remains in the more eternal realm of the beast.

A series of other dogs joined the Freud family soon after. This was in part on account of Marie Bonaparte—a princess, psychoanalyst, *and* dog breeder. (She was a descendant of one of Napoleon's little brothers.) She first came to know Freud when she came to him for treatment, and later she became an analyst herself. She loved and bred Chow Chows—intense, midsize fluffballs that by reputation are merely indifferent to, rather than aggressive toward, strangers. Freud's first Chow was named Lün Yug. After only a year or so, Lün Yug was found dead at a train station near Salzburg, where he had wandered off, and Freud was devastated. In a letter to Ernest Jones, Anna wrote, "I would very much like us to have a new Lün. For the time being my father does not want to hear of it."[5] Seven months later the Freuds took on Lün's sister, Jofi.

Jofi is the lion-maned Chow most often seen in photos with Freud—sometimes in his office, in another one sitting patiently while her master also sits patiently, as his bust is being made. It's Jofi who Freud has in his office with patients. Hilda Doolittle, known as H.D., describes meeting Jofi, and bending down to greet her with an extended hand. Freud tells her not to touch the dog, saying she is difficult with strangers, but H.D., who went by the nickname Cat in analysis, ignores Freud, and Jofi "snuggles her nose in my hand." In other moments, Doolittle complained that Freud was at times more interested in the dog than in her stories. "I think that if the chow hadn't liked me, I would have left," Doolittle said.[6]

The clarity of liking or not liking was something Freud admired in dogs, as he saw them. When Wolf bit Ernest Jones, Freud observed to Jones that it was because dogs instantly knew who liked them and who did not; Jones had an overwhelming fear of wolves. (Freud's mix of liking and unliking seems evident.) Jofi, like Wolf, also became a birthday poet for Freud. On his seventy-fourth birthday, he noted of the ritual that "the nicest little thing is a poem in Jofi's name, from Anna of course."[7] In the poem, which was delivered on a card tied round the neck of a turtle, Jofi imagines an escape and promises to act more restrained in greeting, if only they could be together again. When the Freuds had to flee Vienna to London, Jofi had to spend six months in quarantine. Freud would visit the quarantine quarters. (He also got another Chow while Jofi was away.) The reunion of the dog and human was covered in the news.

Jofi even went so far as to give birth. Not just a substitute child, she revealed herself to Freud as a parent. Of her first litter, only one pup survived. When Freud himself in 1936 was home recovering from a surgery of the jaw, Freud wrote to Marie Bonaparte, "I wish you could have seen with me what sympathy Jofi shows me during these hellish days, as if she understands everything."[8] A year later

he noted in his list-like diary of his final decade, "Jofi in Hospital."
This was for two ovarian cysts, and the expectation was that she
would recover quickly. She died of heart failure a short time later,
having spent seven years with the Freud family. This time a new
dog was brought to the household within a day. This was one of
Jofi's pups, named Lün after the original Lün who had died at the
train station. This Lün had been previously given away, because
Jofi had been seen to be unable to bear having a rival for Freud's
affections. "One cannot easily get over seven years of intimacy,"
Freud said of the loss.[9] Jones said of the quick replacement that
Freud, older now, could not get on without a dog. Freud described
the young Lün as tender.

———

When Marie Bonaparte's dog Topsy became ill with a cancer of
the jaw, she began to write about him:

> Topsy's sentence has been pronounced; under her lip, which is
> again swelling, there is a lympho-sarcoma, a tumour that will
> develop, grow, spread elsewhere, ulcerate, suffocate her, and
> condemn her in but a few months to the most atrocious of
> deaths.[10]

Switching tone from clinical to sentimental to mythic and on,
Bonaparte writes her way through the dog's illness, through the
nearness of death. She takes Topsy for radiation treatment; she
dreams of paradises for nonbelievers like herself; she addresses
to Topsy her thoughts on being a lady with a lapdog while the
streets are filled with labor protesters "clamouring for bread and
leisure." She thinks of the innocence of the dog who was the last
companion of Marie Antoinette. Bonaparte ends the book unex-
pectedly on a happy note; she feels she has saved Topsy's life, and
even more: that Topsy, "lying there by me . . . by her presence
alone must bar the entrance of my room to a worse ill, and even
to Death."

"Does Topsy realize she is being translated?" Freud asked Bonaparte. He was so delighted with the book, which he received a copy of in 1936, that he decided to translate it into German. He wrote to Bonaparte of the book: "I love it; it is so movingly genuine and true. It is not an analytic work, of course, but the analyst's thirst for truth and knowledge can be perceived behind this production, too."[11] Freud worked on the translation of *Topsy* into German through the March 1938 Nazi invasion of Austria, while waiting for paperwork to come through so that he and his family could leave Vienna. Freud was terribly ill as well. With the help of Bonaparte, Freud and his family made it out of Vienna and to London, via Paris, in June. The translation appeared in 1939.

In a letter of condolence to Bonaparte following Topsy's death, Freud included news of his own tumor of the jaw. "The radium has once again begun to eat away at something. . . . My world is what it was previously—a small island of pain floating on an ocean of indifference."[12] Freud had noted of Jofi that when an analysand was depressed, Jofi would rest nearer to the patient, and allow herself to be petted. When an analysand was anxious, she stayed closer to Freud. In the last days of his life, Freud had his dogs near him, and even in his bed. Eventually his tumor formed an abscess that became infected, and ate a hole through his cheek. The putrid smell kept even the dogs at a distance. It was then, after years of pain, that he asked his friend and physician, Max Schur, for enough morphine to exit the world in peace. "Now it is nothing but torture—no comfort—and makes no sense anymore."

Although Freud's dogs wrote poems, they never spoke. Yet Freud's contributions were overwhelmingly based in language, and in observations about the words that others used. Most "slips" he analyzed were verbal slips. When he interpreted his own dreams, he proceeded by analyzing a written recollection of his dream. "So many important things are centered around this one word: trimethylamine," he says, in one of the many almost comically attentive, while also marvelous, moments in what was arguably his most autobiographical work, *The Interpretation of*

Dreams.[13] In another passage of the book, he is detained by a detail in his dream of eating spinach, which reminded him of a kid complaining about the taste of spinach, and that the German word for "taste," *kosten*, was also related to "cost," which he followed out to the idea of being loved without cost. And yet the large emotional and domestic shift in his later years was toward these expressive, nonverbal creatures—whose deaths he had to witness—and who clearly had the most meaningful things to not say.

A NIGHT AT THE FREUD MUSEUM

Susie Boyt

A night at the Freud Museum! The idea appeals. I always think twelve hours the perfect length for any holiday. Philip Larkin at his most likable said, "I wouldn't mind seeing China if I could come back the same day," and I agree.[1] Packing my case, though, my intent feels heavy. There isn't the sense of a spree. I think of the bags I took with me when I went to the hospital to have my daughters: bags of hope, bags of fear. I am braced after a month when, deliberately, there hasn't been a second to think about a thing. I sense the facts vying for position, sour and exacting, after stretches of neglect. Scrutiny beckons, mercilessly. Such a stagey approach to feeling can't be good, but my mood is odd. I've been asking others how I seem, looking in the mirror to try to gauge my state of mind. My dreams have been especially sarcastic.

The museum is situated in the house where Sigmund Freud lived for the last year of his life, with his wife, Martha, and daughter Anna, and their maid Paula Fichtl, after the Nazis drove them out of Vienna on June 4, 1938. The house at 20 Maresfield Gardens is a wide, three-story, red-brick villa. It sits in a prosperous and leafy broad North London thoroughfare, its size and bearing in 2023 rendering it, and the neighboring dwellings, a mini-embassy, a mansionette. It's the kind of address at which fifteen years ago a drawing room owned by internationally acclaimed musicians might boast two grand pianos, primed for duets. It would be too expensive for them now. The road still throbs with high IQs, but it isn't glamorous, or if it is, it possesses a drab sort of glamour, tweedy and sedate, like Celia Johnson's character in *Brief Encounter*, possibly, with an injection of new tech cash.

I am to spend a few hours alone in Freud's study when the museum is closed and then sleep in Anna Freud's bedroom. I've brought sheets and blankets and a pillow. I have use of Anna Freud's bathroom and the kitchen next door. Some supplies have been laid in for me. Leaving my house, I add a box of tissues and a bottle of water to my overnight bag. If I could only get hold of a trailing spider plant, my luggage could pass for a therapist's basic prop kit.

———

At the end of Maresfield Gardens a florist is selling my favorite pale-pink roses—Sweet Avalanche. There's something about a pleasant disaster . . . the idea of good trouble . . . I hope my thoughts strike me like a sweet avalanche tonight. I begin to audition various cares to see which might best suit my august location. I don't want anything routine or banal. There's a recent loss that has gone undermourned, and it's beginning to nip at my ankles. There are slights that I've batted away, trying for elegance, like a lady in a restaurant sending back a half-cooked piece of fish. I've a young friend, brilliant and soaring, but stricken of late, whom I've attempted to help a bit as he explodes his life. He assumes our relationship, from my side at least, is one of unconditional love. It's true I've defended him and made his well-being a priority. But it is an error on his part, I think. We planned to speak recently, at his request, and he sent a message through to ask if we might not speak, after all. It didn't suit that day. He said he was hoping for "a reprieve." That word appears to have broken something. At a literary festival recently, in front of a banner saying *Families; the joy and the misery*, or was it *Motherhood: the pain and the pleasure*, I said I was uncertain about unconditional love, that I thought people spoke of it as though it came as standard and in great supply—but in fact it was rare in the extreme. I cannot always run to it for my own household. (Sigmund Freud said it existed only between mothers and infant sons.) I understand that adolescents need to feel home is a safe place to be your worst self, but to how many can I offer this service? Personally, I showed the best of myself to my parents. It is a theme in my life, currently, that too much of it involves gestures that feel like human sacrifice.

And what if my dreams at the museum let me down? They may be low in content; I don't mean low as in base, for that would in its way be excellent, but humdrum or even slight—I remembered to buy toothpaste! I posted a letter!—and how could I admit to that, even to myself? The night that Sigmund Freud sailed from Calais to Dover to come to London in June 1938 he dreamed, with honor and a burst of courage, that it was not Dover where the ferry docked but Pevensey, where William the Conqueror landed in 1066.

I take the linen to Anna's bedroom, making the bed up carefully as though for an esteemed guest. The sheets and pillowcases are pink and white and frilled, things my daughters have outgrown, comforting in their way. (The state of convalescence is my true homeland, I sometimes think.) I notice there are five tripods in the corner of the room, one with a large black hood like the abdomen of an ant in a diagram we learned at school. Long spiky legs protrude. Oh no! Oh well. My insect phobia is reasonably mild. On the other side of the room there is a large black-and-white poster of Sigmund Freud against a red ground, eight or nine times life size, with the accompanying phrase: "It is said that the twentieth century person was born on Freud's couch." I imagine this scene, and it is a baby in a tiny bowler hat with a furled umbrella and a furled personality that I see.

My father-in-law was psychoanalyzed by Anna Freud for more than two decades in this house. My mother-in-law once told me— in even tones—that when she was first married he used to breakfast every morning with his first wife and their child, then go to see Miss Freud and then on to the *Observer* newspaper building, where he was editor.

Downstairs in Sigmund Freud's study the alarms have been de-activated. I've permission to wander inside the roped-off areas as long as I don't sit on the desk chair, which is weak. The chair, made of reddish-brown cracked leather, was designed by the architect Felix Augenfeld. A present from Freud's daughter Mathilde, it looks Henry Moore-ish, its curves and rounded headrest reminiscent of a slender woman. Augenfeld wrote: "S.F. had the habit of reading in a very peculiar and uncomfortable body position. He was leaning in this chair, in some sort of diagonal position, one of his legs slung over the arm of the chair, the book held high and his head unsupported. The rather bizarre form of the chair I designed is to be explained as an attempt to maintain this habitual posture and to make it more comfortable."[2]

At home in my top-floor office I write in my father's desk chair, a small modern wooden chair on rockers, half-upholstered in beige calico, from some sort of be-kind-to-your-back shop, the fabric bearing quite a bit of flesh-colored oil paint.

In Freud's study I sit and watch the scene before me as though it were a sitcom or stage set, awaiting actors. The couch with its five cushions and carpet-style cover and thin gray blanket with S.F.'s coral-colored appliqued monogram has a great deal of presence. I sit on it for a moment and then lie down and feel foolish. I am aware the museum's security guard is glued to the CCTV. Might he have some sensible advice for me? Anna Freud said to my father-in-law, "I believe in sense as opposed to nonsense," but I'm not so sure. I get up from the couch and take instead a seat in the green velvet chair where Freud sat to listen to his patients. I feel more comfortable there. I am reading La Peau de Chagrin, the novel that made Balzac's name, the last book Sigmund Freud read. A young man, in a state of suicidal desperation, has entered a casino and is "standing there like an angel stripped of his halo, one who has strayed from his path." The casino itself is unpromising. In my experience they are places where people go to feel numb. This one is an icy-hearted arena. "The walls covered with greasy wallpaper up to head height, show nothing that might refresh the spirit. There is not even a nail there to make it easier to hang one-self." It is a place where "grief has to be muted" and "despair must behave in a seemly fashion."[3]

Business as usual, then.

In the study, because there is for the first time in the museum's history a small exhibition of paintings by Lucian Freud, my father, a picture of my grandmother hangs over Freud's couch, to thicken the plot. My father nursed a sort of abstract respect for the serious-ness of psychoanalysis but considered it "unsuited to the lifespan." Still, we sometimes discussed it. He once asked me, when I was sit-ting for him, whether it had any ideas or helpful suggestions when it came to the handling of obsession, whether this was something that had been addressed in my own therapy. He was talking, I knew, about matters of the heart. I was twenty-one at this point, and he was sixty-eight. I was touched by this opening seam of humility. "The thing about obsessions, if you ask me," I began, "is that they tend to occur when there is something else pressing that you're trying really hard not to think about."

"Oh?"

"The trouble is, of course, that the obsession quite quickly can cause more pain and difficulties than the original thing you're trying to avoid." I could tell instantly it wasn't the answer he wanted. I knew he had visited my elder brother at a rehab center recently, where he was trying and trying not to beat a heroin addiction. There my father had attended a small meeting with some gathered sup-port staff where he was told, "Alex's problem, apart from drugs, is that he is addicted to obsessive love."

"But surely obsessive love returned is the finest thing a man can feel," my father hotly defended his son.

———

In the painting above Freud's couch, my grandmother is lying fully clothed—beautifully dressed—on a bed, her arms splayed at her sides in the "Don't shoot" position. It's the attitude in which both my daughters slept when they were newborn. The fabric of her paisley dress looks luxurious, stately; and the material of the bedspread—intersecting white arcs and little textural curved lines of holes as in a hemstitch pillowcase or huck towel—is tender and modest. The bed has iron bars like the beds in a hospital or convent. Sigmund Freud was impressed with my grandmother. They got on well, and she was clever. It meant a great deal to Lucie that her father-in-law admired her and enjoyed her company. It was Lucie who insisted her family leave Berlin in 1933. I met her just once, when I was visiting my father at 36 Holland Park. You rang the bell that discreetly read TOP FLAT, and then there were about seventy steps. I paused and said good morning as I passed her on the stairs. I think I would have been about fourteen. She smiled. Did she know who I was? She looks at home lying here. I get back on the couch again and look up at her in her frame and feel for a moment as though we're about to meet on Zoom.

———

On March 15 the Gestapo raided Sigmund Freud's home at 19 Berggasse. The Professor was recovering from recent cancer surgery, and his wife, Martha, to defuse the stress and terror of the situation, asked the men if they'd care to leave their rifles in the umbrella stand. Might they like to sit down? These friendly and hospitable gestures did help calm things a little. It's a scene I often think of, extreme politeness being a useful resource in dreadful situations. After Freud left his home on June 4, 1938, on the 3:55 Orient Express, traveling first to Paris and then to Dover by ferry and then to London, the Nazis changed the function of his building to "collection apartments," and approximately eighty Jews were imprisoned there to wait for deportation to concentration camps.

———

I knew Freud's study to be grave and masculine, but I had not expected such a climate of sadness. Why hadn't I? Time has a strange quality here. It gallops and leaps when I assumed it would drag. I think of the clock melting in the Terry Johnson play *Hysteria*, which is set in this study. Fifty minutes passes in an instant, then another fifty and another. It's as though there's an impatient quality to the atmosphere. No room for anything inessential. My concerns are trivial here. The study is peopled by a cast of hundreds: the antiquities, heads and figurines that adorn most of the cabinets and surfaces, which arrived from Vienna along with other essentials such as Freud's couch in the first week of August 1938. The figures can't help but make you think of refugees.

The scent is of old leather, and there are wan notes of tobacco or something more mysteriously smoky like Lapsang souchong tea or the remnants of a bonfire, the foggy brown smell that still thickens the air for twenty-four hours after fireworks have been lit. French windows with their long red theatrical curtains almost appear to invite intruders. Freud treated a small number of patients and continued to write here until August 1939. Although his architect son, Ernst (my father's father), installed a small lift in the house, at the end of his life Freud slept in this study and a second couch was purchased for him to lie on, an invalid couch with a vivid botanical print and better orthopedic support, from a specialist shop in Great Portland Street. He liked to look through the windows at the roses in the garden, which delighted him and were not visible from his upstairs bedroom. I try to think about what it would be like to lose your home, your state, your patients, your siblings, the city where your mother tongue is spoken, half your books, and many other aspects of your identity at eighty-two, when you were already suffering the long-term effects, in terms of both symptoms and treatment, of jaw cancer. Even Freud's dog avoided him at the end, disliking the smell of the disease. There was much to be mourned. Arriving in London he wrote to the psychoanalyst Max Eitingon, "The feeling of triumph on being liberated is too strongly mixed with sorrow, for in spite of everything I still greatly loved the prison from which I have been released."[4] Freud died in this room. There are many ghosts here. Four of Freud's five sisters perished in the camps: eighty-two-year-old Rosa, eighty-one-year-old Marie (Mitzi), and seventy-eight-year-old Pauline were murdered at Treblinka in September 1942; Adolfine (Dolfi) died at Theresienstadt, aged eighty. My father's great-aunts.

———

I go upstairs and get into the little childish bed in Anna's room. Sleep is out of the question. The giant insects taunt me; the enormous Professor looms, with loss suspended bleakly in the air between. It is cold, and I am in all my clothes. What do you think you're doing? I ask. I get up, find a cupboard—and this is so unlikely it feels like a mirage—it is stuffed with packets of biscuits! I open a pack of Bourbon creams and eat five very fast. Why not? They were the medicine of my childhood. I redo my teeth and get back into bed, which now smells sugary and has dark crumbs.

My thoughts turn to the woman I used to see three times a week in the adolescent department of a nearby psychoanalytic clinic. I was twenty-one, bereaved, and reeling and felt as though the universe was trying to finish me off. She was high-spirited, rigorous, greathearted, and treated me so well I began to see myself differently. Jeannie, she was called, Jeannie Milligan. She dramatically altered my life chances.

An episode comes back to me in the narrow pink bed. For one of our sessions, the only time it ever happened, she was fractionally late, about one hundred seconds. She apologized and asked me if it would be possible and convenient for us to add the missed portion on at the end. I remember analyzing her words as though they were a poem. (I was a third of the way through an English degree at Oxford but had taken half the year off owing to "circumstances.") Not only was she acknowledging the lateness and apologizing for it—lateness I knew another would scarcely see or feel—she was offering to make reparations. More than this, she did not assume her plan would suit me, for I might conceivably have to be somewhere immediately afterward and be unwilling to pass this infinitesimal lateness on. I could tell she was keen to iron out any possible sting of rejection. Yet there was none of the humiliation that attaches itself to "treatment," no hint I was a tremulous invalid, perched on precarious cliffs. It was merely a putting right, almost automatic, as one might straighten a chair or pat dry a plate. What courtesy! It contrasted so dramatically with a long period in my life when my father used to telephone regularly and ask me if he could speak to one of my older siblings.

Once or twice during the many years I saw Jeannie, she issued sentences of profound approval that still wallpaper the inside of my head. "You were very brave," she said to me. Another time: "However bad you felt, you never stopped working." Medals for courage and grit and grafting! I saw her on and off for three decades, sometimes with gaps of several years. In some respects she was a third parent to me.

Our very last conversation had notes of farce. She was retiring. "I have to ask you something. I am in good health now," she said, "but if I were to die would you like to be notified?"

I nodded. "And if appropriate I'd like to come to your funeral if I may."

"Yes," she said, "yes, after all we've been to each other."

"And . . . and if I should predecease you, would *you* want to be notified?"

"Yes."

"And come to my funeral?"

She nodded, in symmetry.

We peered at each other in the shadows of this extremely odd conversation.

"Well, see you there then!" I said.

I almost added, "I think psychoanalysis is an unrivaled method of human understanding, but I do occasionally wonder if its theories apply a little more to the Freud family than the population at large." But there was no time to introduce new themes.

I Google her from Anna Freud's bedroom on my telephone, wondering if there is any news. I would so love to see her again, but I know it isn't possible. She knew me before I built myself. She saw the tenor of the raw materials; the things that needed to be discarded; the new hardware that had to be acquired. The swathes of unfactual landscape we swept away together!

On the little screen suddenly—there it all is again—no description of upcoming talks and publications, just the facts with their nightmarish proportions. She had perished alone in a house fire, months earlier. I don't open them, but there are films of her burning home on the screen. Our parting agreement, that she would not die without telling me, must have gone up in flames. It was the wrong ending entirely, savage and Victorian, for someone who gave so many young people a magnificent start in life. You can feel guilty of treachery when someone you're crazy about dies. I feel it now. You did everything for me, and I couldn't even spare you this.

But there are also wonderful obituaries and rapturous tributes . . . a pioneer in combining the disciplines of social work with psychoanalysis . . . a loyal colleague and loving friend . . . everything she gave, her sense of humor and her sense of justice . . . tremendous vivacity and glamour . . . the star of the annual pantomime, singing and dancing and acting with sheer brilliance and utter captivation.

I think of wandering down into the study again, but the alarms are on now and all the lights are off, so I gaze up at the picture of Sigmund Freud on the wall, and then I hear myself apologize.

SIGMUND FREUD AND ME

Esther Freud

I was eighteen, in my first term at drama school, when a fellow student asked me on a date. "Is it true that you're related . . ." Someone must have warned him. "Isn't your grand . . . your great . . . ?" He was struggling, blushing, assuming himself to be a fool, so I lowered my voice:

"Sigmund Freud."

The words familiarly surreal.

"What is it that he's famous for, again?"

We looked at each other, hoping for a clue, and when no clue emerged, we set off for the pub.

—

Forty years later, and I am invited to give a talk at the Freud Museum in Vienna. "History, Family, Silence" is the title, and when I mention that not once during my childhood did the subject of my great-grandfather arise, there is an audible gasp. True, this is an audience handpicked for outrage—but it allowed both me and my fellow speaker, Philippe Sands, author of *East West Street*, to focus on the subject of silence, a direct result, for both of us, of history and of family.

I was brought up in the countryside by my mother, a young woman from a Catholic background, who separated from my father—the artist Lucian Freud—when my sister and I were small.

My father remained an almost mythical figure, living in the studio in which he painted, arriving once or twice a year in an antique Rolls Royce, inviting me, as soon as I could pass as presentable (thirteen), to visit him in London, where he took me to members' clubs, to bookies, to restaurants. London was his city; he knew every corner of his favorite quarter—Soho—everyone, from dukes to doormen; he never missed an edition of London's *Evening Standard* or, for that matter, any British paper published, and although he spoke with an inflection, I accepted it simply as his voice—precise, refined, each word, phrase, joke, curse chosen for maximum effect. In fact—and I discovered this only after his death, when I heard him on a rare recording—he had a pronounced German accent. He'd been born in Berlin, the middle son of the youngest son of Sigmund Freud, whose immediate family moved to England in 1933, the same year Hitler came to power. How long before he mastered English? When did his family stop speaking to each other in their mother tongue? How did it feel to address his parents in a new language?

There are so many things I'd like to have asked him, but a direct question wasn't something he encouraged. He lived in the present. Wasted little time on reminiscence. Prided himself on a lack of sentiment. I learned early to keep our conversation buoyant. No whimsy. No nostalgia. Although slowly, circuitously, I found a way to tease out what I needed, catching him off guard in the slow hours when he was painting, with questions about his childhood, his early marriages, his parents, who I'd never met.

His mother, he told me, had caused conflict by preferring him to his two brothers, smothering him with so much interest that he became allergic (his word) to her attention. He described how, at seventeen, he'd stowed away on a ship bound for Newfoundland, relishing the freedom of being out of her bounds. On arrival he'd sent a postcard as proof of his escape. His brothers he barely mentioned. He'd entered into a feud with the younger—they didn't speak for fifty years—although I saw the elder when I met my father for breakfast at a café. A bearlike man, bearded and jowly, heaping anchovy paste onto a croissant. "Who was that?" I asked when he'd left, and he shrugged, dismissive—"Stephen"— conceding, "my brother." In this context it was less surprising that he didn't talk about his grandfather, although one day I did arrive at his studio to find him in a state of near hilarity. A man, small and foreign, had chased him down the street to ask if he was a relation of "Ze Grape Fruit." My father's shoulders shook, his eyes creased into crescents, his laughter so infectious that I had no choice but to join in. "The grapefruit? All right then, I suppose I am."

The Grapefruit was how Sigmund Freud was referred to from then on, albeit rarely, as if the vastness of his reputation was so all-encompassing, there was nothing left to add, which was how I reached the age of eighteen, knowing I was related to one of the most famous men of the last century, unsure who he was.

It was only later that I began to see it wasn't only my great- grandfather who was not discussed; it was the past: the war, my father's Jewish blood, my own; the chasm that divided those who got away and those who were unable to escape. "Are you Jewish?" I was asked on a school exchange to Germany, aged twelve. It was the first time the question had been posed. Yes. It was too compli- cated to explain, but I was unnerved when the father of the family folded me in his arms.

When my sister and I were children, my father would some- times entertain us by looking up Freuds in the telephone directory. I squirmed as he dialed, struggling to breathe as he adopted the strange, flat tone he used when attempting anonymity. "Is this a relation of the Grapefruit?" he'd sometimes try, or: "Is the painter, Lucian, at home?" While mostly there was bemusement, once someone shrieked that No, they had no connection to that filthy pornographer, before slamming down the phone. I didn't ask for an explanation; I was only grateful the list of Freuds was short.

—

Every generation must rebel in its own way, and the less my father told me, the more curious I became. I began to assemble the scraps of stories I'd extracted, small details about his mother's family in Berlin; the country estate, Gaglow, that they'd owned; his grandmother who'd been disapproved of by her daughters; an uncle who was in the army during the First World War. I jettisoned the novel I was working on, my third, and took this as my subject. Surprised by my determination—I searched through institutes, unearthed memoirs, traveled to New York to interview the only relative of whom he was fond—my father began to warm to my endeavors. Careful, I stayed away from the most famous Freud—burrowing instead into his maternal side, moving, sideways, through a subject I had more chance of making my own. And it worked. After *Summer at Gaglow* was published, my father summoned me to his studio, where he presented me with a carrier bag filled with the correspondence of his parents. "I thought you might like to use these." The letters were in fact from his father to his mother. Where were hers to him? But you can learn a lot from one side of a correspondence, and I was able to trace their lives from courtship to marriage, through the births of their three sons, the rise of anti-Semitism in Berlin, the discussions about where they might safely live. Sleuthlike, I trawled for clues as to why my father was so favored and, amateur analyst that I am (aren't we all?), deduced that when the other boys were born my grandfather, Ernst—jealously devoted to his wife—made sure they were cared for by a nanny. When Lucian arrived, his father was due to depart on a "milk cure" to the mountains, something he underwent every two years to help with the damage to his lungs sustained when he caught TB during his years in the army. Lucian was allowed to luxuriate in his mother Lucie's arms. "I want that child out of the bed before my return," Ernst wrote. Too late. The bond had been formed.

I was still reading through these letters when a stray page slipped from a notebook: Prof. Dr. Freud. The iconic address: Berggasse 19, Wien, printed across the top. The date in pen: 9.2.1923. The writing was indecipherable. Black words sliced like rain across the page. *Lieber Ernst*, I managed, and at the very end, *Dein Vater*. I rushed to have the letter translated, imagining it brimming with insightful revelations—a rethinking of the Oedipus complex, a regretful recalculation of seduction theory. *The weather in Vienna has been very bad.* So followed news of his wife. News of his dogs. Affectionate greetings to his daughter-in-law Lucie.

I tucked it back into the notebook, the pages filled with my grandfather's more legible hand, details of dinner parties, people invited, food eaten—*Schalottensuppe mit Leberklösschen*—the flowers that had been arranged. *Pfingstrosen* (peonies) *im Schale* (in bowls) *in alle Zimmer* (in every room). In the back were lists of names. Calmanns, Mosses, Ginsbergs, Samsons, Eisners. Freuds. All numbered. The last entry: 130–131. Kaufman + Frau.

More illuminating was a strand of correspondence in which Ernst was invited to receive an award on behalf of his father. It was clear from the letters Lucie disapproved, insisting he should make the journey only if they were presenting *him* with an award. (He was a successful architect, his practice derailed by the war.) Was this the attitude passed down to my father, who, in turn, passed it on to us? Certainly he had a loathing of posturing, of the reverential, and an anarchic regard for individual merit. He liked to say, in respect of his own children, that his fondness for them had nothing to do with family ties, but was predicated on whether they interested him.

An attitude that kept even his grandchildren on their toes.

I arranged the letters by order of address. Lucie's family home in Charlottenburg. Her married apartment in Regentenstrasse. A holiday house on Hiddensee—the island in the Baltic where they spent the summers. The first London accommodation in 1933, followed soon after by a seaside village in Suffolk, a replacement for the idyll of the Baltic. They were joined here by an array of émigrés and refugees, the Viennese analyst Willie Hoffer, my great-aunt Anna Freud, and later, a new generation of the family, my father's two brothers and their children (typically, my father stayed away), so that when I first visited, in my twenties, the locals nodded familiarly, the postman glancing from my name to my face, in recognition. This would be the setting for my new novel. And it wasn't only the letters I had as an aid. After the publication of *Summer at Gaglow*, material came flooding in. A cousin of my father's sent photographs of the actual Gaglow; a memoir was received from the son of an earlier, acknowledged source; and my father's younger brother—thirty years into their not speaking—asked me out to lunch. Charming, funny, he entertained me with reminiscences, offering possible reasons for the feud, confiding, as we neared dessert, his theory that my father might, in fact, be illegitimate, not a member of the Freud family at all.

I took this information to Lucian, whose shoulders shook with laughter. "I wonder, did he ever meet our mother?" I was glad to have been the bearer of diverting news.

Whereas *Summer at Gaglow* was a difficult book to write, each chapter a marathon of imagination and research, this new novel, *The Sea House*, fell into my hands. I was invited to the Freud Museum in London to a lecture by Walter Freud, another grandson of Sigmund, who re-created for us his experiences as an enemy alien, his work as a Special Operations executive parachuting into Germany in the final months of the war. There I met other members of the family; one Freud, affable, levelheaded, tall, who, it transpired, was not related at all.

Until then this museum was a place I'd been too self-conscious to enter. What if I was thought to be there under false pretenses? What if my father heard about my visit and disapproved? I'd imbibed the message so entirely—nothing must be laid claim to—that sometimes I found it hard to pronounce my own name. Frowd? Frood? Once, a taxi that I ordered arrived for a Miss Forehead. Now, I wandered through the rooms, examining the artifacts, the lithographs and pictures, eyeing the desk clustered with antiquities where one of the greatest thinkers of our age had written his last works, breathing in the smell of the tapestry-covered couch where for the last year of his life the man who had revolutionized the human self-image had treated patients.

———

On the day of our talk Philippe Sands and I walked through Vienna. Like mine, his grandfather, Leon, had been born here. We sat in cafés and talked about the circumstances of Leon's escape, not knowing what was to befall his own mother, Malke, who was left behind. It was only toward the end of his life that he was shown a book with her name on a list of those detained at Theresienstadt, with the detail that on September 23, 1942, she was transported from there to the concentration camp at Treblinka. He took this book and retired to his room, from behind the closed door of which came the sound of his weeping. Of the book, and of Treblinka, he never spoke again.

Decades later, while watching footage of the Nuremburg trials, Sands came across the evidence of a survivor of Treblinka, Samuel Rajzman. Rajzman described the killing there—between ten and twenty thousand a day—on both an industrial and intimate scale. One of the many acts he witnessed: a grandmother accompanying her laboring daughter to the infirmary, made to watch as the newborn baby was slaughtered, then her own daughter, before she herself was shot.

He described how a false railway station had been built several kilometers from the camp. There was an imaginary restaurant, and schedules for departures and arrivals to and from Vienna and Berlin. "Was this created to psychologically reassure arrivals?" he was asked. Yes, he agreed. It was.

He was on this platform when three of Sigmund Freud's sisters arrived. Pauline (Pauli), Maria (Mitzi), and Regina (Rosa). It was September 23, 1942. He saw the commander deal with one of the elderly sisters' request for special treatment.

Alerted by the familiar date, Philippe Sands traced each of the names on the convoy, and alongside Pauli, Mitzi, and Rosa, there, indeed, was his own great-grandmother, Malke. They had been transported from Theresienstadt to Treblinka on the same convoy, on the same day, traveling more than a thousand kilometers east, where they were shaved, ordered to remove their clothes, and led into the gas chambers, together.

———

Before our talk we are given a tour of the newly redesigned museum. Absence is now the central focus of each room. The dents in the plaster where the rug that hung above Freud's couch had been nailed into the wall, the marks where Anna's telephone was installed beside her bed. In each room are photographs of the rooms as they had been. Dense with books and pictures, the artifacts Freud loved to collect.

It was as late as 1938 when Freud realized he would have to leave. In his early eighties, and suffering with cancer of the mouth, he'd been hopeful he might remain in his own home, but when the Gestapo entered the apartment, asking to be shown the contents of the safe, and his youngest daughter, Anna, was arrested, released into the dangerous city in the early hours of the next morning, he accepted it was time to go. After considerable diplomatic and international pressure, and an offer by Freud's friend and former patient Princess Marie Bonaparte to pay a "fugitive tax," introduced by the Nazis—an amount, repaid, that came to a third of Freud's assets—it was agreed the family could leave. They traveled by train to Paris, and on to London where he made his final home.

What I'd never known, or ever considered, was what happened to the apartment after their departure. Now in the museum's newly renovated incarnation I discover it had been used as a *Sammelwohnung*, a "collective" apartment, into which dispossessed Jews were herded, crammed into the rooms where Freud had lived and worked for almost fifty years. Out of sight, they awaited transportation, their names now listed on the staircase, the dates of their births, their inevitable early deaths. Was this discussed within the family? Was it known? And what of the fate of Freud's five sisters, only one of whom survived? Certainly, if it traveled down, my father chose not to distribute it. He was a young man when the war was won, brimming with energy and talent. He put the past behind him. Neither denied nor embraced his heritage. Created himself anew.

Last summer at the Freud Museum in London there was an exhibition of my father's work. *Family Matters*, it was to be titled, before we stepped in to point out the inappropriateness of the phrase. Retitled *The Painter and His Family*, it featured childhood letters, photographs, self-portraits, paintings—a small collection, but a powerful one, in the room above his grandfather's study. This is something that would not have happened in his lifetime, but with loss comes liberation, and a chance to reexamine loyalty. To choose what to inherit.

Sometimes I'm asked if I'll write about the Freud side of the family. I'm not sure. Is there a way to own it? Or has it been too universally owned? What I do know is that through my efforts of investigation I've rooted myself in my own history. I'd needed a family, just as my father had needed to escape from his.

AFTER FREUD

FREUD THE SKEPTIC

Adam Gopnik

Freud is no one's idea of perfection these days. Frederick Crews's demolition of so many Freudian specifics—or Karl Popper's earlier demolition of Freudianism's scientific pretensions—have been left unanswered, or at least unrefuted (though Popper, it should be said, remained fascinated with Freud; I recall that, when I met him in the 1970s, he was absorbed in reading Ernest Jones's biography). As a system builder, Freud, like Marx, can no longer convince us. The Marxist epic of the bourgeoise and the proletariat—even the idea of capitalism as a distinct force, rather than one way of describing a moment in commercial societies—has, for explanatory power, gone the way of the Four Temperaments and the zodiac. (The underlying Marxist premise of economic determinism long ago exploded, and is exploding again every day, as one class in one nation after another acts directly against its own economic self-interest and in favor of its own perceived values and ideals, however bizarre they may seem to outsiders, as in the tragic history of Brexit.)

Freud's parallel epic of ego and id and superego and the rest are equally exploded, as mythological-seeming an explanatory mechanism now as the Greek gods picking winners in the *Iliad*. Yet Freud lingers on—as, for that matter, does Marx—less for his scientific pretensions or systematic explanatory claims than for his tone, stance, point of view, "climate of opinion," as W. H. Auden memorably predicted, which continues to reach us as literature reaches

us: not for its quantifiable certitude but for its suggestive incerti-
tude, for beginning an inquiry that its author can't foreclose.

In part, what has happened is what always happens with
epoch-defining figures: the revolutionary bits now look obvious,
and the false bits just look false. And yet when we read the best
of Freud's writings, wrong though he may be on the facts of childhood development, or as dated as may be his views on homo-
sexuality—or heterosexuality from the woman's side, for that
matter—we don't, I think, feel the sense of exasperation or dis-
belief we often do in the presence of bad ideas with other than
benign consequences. Reading, say, the social Darwinists, or the
eugenicists, or the anti-Darwin rants of proponents of intelligent
design, we feel a sense of disgust and despair that intelligent
people could ever have held, or still hold, views so self-evidently
absurd. Even reading Marx, one senses uneasily the spleen and
bad temper that informed so much of his character, and that was
one of the unhappy legacies infused into his ideas. His hemor-
rhoids are, so to speak, on the page along with his hopes.

But writers' systems need not wholly encompass the world to
be powerful. There are neither Elves nor Ents in existence, but
Tolkien speaks to us still in his ability to crystallize human spirits—
heroic, remote, welcoming—into imaginary kinds. And so, Freud
still speaks to us today, though by now it is Freud's skepticism, not
his system building, that impresses a reader—it is his iconoclasm
that excites us, his skepticism about the pieties that we are forced
to mouth in social life, and his desire to speak candidly about
the raw truths of appetite and desire that lie beneath them, as the
actual engines of our existence.

Darwin, another great writer disguised as a data collector, argues as a scientist argues, through conjecture, general proposition,
specific instances of evidence, potential counterexamples, and
final if tentatively held conclusions. Freud, though he wants to do
this, doesn't. Freud argues as an essayist argues, with a steady flow
of metaphor, erudite and often obscure instance, surprisingly dep-
recating self-scrutiny, appeals to common sense opening onto

extravagant speculative riffs, hesitant but memorable hypotheticals. Though Freud would have wanted to be known first of all as a scientist, he has the essayist's key gifts: an ability to find and follow the right metaphor, and then to clinch the metaphor with a neat aphoristic summary. In plain English, Freud does the work that essayists do and ought to be remembered the way that essayists hope to be remembered: for a tone and point of view on the world, a series of arresting, irresistible metaphors, and for small acts of candor that add up to a larger significant courage.

—

As every historian of the essayist points out, so much that by now it is a bromide, the word *essai* means, in French, originally, a "try" or "attempt"; the speculative impulse doesn't always have to end in certainty to be honorable. So it is important for us to recall that for what one might call the "Auden generation," those writers who came of age in the 1920s and 1930s, when Freud's thought was still burning and alive, the whole idea that human behavior might be driven forward by repressed sexual desire—a desire that might include erotic fascination with one's own parents or siblings, and that, instead of being episodic and occasional, might be the major wind that blew us forward through life itself—was entirely new in the world.

We now take it for granted that these things are so. We say calmly of adolescents that they are sorting out their sex lives, and if the results may—in ways that Freud himself might have disapproved of—include "deviant" sexual choices, our middle-class heads nod in obvious agreement. Of course! Thirteen-year-olds have sexual lives, and so do babies at the breast. When Freud, in his essay on Leonardo, delicately but directly cites fellatio as one of the lurking human impulses roiling the surface of "normal" sexual life, we who are his descendants may not quite recognize the radicalism of his gesture. *People* do *such things?* his time asked, or pretended to ask. Normal *people do such things*, Freud insists—and homosexuals, like Leonardo, are normal in doing them, and dreaming of them, too.

We underestimate, I think, how original this form of inquiry was. People did not—not merely as a rule, but not at all—explain the creative sources of the great painters of the Renaissance by reference to their ambivalent infantile feelings, recalled in maturity, about blow jobs. Freud did. In this way, one has the sense, reading Freud, of passing, so to speak, from the pilots' room on the *Titanic*, where everyone is in Edwardian uniform, manicured and keenly looking straight ahead toward the destination, into the engine room of the ship, where the coal stokers are stripped to the waist and sweating as they curse and shovel fuel into the intolerably hot furnace. This is how the passenger ship, our Psyche, really runs.

Yet Freud's gift as a writer is quite specific, beyond his contribution to ending taboos. In praising him as an essayist above all, I don't merely mean that he was a good literary craftsman or an able polemicist, though he was obviously both of these. I mean that he had the classic essayist's purpose as it descends to us from Montaigne—the caustic, or sometimes humorous, purpose of replacing the pious fictions of received dogma with the human truths of our actual behavior.

That is, despite the charm and cosmetic appeal of Montaigne's tone, *his* real purpose is a radical insistence on a good-humored honesty about human efforts and human intentions. For all his charm and sobriety, what Montaigne hates most of all are the pious fictions people live by. He replaces those pious fictions with recognizable human truth. It is the side of Montaigne that leads right to La Rochefoucauld's aphorisms, with their equally disabused wisdom about the real motives that lie behind polite morals. (Indeed, though I wasn't aware of it when I began this essay of my own, the connection between Freud and Montaigne has been cited often, even taking in the prescient connection between the essayist's play of free association and the psychoanalyst's patients' parallel free association. And Harold Bloom urged us all, in the pages of the *New York Times* in 1986, to read Freud as the Montaigne of the twentieth century.)

A "good-humored" or at least equable tone may seem strangely associated with Freud as a writer—but whatever his drive for power as a psychoanalytic politician, amply documented in his biographies, the tone of his best writing *is* good-humored in the essayist's sense: equable, conscious of error, searching for evidence, capable of seeing the other side of the issue, and arriving at conclusions as much by gestures of spontaneous sympathy as by hard-driven statistical certitudes.

Of these essays let me demonstrate quickly by taking up two, for the not very complicated reason that they are *this* essayist's favorites within the Freud canon. They are the classic 1930 essay called "Civilization and Its Discontents," and that long 1910 essay on the childhood sources of Leonardo Da Vinci's vision, most often called in English "Leonardo da Vinci and a Memory of His Childhood," and translated into English by James Strachey in 1923.

In "Civilization and Its Discontents," one at first finds irresistible the disenthralled—though not disillusioned—tone of debunking. The piece's ostensible point is to establish the theory of sublimation: men want to act rapaciously, unabatedly, freely—and everywhere are met by the restrictions of social life, the need to turn the simple search for physical pleasure into the social work of building things. Concerts and castles, literature and law alike, are the work of human beings who have been emancipated from their baser urges and—Freud's more original point—have, just as much, become enslaved to their "higher" purposes.

Yet how astoundingly the essay passes from the abstract and hazy air of speculation into the crisp specifics of aphoristic summary! To divert us from the sheer suffering of existence, Freud tells us, we have set palliatives: "There are perhaps three such measures: powerful deflections, which cause us to make light of our misery; substitute satisfactions, which diminish it; and intoxicating substances, which make us insensitive to it."

A summary of Samuel Johnson's could not be more succinctly Latinate, or depressingly accurate, balancing nicely between abstract statement and specific knowledge. We can be distracted, or else we can drink. Nothing could be neater.

There are moments in Freud's essay that are, similarly, memorably bland while being as explosive as anything in Darwin, in his annihilation of religion:

> It is asserted, however, that each one of us behaves in some one respect like a paranoic, corrects some aspect of the world which is unbearable to him by the construction of a wish and introduces this delusion into reality. A special importance attaches to the case in which this attempt to procure a certainty of happiness and a protection against suffering through a delusional remolding of reality is made by a considerable number of people in common. The religions of mankind must be classed among the mass-delusions of this kind. No one, needless to say, who shares a delusion ever recognizes it as such.

Yet what is most impressive in the essay is the easy, magisterial passage from the candid confession of the vanity of human wishes, and the transparency of human consolations, to the equally acute appreciation of the necessity of human vanity—of illusion—for us to live decently at all. Freud's speculation, after surveying, as gimlet-eyed as any seventeenth-century divine, all the illusions that we need to sustain us, is that

> the programme of becoming happy, which the pleasure principle imposes on us, cannot be fulfilled; yet we must not—indeed, we cannot—give up our efforts to bring it nearer to fulfilment by some means or other. . . . By none of these paths can we attain all that we desire. Happiness, in the reduced sense in which we recognize it as possible, is a problem of the economics of the individual's libido.

"The economics of the libido" is in itself a phrase touched by genius; and the nobility of the author's effort to balance the budget of his own—at once being brutally brusque in his dismissal of art, science, and religion as mere distractions from our extravagant infantile erotic demands, while at the same time recognizing those "distractions" as the necessary building blocks of civilization—remains inspiring in its mix of candor and exhortation.

In his essay on Leonardo, Freud's mistakes have often been noted by art historians—he mistranslates the name of the bird that Leonardo imagined attacking him in infancy as a "vulture," which, it seems, it is not, and seeks in Egyptian mythology for a dubious analogy to the mythology of woman-as-vulture, a point that cannot be sustained by historical scrutiny—though the larger point that birds often represent mothers is not at all frivolous. (*Owl Babies*, one of the key books of modern American childhood, rests on just this relation of the abandoned children to the mother owl. "And then she came . . . ," the phrase evoking the return of the mother owl to the abandoned nest, is one of the most powerful summations in children's literature, which children grow up to quote in later life.)

But the central insight of the essay—that Leonardo associates the beatific and enigmatic smile of the Gioconda and his Madonnas with the double nature of womanhood, and that he is engaged in a kind of psychological portrait of his own childhood, when he was raised by both his natural- and adoptive stepmother—seems poetically right, persuasive on its own terms. Two women do haunt him. Freud pushes the point further by insisting that homosexual identity begins with "over-identification" with a strong mother, a cliché now exploded, too, since the homosexual instinct may well precede the identification, rather than be produced by it. The point, pushed too far, is not in itself false: some gay men do strongly identify with their mothers, and that identification is part of the inner life of their art. (Auden was one.)

We also may now have to supplement Freud with a "Gombrichian" understanding of the "Gioconda smile" as part of the growing "technology" of illusion in Renaissance painting. Just as the aerial perspective that Leonardo conquers has an illusionistic purpose not easily assimilated to a psychological one, so the famous smile has the effect, in its subtlety and multivalence, of seeming "alive" in ways that the stolid or overanimated expressions of most Renaissance portraiture do not.

But indeed, that very project of increasing ambiguity in order to arrive at illusion is not without a psychological poetic content of its own; a tolerance for ambiguity, as Freud might have put it, is a stage in the psychological development of civilization. The Mona Lisa smile becomes a convincing synecdoche for Leonardo's attempt to transform the neatly turned and fixed grimaces of earlier Florentine painting into ever-compelling possibilities of potentials, an economy of the libido imprinted on the face—an attempt that, we know from Leonardo's own writing, was very much on his conscious mind.

Through Freud's empathetic imagination, the strangeness of Leonardo's picture of the Madonna and St. Anne—and anyone who sees it in the Louvre and is not compelled by its strangeness does not know how to look—is resolved into a convincing human trace memory. It is the landscape of a memory. (It is, of course, doubly eerie that Freud himself seems to have been raised by two mothers—his own and a beloved nursemaid, not at all an unusual combination among the upper middle classes of his Teutonic time and class—and then, the kind of punch line that only history can create, it is triply eerie, not to say hilarious, that our own most famous Leonardo, the actor who also has an "of"-form Italian name, has two mothers as well, both of whom, natural- and stepmother, he brought to the Academy Awards.)

We do not have to be convinced in order to be provoked—the essayist's job is as much to unsettle our imaginations as to persuade our understandings. Anyone who comes away from Freud's Leonardo unprovoked is not capable of provocation. Freud is right to have called it his most beautiful work of writing, and it is beautiful and true in the way that beautiful things can be, as Freud himself knew, through their halo of implication more than their assertion of truth. (Freud made the arresting point that though all our pleasure is genital in origin, the genitals themselves are never thought beautiful. We always find beauty one step removed from its apparent source. What makes an essay beautiful is its halo of implication.)

———

The scientist works with the advancing edge of objectivity; an essayist works, often exasperatingly, with the blunted force of ambiguity. There is no better instance of this than the tale of perhaps the most famous of Freud's positive aphorisms, his supposed insistence that all that matters in life is "Love and Work" and that mental health is simply the ability to pursue both at once, an idea that has inspired the titles of at least two novels.

In a fine piece of literary-psychoanalytic detective work, Alan Elms in a brilliant 2001 article titled "Apocryphal Freud" set out to find the source of this Freudian aphorism. Tracking this elegant formula down, he finds its source in Erik Erikson. Yet he insists that "Erikson does not try to pin the quotation down to a written source, because there is none. The concordance to Freud's published writings in English translation, which indexes every occurrence of every substantive word Freud used[,] identifies no passage in all his writings in which 'love' and 'work' occur together in a sentence or even on the same page. . . . By Erikson's account, Freud said 'Lieben und arbeiten,' rather than writing it; but Erikson does not claim that he himself heard Freud say it."

Searching for a source, Elms discovers that, in a later work, Freud *did* say that daydreams "have two principal aims, an erotic and an ambitious one—though an erotic aim is usually concealed behind the latter too." Recognizing this as the likely origin, we see that "Love and Work" is probably an Americanized euphemism, typical of the more pious Erik Erikson generation's desire to cosmeticize Freud, Freud's own formula of "Desire and Ambition" or, perhaps better put, "Lust and Competition."

A lovely structure of contemplative sincerity collapses as we make the translation. And yet with it comes a hard truth not at all unrecognizable: we *do* live every day in a tapestry of lust and ambition. Desire and ambition are less high-sounding but more persuasive as our motives. Our erotic daydreams, fed so easily by the internet now, make our days.

But the "cosmetic" elevation of desire and ambition into love and work is not entirely wrong, either. For at the end of a day's work, with the phantasms of desire cleared—or, at times, forced away—and with ambition revealed as a substitute for what is at best the perpetual running in place of our existence, we still end in . . . love and work. Sex and ambition *are* love and work, sublimated into the dailiness of things.

Freud's vision of human life as a series of perpetual reconstructed pieties, in need of perpetual disabused candor, is a modern one, and valuable. For it is, even more than optimism about human nature, the best side of the Enlightenment "project." We are such stuff as we make our own dreams on. We are, from birth, carnal, needy, driven, transgressive, appetite-driven creatures. Freud's insight, very much a writer's kind, is that this does not prevent us but in a way *compels* us to do the work of civilized people—to marry, to raise kids, to treat each other decently. He sees that the business of sublimation is not a distraction, but the means to a construction of a better world in which selves can coexist.

It is what gives Freud's frequent invocation of "real things" its peculiar pathetic force. To be in relation to "real things" in the world as it is, is not, for him, the normal foundation of life but the summit of all our efforts, achieved gasping and with difficulty (and to conclude the metaphor, possible presumably only with the help of those trained Sherpas, our therapists).

"We are double in ourselves, and doubt what we most believe," Montaigne wrote. In reconciling us to our own limitless lust and frustrated ambition, Freud did the good work of making sense of our daily transition from our sexual selves into our social ones. We see that engine room of erotic appetite more clearly—which does not mean that the pilot's room is entirely an illusion but rather that it is the coal being shoveled by the naked self below that makes the ship go.

Makes it go for a time, at least. None of our boats—Freud's other lesson and an essential one, too—misses the iceberg. To write a note from the life raft of the sinking ship and put it in a bottle and send it to posterity, imagined as an unknown island, still somehow inhabited, is a hope unknown to scientists. It is peculiar to writers, whatever professional hats they wear.

PLAYING THE GAME

Michael S. Roth

My grandson Luc sits on the floor with me. He is two years old. We are surrounded by small toys, mostly blocks and cars. He stares into my eyes with an impish grin and, without looking down, pushes all the toys behind him so that none are visible. Big smile. "Behind the back," he says to me, looking at the floor in front of him. "Behind the back," he says again with a laugh, as if he has just performed an extraordinary magic trick. I smile back and repeat with him: "Behind the back." We then push the toys out in front of him, and we start again.

I've been reading Freud since I was a teenager. Really. So, while I'm playing this game with my grandson, I'm immediately thinking of the most famous game in all psychoanalytic literature: *fort-da*. WE ARE PLAYING THE GAME, I thought, while playing the game. "Behind the back," Luc said again while he made the toys disappear for a moment. We both were enjoying ourselves.

Freud spent several pages on his grandson and the *fort-da* game in *Beyond the Pleasure Principle*, which was first published in 1920. This is an exceedingly odd book, which after describing a child's game famously introduces the death instinct. More on that soon. Before he describes his grandson ("not at all precocious in his intellectual development") and the game, Freud writes about what he called "the dark and dismal subject of the traumatic neurosis."[1] The Great War had recently ended, and an extraordinary number of soldiers had returned from the front physically but not mentally.

They revisited their painful pasts in intrusive memories and a variety of other symptoms, including flashbacks. Those who suffered from trauma often returned to their painful memories in dreams, and Freud notes, "this astonishes us far too little." He describes the sufferer as being "fixated to his trauma" and wonders about "the mysterious masochistic trends of the ego." Indeed, these are the last words in the text of *Beyond the Pleasure Principle* before Freud describes his grandson's game.[2] Mysterious indeed.

Why does Freud think we should be astonished that people are fixated on their trauma? This will take some undoing, for in the last thirty years or so we have become accustomed to the notion that people get stuck on traumatic events—indeed, that what makes an event traumatic is our very inability to get past it. For Freud, motivation is guided by the pleasure principle, so it made little sense to him that we would unconsciously return to images and emotions that were so painful to reexperience. Remember, for him a primary window into the unconscious is the dream. And he argued that all dreams were fulfillments of wishes. We wish, surely, to escape trauma—in terms of the pleasure principle as he understood it, we are motivated to reduce the tension that the trauma caused us. The pleasure principle should lead us away from the traumatic past—not back to it. But in those who suffer from the aftermath of trauma, the suffering is a magnet for memory; the wish seems to be to relive the pain. Mysterious masochism, Freud wonders.

But just after his brief consideration of trauma, the father of psychoanalysis turns to his grandson and the game. The little boy, whom we now know was Wolfgang Ernst Halberstadt, is described as well-behaved and well-adjusted (if not precocious). Freud wants readers to take the child as fairly typical so that he can feel free to generalize from this child's behavior. The game Ernst (as he was called) plays is to toss something away while cooing *fort* (gone), and then bringing it back (or refinding it) and exclaiming *da!* (there!). Now you don't see it, now you do. Or, in the version of the game my grandson Luc (who is anything but ordinary!) played: "behind the back," followed by "here it is!" Freud understood the game as a reenactment of the departure of the child's mother. From time to time, she had to leave him with a nurse, and the game was a way of reexperiencing loss and then undoing the loss with a "da!" or "here it is!" Freud interpreted the game as a vehicle for attaining mastery over an unpleasant experience. Instead of passively undergoing disappointment when the mother leaves, the little child actively controls loss and return— "behind the back" and "here it is!" Freud's grandson, and mine, were actively restaging losses they had already learned were part of life. Mothers leave; this is painful, but it is important to realize that the world remains even when they are gone. Mothers return, but when they return, now one is already anticipating their departure. During the Covid-19 pandemic, Luc was Ernst's age, and his parents would "disappear" to another part of the house to work. They would say goodbye with "Mama has to go to work now," or "Dada has to go to work now." It all went smoothly (as it usually did for Ernst during his first years of life, despite the ongoing war), but I noticed that when Luc's parents returned, they were soon asked by my very precocious grandson, "Mama has to work?" There were giggles and "No, Mama is here now." But Luc knew already to anticipate loss. Mama has to work; Mama is here. *Fort-da*. Who knows that things we value are bound to disappear? The child knows.

Freud's discussion in *Beyond the Pleasure Principle* of his grandson's game is, we repeat, preceded by some brief comments on traumatic neurosis and the repetition of painful experiences. It is followed by a discussion of repetition in therapeutic work—how it's not enough that patients find themselves in intellectual agreement with an interpretation by the analyst; they need to repeat, act out, elements from the past in the course of therapy. Freud ends that section of *Beyond the Pleasure Principle* by concluding that there is a compulsion to repeat that cannot be explained simply by the pursuit of pleasure. Repetition, he extrapolates by the end of the wildly speculative study, bespeaks a desire for stasis, which he will conclude emanates from what he will call the death instinct. He recognizes that this is conjecture, even "far-fetched speculation."[3]

What has Freud pushed behind the back in the move from traumatic neurosis to the *fort-da* game to speculations on repetition and death? First, there is the sad biographical dimension. Freud's daughter and little Ernst's mother, Sophie, died from influenza before the book was published. It was so sudden! Sophie was ill for just five days, and then (along with millions of others lost in that pandemic) she was gone. She was pregnant at the time, and in addition to Ernst, left a younger son, little Heinerle. We know Sophie was her father's favorite, his "Sunday child," and that he felt the loss acutely. But we don't know this from his text, in which there is only the following footnote:

> When this child was five and three-quarters, his mother died. Now she was really "gone" ("*o-o-o*"), the little boy showed no signs of grief. It is true that in the interval a second child had been born and had roused him to violent jealousy.[4]

In keeping with the tone of the book, Sophie is unnamed in the text, and her status as the author's daughter is unmentioned. She is kept behind the back, as it were (*o-o-o*). But in letters to friends Freud remarked on "the unconcealed brutality of our time" that made it impossible for him and his wife even to be with the family for the memorial and the mourning period. There were no trains just after the war. Little Ernst had become a difficult child, and the family attributed this to jealousy of his sibling. Then a short time later, this rival brother, Heinerle, was taken by the flu. Freud was inconsolable, and it was left to his other daughter, Anna, to help Ernst cope with those things that disappear and never return at all. Anna knew something about losing a favored sibling. The coping may be all the more challenging when we wish for disappearance. It must have been terrible for both. Anna would later become the first psychoanalyst to focus on children, and Ernst would eventually become an analyst himself, changing his last name from

Halberstadt to Freud. The father of psychoanalysis resorts to some jargon in saying that he suffered a "deep narcissistic injury," and he retreats to work. "I work as much as I can, and am grateful for the diversion."[5] Behind the back.

"Inability (unwillingness) to mourn leads to fear of loving," Adam Phillips has written, "which amounts for Freud to an inability to live."[6] Freud's diversion from mourning and love is work. But the work is repetition, and repetition doesn't just lead to mastery. It leads, according to Freud, to death. Here's how the argument goes in *Beyond the Pleasure Principle*. In trauma, in children's games, and in everyday life, human beings gravitate toward repetition. This may be a desire to master whatever it is that is being repeated, but it may also be because repetition itself satisfies something other than the desire for pleasure. It satisfies a desire at least not to move forward, and probably a desire to go back, to return to a prior state. Freud came to this chain of narrative reasoning because the desire to go back was a desire to undo loss, but then, as if to displace loss from the center of his story, he argues that the desire to repeat is really a desire to return to a prior state. A "prior state," we can add, is the state prior to loss. What state is this? The ultimate return is to death—the state of no longer desiring. In the wake of Sophie's death Freud reported that he was reading Schopenhauer.[7] For the German philosopher, to live is to suffer, and we are always already dying. The desire to escape life and to escape desire is a desire for death. Freud called this desire the death instinct.

Biographers have long known that Freud was superstitious about his own demise, expecting it to happen when he was in his early sixties, between 1916 and 1919. He survived this period, of course, but death was everywhere around him. Millions died in the war, and millions more in the flu pandemic. He worried about his sons who were at the front, and he wondered whether the culture he knew before the war would still exist when it was over. Early in the conflict he wrote: "We cannot but feel that no event has ever destroyed so much that is precious in the common possessions of humanity, confused so many of the clearest intelligences, or so thoroughly debased what is highest."[8] He writes that he, like other unsentimental, realist observers, knew that conflict, and even war, remained a possibility in a world such as ours. But, he writes, "we permitted ourselves to have hopes."[9] Hopes that the norms of behavior that countries enforced on their own citizens would have made large-scale, brutal interstate violence less likely. Instead, it had become clear that our brutal tendencies had just been obscured, and that states wanted to monopolize the treachery and violence that they forbade their own citizens in peacetime. One should not complain too much, Freud notes ruefully, to be disabused of one's illusions. We may have put violence and deceit behind our backs, but then we should not be too surprised when they reappear. *Da!* And in the stern, psychoanalytic voice he admonishes: "In reality, there is no such thing as 'eradicating' evil."[10] But don't let that disappoint you too much, he says: "In reality our fellow-citizens have not sunk so low as we feared, because they had never risen so high as we believed." *Fort!*

There is no such thing as eradicating evil because what we call "evil" is just the human drives that civilization denies or deflects. When a civilization turns to war, it calls on these drives, these passions, and what would have been called pathological in peacetime becomes normal. Killing, cruelty, excessive confidence in one's own compatriots, and hatred for the other—cultures fall into these behaviors because the capacities for them have always been there . . . waiting to be satisfied. They can't stay behind the back forever. "When it becomes a question of a number of people," Freud concluded, "all individual moral acquisitions are obliterated, and only the most primitive, the oldest, the crudest mental attitudes are left."[11]

Freud called that force in our lives that disrupts all attempts at knowing and understanding the "death instinct": the force that leads us to want to bury ourselves, sometimes with the result that we reemerge in totally unexpected ways. It is the death instinct—the worm within us—that would undermine any coherent life story we try to frame for ourselves and for others. To acknowledge this force against coherence and understanding is also to recognize our capacities for change. Change and loss are fundamentally entangled, for Freud, but in *Beyond the Pleasure Principle* he considers something more disturbing, more radical: that we desire the losses, or that we hold onto suffering, repeating it. We revisit our traumas in dreams, and we reenact pain in ways that push us back to "an earlier state of things."

These reenactments, at least from Freud's perspective after writing *Beyond the Pleasure Principle*, are an expression of the death instinct. Our erotic drive pushes us forward, moves us toward combinations and constructions, while the death drive pulls us back, moving us to tear things apart in the service of return. When we anticipate loss (and when do we not?), we can play with its possibility—put things behind the back, out of our lives, because we know that we will be able to bring them back. But when we suffer loss, serious loss, we have to find ways to disconnect ourselves from what we miss. We humans have burials, cremation, and a variety of mourning rites to mark the loss of crucial attachments. Through these rituals we prevent ourselves from going too far in staying connected to what is no longer available to us. Some mourn so that they do not fall ill. "In mourning it is the world which has become poor and empty," Freud wrote; "in melancholia it is the ego itself."[12] He described his magnum opus *The Interpretation of Dreams* as a reaction to his father's death, the kind of loss that "causes a revolution in one's soul." Freud suffered from anxiety, migraines, and worse after losing his father, and it wasn't until he was able to face some of his ambivalence toward "the old man" that he was really able to get on with what he called the "work" of mourning. What kind of labor is it to learn to live with loss? And when one stays "stuck" in an attachment to the dead, what kinds of solace and satisfaction are being derived from that connection?[13]

In "Mourning and Melancholia," Freud explored the connections between what feels like inescapable sadness and the process through which one lets go of an attachment to a loved one. In melancholia (what we would today call "depression"), the loss remains unconscious, and aggression is turned inward. In grief, one feels the world to be poor and empty, like an abandoned house. Melancholics feel themselves to be abandoned. While mourners may rebel against a world missing their loved one, melancholics rebel against themselves for being unworthy of love, for remaining present. The mourner's memories are all painful, Freud wrote, because the "verdict of reality" comes again and again: the loved one is no more.

Freud considers mourning to be work, a process through which the libido "should be withdrawn from its attachments to this [the loved] object." This withdrawal requires labor because "people never willingly abandon a libidinal position." The beloved is sought for but is no more; in response to the longing of the survivor, reality is firm, its orders clear: your desire is for nothing here; turn away. Mourning rituals lead us through turning away, again and again; this, too, I must learn to live without, and this, and this. The confrontation with and turning away from loss in mourning is a repetitive task, and thus "the existence of the lost object is prolonged." *Fort! Fort! Fort!* It is through this repetitive turning away, painful though it is, that the "ego becomes free and uninhibited."[14] Put some things behind the back, so as to move forward.

Freud himself found solace only by turning to psychoanalytic work following Sophie's and his grandson's deaths. His cherished daughter was snatched from the world, but as an ardent unbeliever he noted, "I have no one to blame, and I know there is no place where one can lodge a complaint." The "verdict of reality" was all too clear. And so he put on the harness and went back to writing and seeing patients. "Work and the free play of the imagination," he told Oskar Pfister, "are for me the same thing, I take no pleasure in anything else." Behind the back? When his grandson Heinerle died a few years after Sophie, he wrote he was "obsessed by impotent longing for the dear child" and with nothing to invest in the world. "Fundamentally," he wrote, "everything has lost its meaning for me."[15] Once again work provided a way of reconnecting to the world. He imagined the searing pain of death and loss as part of a cosmic pattern, the awful return to an earlier state of things. He had written years before that after early childhood "every finding is a re-finding," and he refound meaning by working toward a new theory of instinct and psychology, one in which loss has a place equal to desire.[16]

Freud had long had a theory of why we put things behind the back. The concept of repression, which he'd described as the "cornerstone" of the psychoanalytic edifice, explained that we become unaware of things, consign them to unconsciousness, because we can't bear the desires with which they are associated. Mental conflict arises because it takes real psychic energy to maintain our unawareness of these desires, to keep them at bay. This he understood from his early work on hysteria at the end of nineteenth century, and it was the spine of his theory of why, in dreams (when our energies are relaxed), there is some leakage of desires, distorted expressions of our wishes fulfilled. Symptoms, too, are expressions both of our desires and of our efforts to repress them. Repression can never be entirely successful ("evil cannot be annihilated"), and so we suffer.

During the years of World War I, and especially after the deaths of Sophie and Heinerle, Freud was increasingly drawn to the question of why we return to our suffering, why we stage our unhappiness again and again. This was, he thought, what little Ernst was doing in playing his *fort-da* game—staging the disappearance and then reappearance of his mother. A psychiatrist friend of mine suggested by way of an alternative interpretation that a child of that age is playing with his new understanding of object permanence, realizing that some objects are still somewhere when they are out of sight. The pleasure of playing with a recently developed skill made perfect sense to my friend. Why bring death into this happy, developmental picture?

But Freud emphasized the flip side of the pleasure one takes from this developing skill. We also develop, like it or not, ways of coping with the fact that the "objects" of our desire, of our love, are impermanent. They go missing on us. Sure, we develop sensory abilities (like depth perception and notions of object stability) just as we develop moral capacities (like empathy and ideals of behavior) as part of our maturation as human beings. But psychoanalysis warns us not to be fooled by stories of developmental progress at either the individual or societal level. Although we gain confidence that objects have permanence even when we are not looking at them, we never fully leave behind those stages of confusion about whether the things right before our eyes might suddenly disappear. When we play with loss, when we put things "behind the back," we are containing our confusion, controlling the emotions aroused by the threat that the things we care about might disappear. During the World War I years, Freud realized that we repetitively play with impermanence as a way of coping with loss, of returning to feelings prior to the recognition that what we love will disappear. He also sadly recognized that we repetitively reenact our premoral rage and hatred. No matter how much we develop as individuals, no matter how far we seem to have progressed as societies, we probably have "never risen so high as we believed."

But there is more. Freud tied the death drive to aggression, to tearing things apart. This is how the death drive pushes forward, he argued, creating destructive conflict. But the death drive also pushes backward, as it were, to trauma. When he wrote *Beyond the Pleasure Principle*, the return to trauma was anomalous, and Freud found it difficult and important to answer the question of what we were getting out of the turn to trauma in dreams and in play. In the twenty-first century, by contrast, trauma is everywhere, and the traumatized have been elevated morally and politically. Only the privileged would claim some escape from "the dark and dismal subject" of trauma. And no one wants to admit to being privileged. To quote Freud once more, "this astonishes us far too little."

I'd like to think that Freud would ask what we are putting behind our backs as we focus more and more on trauma in popular culture, in academia, and in politics. What desires are satisfied or obscured by the embrace of the traumatic? Has the "mysterious masochism" that he wrote about in the second decade of the twentieth century become a "moral masochism" in our time? Freud turned to a theory of death as a way of understanding the murderous culture all around him, and as a way of processing the heartbreaking losses of his daughter and grandson. He put himself to work on a new theory of the mind to put those events behind his back. What work awaits us in the wake of our fascination with trauma and the stories it generates?

AGAINST INTERPRETATION

André Aciman

To illustrate an aspect of Sigmund Freud's *The Interpretation of Dreams*, let's take an example drawn from the Second World War. Had the Germans known that the British had discovered an Enigma machine in a scuttled German submarine and had broken the German Enigma code, the first thing that even the lowliest-ranked German cryptographer would have done is to change the code immediately and never use the same machine itself. This explains why it was of vital importance for the enemies of the Reich not to let the Germans suspect that their code was cracked. Thus, once the British decoded a message revealing German plans to bomb the city of Coventry in central England, they had to face the very difficult choice of not sparing Coventry from the imminent German raid to avoid revealing that they had decoded the German code. Or so goes a disputed version of the story.

Now, apply the logic of the British code breakers at Bletchley Park to Freud's *Interpretation of Dreams*. Unless the subconscious really wants its cryptic language decoded or, alternatively, unless its language is not even coded but just a labyrinthine garble meaning nothing, it would be reasonable to assume that the first thing the subconscious might do, if it aims to remain *sub*conscious, is to change its code or stop dreams altogether. We could attempt to keep secret our forays into its coded language, just as the British did with the German code at Bletchley Park, but there is an important difference between Alan Turing, the principal decoder in England,

and Sigmund Freud. Freud cannot keep his reading of his own dreams from leaking to his subconscious, because the very mind attempting to penetrate the language of the subconscious is itself the carrier of that selfsame subconscious. In other words, the subconscious is perpetually apprised of what its code breakers are attempting to do. This, to return to our war parallel, would be as though Bletchley Park were home to English code breakers perpetually leaking their findings to German encoders across the Channel.

To repeat: unless our dreams want to be decoded or unless they are just a mass of gobbledygook, it would stand to reason that the first thing the subconscious might do to remain *sub*conscious is to modify its code or stop dreaming altogether. When informed time and again that its coded dreams have been interpreted, the subconscious might continue to operate as usual by using its by-now superannuated, encrypted symbols: cigar = phallus, urn = vagina, and so on. Or, on hearing that these can be easily read and therefore no longer retain their coded status, the subconscious might change symbols, either by swapping pencil for cigar and cave for urn, or by changing symbolic coding altogether, as the Germans attempted to do when they added a fourth rotor to their three-rotor Enigma machine and paralyzed for a while the Ultra code breakers at Bletchley Park. Thus, the phallus, let us say, is no longer represented by a cigar or a pencil but by a scale; similarly, the vagina is not an urn or a cave but a pair of glasses. (My own new symbols are themselves, of course, open to Freudian interpretation!) The analyst, in short, can no longer decipher and unmask a dream's symbolic language with what he's been taught in his training. He needs to reinterpret his interpretation with the suspicion that the subconscious may always be one step ahead of him.

Even the process of free association can no longer be so free, since the ability to associate one seemingly harmless word with its hidden, underlying content is now compelling the subconscious to revise and censor itself and be particularly cautious of a mechanism that, for more than a hundred years now, seemed to pry open the portals of the psyche. Knowing more or less how free association works encourages the patients to veil, repress, or intentionally miscast the link triggered by the one word thrown at them by their analyst. An educated patient today is not a patient of one hundred years ago. Today one uses all manner of pseudopsychological jargon while having coffee with a friend. Freudian terms are part of everyone's vernacular.

The very prospect of what is called "interpretation" has been totally upended and disrupted once the subconscious, aware of the analyst's tracking devices, might have a second-, or third-, or fourth-degree coding, riddled with more decoys and labyrinths than Freud suspected.

The subconscious can no longer use one set of symbols and substitute them with another that is more intractable, the way parents, who do not want their English-speaking children to understand what they say to each other, will use French, for instance, instead of English, only to observe, with the passing of time, that the children are able to understand enough French to piece together their parents' mysterious conversation. This might be why parents spell out words in English when the children are still too young to read, only, once again, to discover that the children can read their spelled words. If only to belabor the point, parents could resort to a mix of Proto-Indo-European and Dravidian languages, or simply abandon the very concept of a language, abandon even the temptation to use cuneiform instead of hieroglyphics, and turn to cloud signals instead of good old English or just Quipu, the Andean language of talking knots.

If the subconscious is to remain *sub*conscious it cannot be interpreted; it refutes interpretation. It is not a fossil or a dead language. It is constantly evolving, and like the German code, constantly adding rotors to its Enigma machine. But if it is true that we need to interpret our dreams, which subsumes that dreams are coded and therefore may not want to be interpreted, then the moment we are fairly sure to have interpreted our dreams is the moment when dreams will need to find a new, post-Freudian idiom.

Either this or the subconscious can refuse to alter its language and, like a testy old person, is set in its ways, doesn't care to learn new tricks, and refuses to be reeducated.

Which is where psychology is today. It assumes that the subconscious is a dead language. And it needs to assume this because, otherwise, dead languages like Latin and Ancient Greek could suddenly flourish and morph in new, unpredictable ways and borrow inflected idioms from, say, argot French or millennial English.

Either this or its code was never broken at all. The code just allowed us to think it was broken.

Or it operates not by analogical imagery (pencil = phallus, or seven lean cows = seven years of famine) but on an altogether dyslogical and more primitive plane, which is often how superstitious folk interpret oneiric events. Thus, dreaming of a baby (allegedly a happy prospect) augurs terrible news, the way dreaming of gold presages nothing short of penury.

Dreams, in short, are not open messages from one faculty within us to another faculty equally within us. This much Freud suspected. Hence his need to interpret these so-called messages. What he didn't know, or refused to know, was that these messages were constantly being recoded precisely because someone was intercepting them.

The issue here is that our dreams do not want to be interpreted and are continuously resisting our probes and continuously throwing us off. Why should they be coded or assumed to be coded if the code ultimately can be decrypted, usually either to satisfy our predetermined reading or to please our sleuthing instincts, which is what happens when tea leaves or ground coffee sediments are read.

Let us for a moment imagine that the ever-scheming German cryptographers may have "planted" the Enigma machine in the captured submarine, hoping that the Allies, after strenuous efforts, might believe they had finally broken the code. Meanwhile, the Germans might have been already communicating in another code, which the Allies never intercepted or suspected, since the

Germans continued to broadcast via Enigma the better to placate the Allies who believed they were eavesdropping on vital, up-to-the-minute information. After all, the Allies had done no better with Operation Mincemeat when they too "planted" a dead person carrying false messages about Allied invasion plans, which the ever-suspicious and guarded Germans seemed to have gobbled up, in Churchill's words, "rod, line, and sinker."[1] Wars, as is frequently repeated, are won not by superior strategies or better military deployments but by the commission of fewer bungles, that is, by one army being just slightly less incompetent and possibly luckier than the other.

The entire notion of decoding the subconscious could have been a setup on the part of the subconscious itself the better to remain inviolable. In that sense, the dead British soldier carrying Allied disinformation in his briefcase and whose body was thrown off on the Gulf of Cádiz—read or see Ben Macintyre's *Operation Mincemeat* (book 2010, film 2021), or the earlier version of the tale in the 1956 film *The Man Who Never Was*—was functioning exactly as does the subconscious. The dead man's briefcase, once intercepted by the Germans, ended up revealing false information, persuading the Germans, who had expected the Allies to land in Sicily, that the Allied attack would come from Greece, not Sicily, thus compelling them to divert their forces to Greece and leaving Sicily totally vulnerable.

Dream interpretation is the act of postulating meaning to something that means to seem meaningless.

But the opposite is equally true. *Dream interpretation is the act of postulating meaning to something that does not mean to seem meaningless.*

We are back to the English double-dealings with the Germans.

Not all interpreters are equally gifted interpreters. Joseph in Pharaoh's court is, of course, the ultimate exception.

But this brings an important question: Is there ever a mistaken Freudian interpretation of a dream? Can there be an interpretation that is entirely wrong?

Or to put the same question differently: Can there be more than one interpretation of a dream? Can an interpretation of one analyst be incompatible with another analyst's interpretation, though both are persuasive enough and both have arguments in their favor? And how should we measure the difference? What if Joseph's "fatfleshed kine" devoured by "leanfleshed kine" meant something entirely different and only accidentally and retrospectively coincided with lean years?

Which brings us to the most important question of all: Why do we need to have our dreams interpreted, why the belief that a dream whispers a hidden and elusive meaning? Is it to understand better the tussling within our psyche or, as more primitive minds are wont to do, do we need to interpret dreams in the hope of uncovering, say, a traitor, or a year of dearth, or a winning lottery number?

In this, I am reminded of the elaborate history of people attempting to decipher the Egyptian hieroglyphs. Everyone could tell that these were symbols that needed to be decoded, but among the many who attempted to decode Egyptian letters before Jean-François Champollion (1790–1832) was the Jesuit scholar Athanasius Kircher (1602–80), one of the most learned men of his time, who was persuaded that he had indeed decoded Egyptian hieroglyphics. How could he have been led to believe he had deciphered them when he clearly had not? Yet many were persuaded that he had indeed cracked the silent hieroglyphics.

Not dissimilarly, Freud was persuaded that he had taken significant steps in studying the essence of the dream work and indeed postulated the theory that dreams are made of manifest content and latent content. But he also understood that the two were intricately braided, the way that Champollion had finally understood that hieroglyphics consisted of both logographic and phonetic signs operating simultaneously on the same stone. The reason hieroglyphics were difficult to read was no different from the reason dreams needed Freud to read the subconscious in them: the messages seemed corrupted, distorted, amorphous; they weren't just censored but seemed intentionally juggled and en-crypted the better to confuse and remain impenetrable. Freud, after all, might have been trying to provide or, at best, bypass a Euclidian solution to a problem that quantum thinking itself would have been equally unable to resolve. His genius was in understanding that dreams are intractable to ordinary logic, that interpretation itself had to proceed along a pathway no less tor-tured, twisted, and at times as casual and intractable as were dreams themselves.

In this connection, I cannot resist quoting the words of the French moralist François de La Rochefoucauld (1613–80) spoken about self-love and pride, what we call by the slightly pejorative term of ego. La Rochefoucauld might just as well have been speak-ing about Freud's subconscious, when it resists analysis. As he writes in his first suppressed maxim in *Reflections; Or Sentences and Moral Maxims*:

[Self-love] exists at every stage of life and in every walk of life. It lives everywhere; it lives off everything—or nothing; it adapts to anything—or the loss of anything. It even enlists among those who wage war against it; it participates in their plans; and, most remarkably, it hates itself just as they do, it plots its own downfall, it even toils to bring about its own ruin. In fact, all it cares about is existing; and as long as it can exist, it is quite willing to be its own enemy. So there is no reason to be surprised if it sometimes joins forces with the harshest aus-terity, in whose society it sets out boldly to destroy itself—because while it is crushing itself on one side, it is recovering on another. When we think that it has abandoned one of its pleasures, it has only adjourned it—or exchanged it for some-thing else. And even when it is defeated and we think we are rid of it, it reappears glorying in its own defeat. That is the portrait of self-love, whose entire life is merely one big long flurry of agitation. The sea is a tangible image of it; and in the perpetual ebb and flow of the waves, it finds a faithful picture of its own eternal restlessness and the turbulent succession of its thoughts.[2]

The restless subconscious is indeed in eternal motion—flux and reflux—always changing courses, siding both with and against us, speaking in many tongues and many symbols, but always a step ahead of us, even when we're persuaded, no differently from the misguided Athanasius Kircher, that we've decoded it.

Yet, in keeping with La Rochefoucauld's twisted reading of the psyche and in thinking of how the subconscious behaves, everything I have said here could be easily invalidated. So far, I have assumed that the subconscious does not want to reveal itself, that it speaks with a forked tongue precisely because it means to resist our efforts to penetrate its secret language. But, as I've hinted twice above, what if the subconscious wishes to reveal itself, what if it wants to tell us things about itself, and hence about us, but doesn't know how to do so, or it is we who are unwilling or incapable of heeding its messages? What if we are the ones who pretend it is intractable, we the ones who want to shut it out, we the villains, while the amiable subconscious, eager to reveal itself, is being almost muffled into a vaporous silence like cloud signals and Quipu?

La Rochefoucauld saw this baroque cat's cradle clearly enough. The constant switching of roles is typical of the subconscious: it slips into our very thinking once we are awake to let us suspect that it is our foe and we its friend, only then to correct our thinking to make us its foe and it our friend, but then corrects our thinking once more by making us realize that this is indeed its fundamental stratagem: to keep slipping in and out of our grasp, to remind us that thinking is itself a corruptible vehicle, that thinking redresses itself only to reveal its faults the better to fool us into seeing that we have broken the secrets of the subconscious, only then, again and again, to tell us that we are not even split in half with one part trying to decode the other, but that we are at war with ourselves, though with constant, secret, under-the-radar embassies meant to undermine a declared state of hostility where the enemy of my enemy could be, then, but may not be my enemy still.

Operation Mincemeat praises Colonel Alexis Freiherr von Rönne, Hitler's spymaster and trusted right-hand man, by alleging that von Rönne was in fact an anti-Nazi who, knowing all along that the British body floating on the Gulf of Cádiz was nothing more than a plant, intentionally helped persuade the Führer that the Allies were planning to land in Greece, not Sicily. "Whatever his reasons, and despite his reputation as an intelligence guru," writes Ben Macintyre, "by 1943 von Rönne was deliberately passing information he knew to be false, directly to Hitler's desk." When MI5 debated why the German had fallen for the British canard, their only conclusion was to suppose that Von Rönne was indeed trying to help defeat Hitler from within.[3]

To reprise the analogy between the war and the subconscious, von Rönne took the bait but by doing so was one step ahead of the English. He wasn't fooled, but the British were convinced he'd been fooled, except that by a further torsion, the English realized that their inside man in Germany was not a British spy but a member of the German command. As Ewen Montagu says in the film, "Either that's true or it's a fiction we want to be true." Freudians are far from engaging in such complex double-dealing where the subconscious stays encoded the more we attempt to decode it.

We are in the realm of quantum thinking again, where things are both true and untrue, where what we believe the subconscious is muttering in our dreams is a sealed book but open to all manner of interpretations, so that Athanasius Kircher's hieroglyphics could turn out to be no less accurate than Champollion's, and where Freud's symbols may end up being spot-on with a very good chance of being entirely wrong.

FREUD THE ESSAYIST

Phillip Lopate

It is puzzling to me that I feel compelled to defend Sigmund Freud as a towering figure when his name is dismissed in polite conversation. Of course there are scholars and scientists who have serious objections to Freud, but what I have encountered more often are people who have never read even a page of him, who dismiss him with a knowing comment such as "He got many things wrong, especially women," on the assumption that this is the received wisdom, which says a lot about the way so-called educated people's opinions can arise from cocktail party consensus and circulate lazily. Very well: But why should it bother me so that I rush to defend Freud's honor? Certainly I find it an infuriating measure of ignorance that the dismissive person fails to understand to what degree his or her mental outlook has been shaped by Freud (however unconsciously). Still, that would not be enough to explain my personal investment in upholding his importance at all costs.

Part of the reason may be my loyalty to Freud as a Jew, for I regard Freud as a great *Jewish* thinker, his analyses the direct descent of rabbinic explication and midrash. I grew up in Jewish Brooklyn when Freud was spoken of reverentially. My own mother, though working-class, managed to scrape together enough dough for her weekly therapy sessions and, coming back from them, would explain to us her children such concepts as projection and the Oedipus complex. So I imbibed the basic doctrine of Freudianism like mother's milk, as it were. And when his star began to decline, I felt sorry for him; he became an underdog who needed my championing, all the more because some of that effort to cut him down to size seemed faddish and intellectually shallow. The fact that various notions of his struck even me as far-fetched or suspect, I don't dispute; but I read him more or less as one does a poet, for his allusive lyricism. I read him the same way I did Roland Barthes, Walter Benjamin, and Theodor Adorno, not so much in total agreement or even understanding their systems, but stimulated by their glints of aphoristic sublimity.

With Freud, it went further: I was charmed by his voice, his rhetorical syntaxes so reasonable sounding and engaging on their way to being shocking. In college I took a seminar that would profoundly influence my future writing style: "Nietzsche, Freud, and William James." I was too young to appreciate the heavenly William James, but the first two marked me forever: Nietzsche by his mischievous, pouncing, wittily aggressive delivery; Freud by his reassuringly commonsense openings that led to the most radical conclusions. Both Nietzsche and Freud were rejecting conventional society's bland assurances and delivering the bitter truth—that truth of disillusionment I needed so badly as an adolescent, in order to make my way into adulthood.

So it was Freud the writer, the literary stylist, that I came to admire. Not being a psychoanalyst in training, I would never be able to follow the more arcane details of the psychic mechanism of that science (or pseudoscience—I was willing to go either way), but I could still delight in the chase. While others might dismantle this or that technical assertion by Freud, I was happy to share his pleasure and excitement in making fresh discoveries. He was the explorer, a bearded Moses leading his people (myself included) into the Promised Land of psychological clarity.

I continue to be attracted to Freud's rhetorical means of persuasion. His conversational style is that of a classical personal essayist. He addresses the reader with regularity, anticipating resistances to his argument and heading them off at the pass. Nowhere is this conversational manner more evident than in his *Introductory Lectures*

on Psycho-analysis, delivered orally in two sets and published in
1916–17.[1] He begins by apologizing that, unlike a medical teacher who
can demonstrate on his patients, all he has to offer are words. "In
psycho-analysis, alas, everything is different. Nothing takes place
in the psycho-analytic treatment but an interchange of words between the patient and the analyst. The patient talks, tells of his past
experiences and present impressions, complains, confesses to his
wishes and his emotional responses. The doctor listens, tries to
direct the patient's processes of thought, exhorts, forces his attention
in certain directions and observes the reactions of understanding
or rejection which he in this way provokes in him." Still, words are
not nothing: "Words were originally magic and to this day words
have retained much of their magical power. By words one person
can make another blissfully happy or drive him to despair, by
words the teacher conveys his knowledge to his pupils, by words
the orator carries his audience with him and determines their
judgments and decisions. Words provoke affects and are in general
the means of mutual influence among men. Thus we shall not de-
preciate the use of words in psychotherapy." By this preliminary
note Freud is not only explaining the practice of psychotherapy
but also covertly expressing his ambitions as a writer.

He does something else early on in these talks: he defends his
attention to the small. Beginning his lectures with a discussion of
what he calls parapraxes (slips of the tongue, accidental misplace-
ments of objects, etc.) and anticipating that the audience will "protest with some annoyance" at spending so much time on these
"trivialities," he counters:

> I should reply: Patience, Ladies and Gentlemen! I think your
> criticism has gone astray. It is true that psycho-analysis cannot
> boast that it has never concerned itself with trivialities. On the
> contrary, the material for its observations is usually provided
> by the inconsiderable events which have been put aside by the
> other sciences as being too unimportant—the dregs, one might
> say, of the world of phenomena. But are you not making a

confusion in your criticism between the vastness of the problems and the conspicuousness of what points to them? Are there not very important things which can only reveal themselves, under certain conditions and certain times, by quite feeble indications? I should find no difficulty in giving you several examples of such situations. If you are a young man, for instance, will it not be from small pointers that you will conclude that you have won a girl's favor? Would you wait for an express declaration of love or a passionate embrace? Or would not a glance, scarcely noticed by other people, be enough? a slight movement, the lengthening by a second of the pressure of a hand? And if you were a detective engaged in tracing a murder, would you expect to find that the murderer had left his photograph behind at the place of the crime, with his address attached? or would you not necessarily have to be satisfied with comparable slight and obscure traces of the person you were in search of?

In this paradigmatic essayist's move from the general to the particular, I'm noticing that Freud draws his two examples or vignettes from courtship and from Sherlock Holmes, since he is never far from thinking about Eros and his case histories have often been compared to detective stories. Still, what really catches me is a phrase at the end of the paragraph, which I italicize: *"since everything is related to everything, including small things to great,* one may gain access even from such unpretentious work to a study of the great problems." This idea, that everything in the universe may be seen as linked, echoes almost word for word an assertion by Michel de Montaigne, the founder of the modern essay. And the territory of the small, the supposedly trivial, the everyday, has been claimed by countless essayists, from Charles Lamb to Fanny Fern to E. B. White.

Freud's method in these introductory lectures is to lead his audience from parapraxes to dream interpretations to a general theory of the neuroses, including the stages of sexual development (oral, anal, genital), to resistance and repression, the formation of neurotic symptoms, anxiety, narcissism, and transference. All along, he implants tensions regarding problems that will have to be resolved somehow or other (another classic essayist move), as when he says, tweaking his audience: "I shall not hold you, your education or your attitude of mind responsible for the next difficulty. Two of the hypotheses of psycho-analysis are an insult to the entire world and have earned its dislike. One of them offends against an intellectual prejudice, the other against an aesthetic and moral one." The two hypotheses he is referring to are the existence of the unconscious and the sexuality of children. He is well aware of the harsh criticisms directed at him by colleagues and the public regarding these matters, and his response is to acknowledge them openly as minefields. He is in turn bringing unwelcome news, and reassuring ("I will try to console you") by explaining how it all fits into a logical system, which, if one can accept it, will illuminate some dark corners of the psyche. It may also injure one's vanity or self-esteem, this discovery that we are scarcely in control of our lives; fragmented, self-divided, ruled as much by unconscious, irrational instincts as by reason and our egos. In a moment of forgivable hubris, he even compares this devaluation of human beings to Copernicus and Darwin, both of whom diminished *Homo sapiens* in the larger scheme of things. But he never loses sight of a likely persistent skepticism on the part of his audience: "Nor can you guess what development led to a denial of the unconscious— *should such a thing exist*—and what advantage there may have been in that denial" (my italics).

Though Freud could be disturbingly provocative, he averred that he had no wish to engage in a fight: "I take this opportunity of assuring you that in the course of these lectures I shall indulge in very little controversy, especially with individuals. I have never been able to convince myself of the truth of the maxim that strife is the father of all things." Thus he restores some balance to offset the anxiety his ideas may arouse—a rhetorical side of Freud that is often overlooked.

It strikes me how often the essayists I revere have been the bearers of disenchantment, stripping away some anodyne notion of its sentimental underpinnings: Hazlitt diagnosing the pleasure of hating, Lamb confessing the limits of his imperfect sympathies, Nietzsche locating Judeo-Christian morality in weaker beings' resentment of the strong, Orwell admitting his ambivalence and shame in killing an elephant, Baldwin and Fanon confronting the internal scars of racism, Sontag debunking the satisfactions of interpretation, Adorno alerting us to the injustices of the liberal consensus, Gombrowicz shattering the pretenses of poetry. What is it about the essay as a form that so often goes to this place of contrariety? Is there not something sadistic in this ripping off of bandages? And yet I have always found it exhilarating, the puncturing of false hopes as a path to stoical wisdom. If you could still be standing after hearing the Bad News, even energized by this refreshing negativity—if it does not kill you, as Nietzsche said, it will only make you stronger. I have tried to offer the same sort of invigorating disillusionment in my own essays, such as "Against Joie de Vivre" and "The Limits of Empathy," which if nothing else try to console other discontented naysayers that they are not alone. And whenever I was asked to write something and found myself unable or unwilling, I have analyzed my own resistance, as in "Resistance to the Holocaust" and "Terror of Mentors." In this, too, Freud has been my mentor.

He playfully invites his listeners and readers to speculate, just for the sake of scientific curiosity: "I will put a suggestion to you. . . . Let us take it as a premise from this point onward that dreams are not somatic but psychic phenomena. You know what that means, but what justifies our making the assumption? Nothing: but there is nothing either to prevent our making it. Here is the position: if dreams are somatic phenomena they are of no concern of ours, they can only interest us on the assumption that they are mental phenomena. We will therefore work on the assumption that they really are, to see what comes of it. . . . If you feel inclined, then give up the attempt! But if you feel otherwise, you can accompany me further." He emphasizes the necessity of skepticism and doubt, key premises of Montaigne, whose motto was famously "What do I know?" Montaigne says: "I do not teach, I tell." Freud says: "I do not wish to arouse conviction; I wish to stimulate thought and to upset prejudices." He says about his patients: "The attitude we find the most desirable in them is a benevolent skepticism." About these lectures: "what I had in mind was nothing in nature of a presentation *in usum Delphini* [for the use of the Dauphin, i.e., bowdlerized], which would give you a smooth account with the gaps filled in and the doubts glossed over, so that you might believe with an easy mind that you had learned something new. No, for the very reason of your being beginners, I wanted to show you our science as it is, with its unevennesses and its roughnesses, its demands and hesitations." He is not imposing a dogma; he is giving readers the freedom to disagree. If R. P. Blackmur called the essay "a form of unindoctrinated thinking," then Freud is practicing that form. He is also in continual dialogue with himself, thinking against himself, catching himself: "Ladies and gentlemen, I have the impression that we have advanced too quickly. Let us go back a little." And: "I beg you, however, not to try to understand too much of what I tell you."

Yet always, he makes the attempt to recapitulate the steps, to show how we got to this point and to coax the reader, therefore, to sign on to his underlying premise (in this case, that the unconscious exists): "If, now, you consider further that the state of affairs which we have established in our two cases is confirmed for every symptom of every neurotic illness—that always and everywhere the sense of the symptoms is unknown to the patient and that analysis regularly shows that these symptoms are derivatives of unconscious processes but can, subject to a variety of favorable circumstances, be made conscious—if you consider this, you will understand that in psycho-analysis we cannot do without what is at the same time unconscious and mental, and are accustomed to operate with it as though it were something palpable to the senses." It's not a particularly lovely sentence; maybe it sounded better in German; but I wish only to draw your attention to this If-if-if-then syntax as one of the ways Freud undertakes to induce agreement.

With characteristic cheek, he will suddenly announce: "I notice now, Gentlemen, that I have been talking to you about a number of things which you are not yet prepared to understand." He will make confident pronouncements that seem cockamamie, to have come out of nowhere, such as: "And finally, remember that we must always interpret 'dreams with a dental stimulus' as relating to masturbation and the dreaded punishment for it." We see that, in addition to his healthy skepticism, he was capable of drawing on a tone of assertion that may be just as necessary for an essayist as are humility and doubt.

Freud boasts of this aplomb, noting, in *An Autobiographical Study*, about his former research partner and coauthor of *Studies in Hysteria*, Josef Breuer: "he was affected by the reception which our book had received both in Vienna and Germany. His self-confidence and powers of resilience were not developed so fully as the rest of his mental organization. When, for instance, the *Studies* met with severe rebuff from Strümpell, I was able to laugh at the lack of comprehension which his criticism showed, but Breuer felt hurt and grew discouraged." Obviously, Freud did not lack for self-confidence or an assertive tone that could cut to the essence. It went a long way toward accounting for his law-giving, aphoristic style.

But he also took the reader into his confidence and expressed doubts about his writing process. Deep into his *Introductory Lectures*, he says:

Why did I not begin my introduction with what you yourselves know of the neurotic state and what has aroused our interest— with the peculiar characteristics of neurotic people, their incomprehensible reactions to human intercourse and external influences, their irritability, their incalculable and inexpedient

behavior? Why did I not lead you step by step from an understanding of the simpler, everyday forms of the neurotic state to
the problems of its enigmatic, extreme manifestations? Indeed,
Gentlemen, I cannot even disagree with you. I am not so enam-
ored of my skill in exposition that I can declare each of its artistic
faults to be a particular charm. I think myself that it might have
been more to your advantage if I had proceeded otherwise; and
that was, indeed, my intention. But one cannot always carry out
one's reasonable intentions. There is often something in the
material itself which takes charge of one and diverts one from
one's first intentions. Even such a trivial achievement as the ar-
rangement of a familiar piece of material is not entirely subject
to an author's own choice; it takes what line it likes and all one
can do is to ask oneself after the event why it has happened in
this way and no other.

Spoken like a true writer. As every writer knows, language has
a will of its own and sometimes guides you, rather than you it.
It is not news that Freud was a celebrated prose stylist: his ap-
pealing, seductive, literary manner had a great deal to do with the
rapid proliferation of his ideas. So Stanley Edgar Hyman long ago
argued in *The Tangled Bank*. Thomas Mann even nominated Freud
(unsuccessfully, alas) for a Nobel Prize in Literature. He was in fact
awarded the Goethe Prize in 1930. Whether his conclusions hold
up, whether they are replicable or not, are issues beyond my ken; but
even if they are too idiosyncratic to pass muster as hard science,
all the more reason to regard him as an imaginative writer, with an
allusive suggestiveness that meshes well with the humanities. I can
imagine a time (it may already be here) when Freud will be at most
consigned to a footnote in psychology classes, while continuing
to tantalize literature departments indefinitely.
Of course there has been considerable argument about the degree of sexist or patriarchal assumption underlying his analyses of
women. I am aware that there are female thinkers on both sides of
the debate, pro- and anti-Freud, as well as many who are simply

indifferent to him. All I know is that some of his best writing occurred in his case histories, such as *Dora: An Analysis of a Case of
Hysteria* and *The Wolf Man*. In *Dora*, we witness a cat-and-mouse
game between analyst and patient that many critics have compared in its organization to a novella. I would argue that it also
bears resemblance to that subgenre of the personal essay I have
called "the double portrait," in which narrator and subject are both
revealed through their interactions.

Freud was also essayistic in his techniques of elaboration and
aphorism. In a startling paper, "The Most Prevalent Form of Deg-
radation in Erotic Life," written in 1912, Freud gave full rein to his
epigrammatic tendencies. He described certain male patients who
could not achieve potency with women they revered and felt ten-
derly toward, because of an incest taboo identification with their
mothers or sisters. "Where such men love they have no desire and
where they desire they cannot love," he aphorizes. "Hence comes
his need for a less exalted sexual object . . . who does not know the
rest of his life and cannot criticize him." Clearly, Freud is speaking
here about a narrow sociological slice, the bourgeois male who
sleeps with lower-class women and prostitutes or frequents the
pleasure quarters. But he keeps pushing his hunches to more in-
clusive generalities: "It has an ugly sound and a paradoxical as well,
but nevertheless it must be said that whoever is to be really free
and happy in love must have overcome his deference for women
and come to terms with the idea of incest with mother or sister."
That warning phrase "but it must be said" epitomizes Freud's
stance that it gave him no pleasure to administer a bitter truth. He
goes on to make a broader assertion, offered as a potential general
law: "However strange it may sound, I think the possibility must
be considered that something in the nature of the sexual instinct
itself is unfavorable to the achievement of absolute gratification. . . . So perhaps we must make up our minds to the idea that
altogether it is not possible for the claims of the sexual instinct to
be reconciled with the demands of culture, that in consequence of
his cultural development[,] renunciation and suffering, as well as

the danger of extinction at some far future time, are not to be eluded by the race of man."

Here, he is well on his way to the speculative manner that would culminate in his 1930 masterpiece *Civilization and Its Discontents*. I know of no book that more directly encounters the crucial question: Why is human happiness impossible, except for brief moments? It is a question I at one time desperately needed an answer to. Its opening line begins "It is impossible to escape the impression . . . ," which characterizes both the proximity of an unwelcome thought and the need to work through it. He often seems to be in the middle of thinking about something. Addressing both the common reader and his colleagues, he contemplates the sources of humanity's discontent with plausibility and a dispassion that seems almost Buddhist. "One feels inclined to say that the intention that man should be 'happy' is not included in the plan of 'Creation'. What we call happiness in the strictest sense comes from the (preferably sudden) satisfaction of needs which have been dammed up to a high degree, and it is from its nature only possible as an episodic phenomenon. When any situation that is desired by the pleasure principle is prolonged, it only produces a feeling of mild contentment. We are so made that we can derive intense enjoyment only from a contrast and very little from a state of things."

Curiously enough, in this eloquent, audacious book, he periodically expresses doubt that he is saying anything more than common sense. "Our enquiry concerning happiness has not so far taught us much that is not already common knowledge." It is as if the Goethe-quoting poetry lover / humanistic philosopher side of him feels guilty toward the scientific researcher side of him, who had so often explicated neurotic discontent in technical terms. In *Civilization*, some of his postulations come very close to sounding like Schopenhauer and Nietzsche. For instance, his digression questioning the soundness of the Christian admonition to love one's enemies has a very Nietzschean ring. In one of his other books, *An Autobiographical Study*, he states somewhat defensively:

"I read Schopenhauer very late in life. Nietzsche, another philosopher whose guesses and intuitions often agree in the most astonishing way with the laborious findings of psycho-analysis, was for a long time avoided by me on that very account; I was less concerned with the question of priority than with keeping my mind unembarrassed." This strikes me as faux naive: the ideas of Schopenhauer and Nietzsche were much in the air in Vienna, however little he may have read them. Moreover, Freud would not be the first author to deny acquaintance with some suspected influence. What goes around comes around: Eugene O'Neill, America's most gifted psychological dramatist, kept insisting to the press that he had never read Freud!

An Autobiographical Study, whose title promises much in terms of revealing the intimate Freud, proves rather disappointing. He sounds grumpy, having been asked to explain one more time the genesis and gist of his theories. In its postscript, he goes so far as to say: "And here I may be allowed to break off these autobiographical notes. The public has no claim to learn any more of my personal affairs—of my struggles, of my disappointments, and my successes. I have in any case been more open and frank in some of my writings (such as *The Interpretation of Dreams* and *The Psychopathology of Everyday Life*) than people usually are who describe their lives for their contemporaries or for posterity. I have had small thanks for it, and from my experience I cannot recommend anyone to follow my example."

So if I were to argue here that Freud was not just an essayist but a personal essayist (my own bailiwick), my linking him with that form had less to do with his being forthcoming about the details of his life than with his injection of warmth and character into every sentence, which allowed us to form a clear notion of the man behind the prose. Since his death, ironically, a brigade of Freud scholar sleuths has been hunting out his personal secrets, to ascertain whether he had this or that shameful extramarital affair or fudged his research methods improperly. At the same time, we can slake our curiosity about Freud's life by reading Ernest Jones's and

Adam Phillips's excellent, admittedly sympathetic biographies of him. Having read both, I conclude that I simply like the man. I am drawn not only to his prose style but to his courage, his curiosity, his willingness to entertain the most unsettling notions. Do I identify with him? Perhaps a little. Another Jewish kid who set out to conquer the world with his brains. But he was a genius as I am not; I stand in awe of his energy and intellectual reach. Freud is my superhero. I am drawn to the way he reluctantly jettisoned hypnosis in his practice for the more open-ended tool of free association (that writerly technique); to his discovery of the importance of resistance, transference, the Oedipus complex, and the sexuality of children; to his discerning the clash between the pleasure principle and the reality principle; to his championing of sublimation (the artist's path) and the legitimate sacrifices that civilization exacts; and to that final, profound battleground between Eros and Thanatos. Increasingly, we have come to see that the death instinct is real, and must be understood alongside the claims of sexual liberation from repression. All these concepts, which are more or less commonplaces by now, these ways of looking at the world that I've taken deep into my soul, have made me an unregenerate Freudian. And I wonder how much those who denigrate him whenever I introduce his name in conversation are, for better or worse, his disciples as well. Are we not all Freudians, at this point?

FREUD NOW?

Siri Hustvedt

There are many ghosts of Sigmund Freud stalking the twenty-first century. His phantoms appear in multiple guises—the innocuous cartoon character, the brilliant writer whose thought has no scientific merit, the great neuroscientist born too early, and the cocaine-addicted, malevolent fraud. It is hard to think of a figure who has aroused as much devotion, ambivalence, and venom as Sigmund Freud. Why?

Although there are thinkers singled out as particularly original or influential in the history of ideas in the West, and Freud is surely among them, the texts these anointed people produced, whether scientific, philosophical, or literary, are often regarded as the products of a single hermetically sealed mind. This is of course never true. Ideas are made in collective reality through ongoing dialogues with other texts and other human beings in particular intellectual and social milieus with their entrenched hierarchies. Ideas are social, and which ideas are accepted and which are discarded cannot be isolated from the structures of authority in a given culture. Contentious ideas inevitably involve power struggles and perceptions of threat to deeply held beliefs that reinforce the status quo.

The caricature of Freud—the white-bearded, bespectacled Viennese doctor—still appears regularly. A "Freudian sips" mug can be purchased from the Unemployed Philosophers Guild, which also sells an eleven-inch Sigmund Freud plush doll along with huggable versions of Einstein and Beethoven. While the last two continue to serve as unqualified signifiers of "genius" in the culture, the headlines pop Freud inspires tell a different story: "Why Sigmund Freud Still Matters When He Was Wrong about Almost Everything"; "Was Freud Right about Anything?"; "What Sigmund Freud Got Wrong about Psychology (and Your Mother)."[1] Most of these articles betray no evidence that their authors have ever read a sentence by Freud. I have discovered that countless people, including psychiatrists, psychologists, and scientists, pronounce Freud's ideas "pseudoscience," but when I ask them how they arrived at this conclusion, it becomes clear that the ghost to which they refer was never encountered on the page.

Whether he was right or wrong is a question obsessively asked about Freud. No one argues that Hegel's thought should be jettisoned in its entirety because he wrongly believed the synthesis of his historical dialectic arrived with the Prussian Empire. Einstein was apparently wrong about quantum entanglement, but his reputation isn't tarnished by it.

I think Sigmund Freud was wrong about women. When I was fifteen, I read commentaries on Freud in Kate Millett's *Sexual Politics* and Simone de Beauvoir's *The Second Sex* before I ever read the man himself. They pushed me to the source. In college, I steeped myself in the psychoanalyst Karen Horney's objections to penis envy. Freud's ideas about femininity did not end my fascination with his work, however, which I have continued to read ever since.[2] In *Freud, Race, and Gender*, Sander L. Gilman makes the argument that the biological racism of the late nineteenth century and its corrosive anti-Semitism, which framed the Jewish man as disease prone, feminized, and marked by circumcision, had a powerful effect on Freud, who projected this internalized vision onto another Other—woman.[3] Gilman's insight doesn't result in a demolition of Freud, however. But then, Gilman is a cultural historian. Freud thrives in humanities departments. The right-wrong, true-false question turns on science.

———

"Freud bashing" in the United States survives chiefly through lavish media attention given to those who make their names by vituperation. In 2017, the literary scholar Frederick Crews published seven hundred pages of moral outrage in *Freud: The Making of an Illusion*. George Prochnik, a reviewer of the book in the *New York Times*, always a reliable barometer of received opinion, articulated a widely accepted view: Why bother? "Medical authorities have broadly recognized the faulty empirical scaffolding of psychoanalysis and its reliance on outmoded biological models. Mainstream American psychologists moved on decades ago."[4]

This breezy assessment of what "medical authorities" and "mainstream American psychologists" believe deserves examination. Freudian thought was ascendant among *psychiatrists, not psychologists*, in the middle of the last century in the United States. Psychoanalytic authority began to dissolve with the advent of pharmacological treatments in the 1950s, their growing availability in the 1970s, and a sharp turn, or rather return, to a reductionist biological model of psychiatric illness, which reigned in Europe in the late nineteenth century, the world in which Freud was educated as a scientist and physician. In 1980, the third edition of *The Diagnostic and Statistical Manual of Mental Disorders* (DSM III) attempted to impose classificatory rigor on mental illness by accumulating lists of symptoms, a throwback to the nosology of the German psychiatrist Emil Kraepelin (1856–1926). The explosion in brain research that began in the 1960s, followed by new brain-scanning technology, turned mental illnesses into brain diseases that were to be treated by new pharmacological remedies. This became the age of media neurodelirium: "God spots" in the brain, "hard-wired" male and female brain differences, and depression as "a chemical imbalance." Neuro mania was paralleled only by gene mania. The "blueprint" or "code of life" would soon reveal genes for schizophrenia, bipolar disorder, aggression, and suicide.[5] After over five decades of research, not a single clinically useful bio-marker for any psychiatric diagnosis, neither neurobiological nor genetic, has been discovered.

In 2017, Thomas Insel, former head of the National Institute of Mental Health, said, "I spent 13 years at NIMH really pushing on the neuroscience and genetics of mental disorders, and when I look back on that, I realize that while I succeeded in getting some really cool papers published by cool scientists at fairly large costs—I think 20 billion—I don't think we moved the needle in reducing suicide, reducing hospitalizations, improving recovery for tens of millions of people with mental illness."[6] Why?

Despite Freud's wandering into broad cultural and philosophi-cal terrain, he believed fervently in the biological fundament of mental illness: "We must recollect that all of our provisional ideas in psychology will presumably one day be based on an organic substructure."[7] His was a "biological psychology": "We are study-ing the psychical accompaniments of biological processes."[8] Freud began his career as a neuropathologist working on the histology of the nervous system in Ernst Brücke's laboratory in Vienna. He published five scientific papers, in which he focused primarily on the nerve cells and nervous systems of fish and crustaceans. In 1884, at the Vienna General Hospital, while researching the medulla oblongata in the human brain, he developed a new histological staining technique that allowed for a clearer resolution on micro-scope slides. Although these contributions are firmly embedded in the history of neurology, they do not appear in *The Standard Edition of the Complete Psychological Works*, nor does the book Freud wrote on aphasia, the language problems that afflict patients with brain lesions.

In 1895, the same year Freud and Josef Breuer published *Studies on Hysteria*, in which Freud confesses rather sheepishly that his cases read like "short stories" and "lack the serious stamp of science," he wrote *Project for a Scientific Psychology*.[9] After burning with excitement about this new work, Freud wrote to Wilhelm Fliess, "I no longer understand the state of mind I was in which hatched the psychology; and cannot conceive how I could have inflicted it on you."[10] It was not published until 1950, eleven years after Freud's death.

This dense work has been subject to ongoing debate, not only about why Freud abandoned it but about its meaning for psychoanalysis as a scientific discipline. Its opening sentence delineates the author's ambition: "The intention is to furnish a psychology that shall be a natural science: that is to represent the psychical processes as quantitative determinate states of specifiable material particles, thus making those processes perspicuous and free from contradiction."[11] Freud wanted to uncover the neural workings of psychic states and quantify them. The psychiatrist and psychoanalyst Zvi Lothane writes, "In the *Project*, Freud returned to the brain, thus making temporary detour from mind to brain, an historical example of recurrent problems in mind-body philosophies."[12] Lothane's understatement allows us to return to Insel on philosophical ground. The question is not whether one needs a brain or genome to have a mind. The answer to that is a resounding yes. The real question is: Are "mind" and "brain" the same thing? Can shifting, subjective, psychological states be reduced to brain areas, the genome, or any other biological functions? And further, what does it mean to quantify or measure these states? Freud's position on the mind/body problem is complex, and it mutated over time.[13]

Despite the failure he oversaw, Insel does not blame the scientific model used in the research to uncover mental illness, which stands or falls on the mind/body problem. What are psychiatrists treating, whole person or body part? Mind or brain? Can mind be reduced to brain? The biomedical model assumes this reduction. Every patient can be broken down like a machine. If the damage can be located to a region of the brain or attributed to a genetic mutation, then it can, theoretically at least, be fixed. In his

2022 book, written for a popular audience, Insel writes, "People with mental illness deserve the same kind of biomarkers we have for diabetes or heart disease."[14] He admits there are no markers of this kind but recommends measuring psychosis and depression on "scientific" scales, despite the fact that neither can be quantified as if it were blood sugar or resting heart rate. Insel's eagerness to quantify what resists quantification is a form of "physics envy." The mathematical structure of physics has a "hard" precision and predictive power to which biology and "soft" sciences, such as psychology and sociology, can only aspire. Physics is also perceived as the *purest* and most *masculine* of the sciences, a disembodied, neutral, Platonic field cleansed of messy subjective values. The joke runs deep: Freud had physics envy too.

When Freud wrote *Project for a Scientific Psychology*, prominent German scientists were working toward an explanation of biology through the laws of physics. In the *Project*'s first paragraph, Freud introduces Q for quantity of neuronal energy, and declares it "subject to the laws of motion."[15] Heavily influenced by his idol, the biophysicist Hermann von Helmholtz, and his work on "free energy" in a closed system, Freud posited a dynamic, energic brain modeled on the first two laws of thermodynamics. The problem is there are no laws in biology as there are in physics and chemistry.[16] There are regularities and patterns, but there are too many exceptions for there to be laws.[17] Some physicists agree that the predictive strategies possible in physics do not apply to biology.[18] Freud had no access to later knowledge about organisms and their exchange of energy and matter with their environments, which limits the scope of his *Project*, but fascination with it has not ended. If Freud were writing now, could he have finished it?

In 1965, the late Karl Pribram, who trained as a neurosurgeon and became a professor of psychiatry and psychology at Georgetown University, published a paper in which he revived Freud's model in the *Project* and updated it.[19] In 1999, the neuroscientist Eric Kandel published "Biology and the Future of Psychoanalysis: A New Intellectual Framework for Psychiatry Revisited." A year later, he won the Nobel Prize in Physiology or Medicine for his research on memory. The neuroscientist Antonio Damasio argued in *The Feeling of What Happens*, "I believe we can say that Freud's insights on the nature of affect are consonant with the most advanced contemporary neuroscience views."[20] In 2013, the neuroscientists Cristina Alberini, François Ansermet, and Pierre Magistretti published "Memory Reconsolidation, Trace Reassociation and the Freudian Unconscious." They discuss the neurobiological evidence for Freud's idea of labile memories and his anticipation of the discovery in the 1970s of long-term memory potentiation, which, they write, "is now believed to represent the cellular mechanisms underlying memory formation."[21] Karl Friston, a neuroscientist and psychiatrist who has been described in popular media as "a genius" with "revolutionary impact," has proposed a complex energic, computational model of the brain, influenced by Helmholtz, Freud, and the eighteenth-century statistician Thomas Bayes.[22] In 2010, Friston coauthored a paper, "The Default-Mode, Ego-Functions and Free-Energy: A Neurobiological Account of Freudian Ideas."[23] In 2020, the neuroscientist Mark Solms, who founded the discipline neuropsychoanalysis, a field that integrates the findings of neuroscience with psychoanalysis, published his *New Project for a Scientific Psychology*, in which he rewrites Freud's *Project* line by line in light of contemporary brain research and Friston's theory.[24] Not all "authorities" have thrown out Freud's biology.

The dream of quantifying mental states was not unique to Freud. Since the late nineteenth century, psychologists have hoped to mathematize forms of madness and degrees of intellectual ability. In the United States, this history is tied to eugenic science that began with Francis Galton, who coined the term *eugenics*, conducted the first twin study, and firmly believed that mental capacities were inherited and could be quantified statistically. After Galton, the disciplines of eugenics, genetics, and statistics were tightly entwined. Statistical innovators developed strategies to codify abstractions, such as "general intelligence," and procure its measurement in IQ tests, which were then used to "prove" the hereditary intellectual inferiority of women as well as all non-Nordic Others, including Jews, Blacks, Mexicans, Italians, and Greeks. Eugenics of varying kinds attracted right-wingers and progressives alike, but its scientific status and popularity were dependent on faith in data collection and statistics. That these statistical operations resulted in innumerable scientific papers that validated racism and sexism should give us pause.

Popular consensus has relegated eugenics to a pseudoscience of the past, which reached its horrific climax in the Nazi death camps, and yet, although the word *eugenics* is now used as a term of opprobrium, the thought that fueled the science lives on. Ideas of heredity and neuropathological racial taint were broadly accepted in the sciences long before Freud fled Vienna in 1938, four of his five sisters were murdered in the camps, and the Nazis exiled psychoanalysis as a degenerate Jewish science, exactly the fate the discipline's founder had most feared. Its heyday in American psychiatry and its subsequent marginalization are permeated with ironies that turn on which ideas live and which die. A positivist model of mind that reigned in the late nineteenth century and influenced Freud, who both borrowed from and resisted it, returned in the late twentieth century: mental illness can be reduced to biochemistry and genetics. This model—which divorced the patient from her world; from other people in it; and from her own personal history, her memories and feelings—would discredit Freudian ideas. Freud's model of the mind, with its dynamic unconscious, the dialogue inherent to psychoanalysis about a person's past, and the drama of transference it initiates, is founded on the idea that through the talking cure, the patient can change and find new freedom.[25] In a 1906 letter to Jung, the Protestant he hoped would save his discipline from a Jewish fate, Freud wrote that psychoanalysis "is a cure affected by love."[26]

The mantra of eugenics, on the other hand, was articulated by the statistician, socialist, and student of Galton, Karl Pearson, in 1892: "No degenerate and feeble stock will ever be converted by the accumulated effects of education, good laws, and sanitary sur-roundings."[27] In 1998, Linda Gottfredson, professor emeritus of psychology at the University of Delaware, echoed Pearson in *Scientific American*: "No amount of social engineering can make people with widely divergent mental aptitudes into social equals."[28] The same born-that-way message was delivered by Rich-ard J. Herrnstein and Charles Murray in their book *The Bell Curve* (1994). Eugenics' disciplinary heirs—large swaths of mainstream psychology, with its scientific pretensions and statistically derived five-factor personality traits (the Big 5); and behavior genetics, with its twin and family studies, heritability statistics, and dogged faith in IQ—have marched on. Penis-physics envy never ends. The psychologist and IQ researcher Ian Deary admits sadly, "There is no such thing as a theory of human intelligence differences—not in the same way grownup sciences like physics and chemistry have theories."[29]

This small-boy science must further rely on an inert, dry, statis-tical biology because it makes no reference to living, moving, de-veloping bodies—to the wet, material reality of genome, cells, or systems. Every organism's biological processes are dynamic and dependent on its relations with what is around it. It is absurd to separate "nature and nurture," as Galton, who coined the phrase, did.[30] Experience alters the brain and influences gene expression. Freud did not have access to research in neuroplasticity or epig-enomics, but his biology is closer to a number of models in contemporary neuroscience than to the biologically improbable mind "modules" of evolutionary psychology, each of which sup-posedly evolved for a specific purpose.[31] And yet, genetic destiny as a statistical percentage based on twin studies, which began with Galton, has been aggressively marketed in media and by evolu-tionary psychologists, such as the bestselling author Steven Pinker.

In *The Blank Slate: The Modern Denial of Human Nature*, Pinker echoes his eugenic predecessors, "Heredity, not their experiences in their childhood home, is what makes children of divorce more likely to fail in their own marriages." He claims that nicotine and alcohol dependence, how much TV a person watches, are all "heritable" traits. Although the word *heritable* suggests that genes play an important and measurable role in a particular person's trait, whether it's eye color or hours of TV consumed daily, heritability is a statistically derived percentage that estimates the degree of variation in a phenotypic trait in a specific population, not an individual, that is ascribed to genetics, and it changes over time. Pinker writes, it "is a *correlate* or an *indirect product* of the genes" (my italics).[32] A correlation, however, is not a cause, and these statistics have been widely criticized.[33] Even a prominent figure in behavior genetics, Eric Turkheimer, has stated that the heritability of divorce does not mean it is "a biological process awaiting genetic analysis."[34] Just as George Prochnik, the *New York Times* reviewer of Frederick Crews quoted above, summons "mainstream" thinking in psychology to dismiss psychoanalysis, Pinker calls on "mainstream science" as his authority, as if a bulwark of consensus actually exists in the fractious world of multiple "sciences": "Psychoanalysis falls outside mainstream science—its claims are not empirically tested; it doesn't mesh with the rest of biology."[35]

—

In fact, in 2007, when Pinker made that statement, there were, and continue to be, more and more evidence-based, empirical studies that demonstrate the effectiveness of psychodynamic psychotherapy, the contemporary heir to psychoanalysis. Researchers administer psychometric tests, gather data, and employ statistical methods to arrive at this conclusion.[36] A measurement of "feeling better" after therapy, however, no matter how rigorous the method, is not like quantifying temperature, mass, or speed. It is good to recall the often quoted words of the statistician George Box: "All models are wrong, but some are useful." In the sciences and in fields that don the trappings of science, there is a tendency to reify models, to mistake the model for what it represents and to forget that in order to represent some aspect of the world, a model is always a simplification of it. Psychoanalysis has hardly been immune to this—treating an abstract concept, ego, for example, as if it were a concrete thing—what Alfred North Whitehead called "misplaced concreteness."[37] Even the most sophisticated models of mind, such as Friston's, have been criticized for this confusion.[38] His model's relation to actual neurobiology is uncertain.

The idea weather is changing. The global Covid-19 pandemic has exposed the grotesque inequalities of class and color and the perils of isolation to human health. It has cast doubt on the you-are-a-chemical-imbalance and the you-are-your-genes messages. Vulnerability to illness depends in part on a person's position in the social hierarchy and her particular circumstances. Is she lonely or surrounded by friends and family? In his book, written during the pandemic, Thomas Insel openly acknowledges that "social support" and human "connection" play crucial roles in psychiatry and that psychotherapy is an effective treatment, although he seems unaware of studies that suggest cognitive behavioral therapy is inferior to psychodynamic psychotherapy, particularly for depressed patients.[39] On October 29, 2021, the American Psychological Association adopted a resolution: "Apology to People of Color for APA's Role in Promoting, Perpetuating, and Failing to Challenge Racism, Racial Discrimination and Human Hierarchy in U.S." In 2022, the journal *Nature* apologized for its contribution "to science's discriminatory legacy."[40] The disciplines of genetics and statistics have begun to examine their eugenic past. Even the sacred principle of statistical significance is being questioned.[41] Psychiatry is grappling with its failed, reductionist, biomedical model that treats the wounded psyche as an isolated brain machine, the broken parts of which can be repaired without much attention to the patient's past or present situation. What was once "mainstream" seems to have shifted.

Freud's thought evolved, and psychodynamic therapies have evolved significantly since Freud. Nevertheless, he understood that what we call mind is embodied and dynamic and that much of what it does is unconscious. Human beings are in states of continual physiological adjustment and readjustment to inner and outer stimuli, and our development is radically dependent on other people. We are biopsychosocial beings in motion until we die. Human experiences and the feelings they generate matter. Our behaviors, thoughts, memories, and forgetting have patterns and meanings, patterns and meanings that often escape us. Speaking freely in the presence of another person trained to listen has healing properties.

Freud's most powerful ghost is a listener. It haunts clinical rooms because he was the first to codify the therapeutic encounter. The therapist tolerates what others do not want to hear, and she answers without judgment. The cure happens between two people in the "intermediate area" through a tumultuous back-and-forth of words and feelings.[42] In the room, the details of a person's life stories are crucial, not incidental. The person is not reduced to his brain, genome, or diagnosis. He is not one of thousands in a population statistic or a single dubious number that stratifies his "intelligence" on a bell curve. Maybe truisms about what "medical authorities," "mainstream psychologists," and "mainstream science" have to say about Freud's legacy are intimately linked to the hierarchies that preserve the myth of "mainstream authority." Maybe in light of spectacular debacles in psychiatry and psychology that were guided by the mainstream thinking of the moment, it is time to listen to a ghost still listening to patients in this country and around the world. Maybe this ghost is a Freud for now.

NOTES

Preface

1. W. H. Auden, "In Memory of Sigmund Freud," *Selected Poems*, revised ed., ed. Edward Mendelson (London: Faber and Faber, 2009).

Penis Envy

1. Sigmund Freud, "Über infantile Sexualtheorien" [On the sexual theories of children], *Sexual-Probleme* 4, no. 12 (December 1908): 763–79.

2. J. K. Rowling, "J.K. Rowling Writes about Her Reasons for Speaking out on Sex and Gender Issues," June 10, 2020, https://www.jkrowling.com/opinions/j-k -rowling-writes-about-her-reasons-for-speaking-out-on-sex-and-gender-issues/.

3. J. K. Rowling, *Harry Potter and the Goblet of Fire* (New York: Scholastic Press, 2000).

4. Rodgers and Hammerstein, "I'm Gonna Wash That Man Right Outa My Hair," *South Pacific*, Columbia Masterworks 1949.

On "Mourning and Melancholia"

1. All subheads in this chapter are from Sigmund Freud, "Mourning and Melancholia," in *The Standard Edition of the Complete Psychological Works of Sigmund Freud*, trans. and ed. James Strachey (London: Hogarth and the Institute of Psycho-Analysis, 1953–66), 14:243–58.

2. Sigmund Freud, "Remembering, Repeating, and Working-Through," in *The Standard Edition of the Complete Psychological Works of Sigmund Freud*, trans. and ed. James Strachey (London: Hogarth and the Institute of Psycho-Analysis, 1953–66), 12:145–57.

Sigmund Freud, Private Investigator

1. Most notably, in *The Seven-Per-Cent Solution*, by Nicholas Meyer, Holmes visits Freud to seek help for his cocaine addiction.

Freud and the Writers

1. Peter Gay, *Freud: A Life for Our Times* (New York: W. W. Norton, 1998), 347–48.

2. Thomas Mann, "Thoughts in Wartime" (1914), in *Reflections of a Nonpolitical Man* (New York: New York Review of Books, 2021), 495.

3. Quoted in Hermann Kurzke, *Thomas Mann: Life as a Work of Art* (Princeton, NJ: Princeton University Press, 2002), 217.

4. Sigmund Freud, *Reflections on War and Death* (New York, 1918), 14.

5. Freud, *Reflections on War and Death*, 13.

6. Leon Edel, ed., *The Letters of Henry James, Volume IV: 1895–1915* (Cambridge, MA: Harvard University Press, 1984), 718, 725.

7. Edel, *The Letters of Henry James*, 729.

8. Edel, *The Letters of Henry James*, 729.

9. Philip Horne, ed., *Henry James: A Life in Letters* (New York: Penguin, 1999), 433.

10. Sarah Bird Wright, ed., *Edith Wharton Abroad: Selected Travel Writings, 1888–1920* (New York: St. Martin's, 1996), 136.

11. Edel, *The Letters of Henry James*, 742.

12. Edel, *The Letters of Henry James*, 758.

13. Edel, *The Letters of Henry James*, 758.

14. Edel, *The Letters of Henry James*, 764.

15. Hans Wysling, ed., *Letters of Heinrich and Thomas Mann, 1900–1949* (Berkeley: University of California Press, 1998), 121, 123.

16. Richard Winston and Clara Winston, eds., *Letters of Thomas Mann, 1889–1955* (Berkeley: University of California Press, 1990), 69.

17. Donald Prater, *Thomas Mann: A Life* (Oxford: Oxford University Press, 1995), 99.

18. Marcel Reich-Ranicki, *Thomas Mann and His Family* (New York: HarperCollins, 1999), 130, 31.

19. Sigmund Freud, *Beyond the Pleasure Principle*, in *The Standard Edition of the Complete Psychological Works of Sigmund Freud*, trans. and ed. James Strachey (London: Hogarth and the Institute of Psycho-Analysis, 1953–66), 18:18.

20. Gay, *Freud*, 579, 581, 586.

21. Gay, *Freud*, 588.

22. Gay, *Freud*, 590–91.

23. Gay, *Freud*, 591.

24. Gay, *Freud*, 592.

25. Freud, *Reflections on War and Death*, 1.

26. Mann, *Reflections of a Nonpolitical Man*, 194.

27. Mann, *Reflections of a Nonpolitical Man*, 35.

28. Mann, *Reflections of a Nonpolitical Man*, 456–57.

29. Freud, *Reflections on War and Death*, 2.

30. Freud, *Reflections on War and Death*, 3.

31. Freud, *Reflections on War and Death*, 3.

32. Freud, *Reflections on War and Death*, 3.

33. Freud, *Reflections on War and Death*, 5.

34. Freud, *Reflections on War and Death*, 6–7.

35. Freud, *Reflections on War and Death*, 14–15.

36. Freud, *Reflections on War and Death*, 8.

37. Freud, *Reflections on War and Death*, 11.

38. Freud, *Reflections on War and Death*.

39. Freud, *Reflections on War and Death*, 19.

40. Freud, *Reflections on War and Death*, 23–24.

41. Freud, *Reflections on War and Death*, 28–29.

42. Thomas Mann, *Essays of Three Decades* (New York: Knopf, 1948), 412.

43. Mann, *Essays of Three Decades*, 414–15.

44. Edel, *The Letters of Henry James*, 597.

45. Edel, *The Letters of Henry James*, 596.

46. Leon Edel, *Henry James, the Master: 1901–1916* (New York: Lippincott Williams and Wilkins, 1972), 452–53.

47. Winston and Winston, *Letters of Thomas Mann*, 72.

48. Freud, *Reflections on War and Death*, 3.

49. Winston and Winston, *Letters of Thomas Mann*, 607.

50. Freud, *Reflections on War and Death*, 3.

The Open-Armed, Beckoning Embrace

1. http://www.ricorso.net/rx/az-data/authors/y/Yeats_WB/quots/quot4.htm.

2. Thomas Lynch, *Bone Rosary—New and Selected Poems* (David R. Godine, 2021).

3. Noel Paul Stookey, "No Other Name," *Album 1700*, Warner Bros. Records 1967.

4. Tim Buckley, "Song to the Siren," *Starsailor*, Straight Records 1970.

My Oedipus Complex

1. Sigmund Freud, *The Ego and the Id*.

2. Kathleen Tynan, *The Life of Kenneth Tynan*.

3. Richard M. Cook, ed., *Alfred Kazin's Journals*.

4. Quoted in Lawrence S. Wrightsman, *Adult Personality Development: Theories and Concepts*.

5. Quoted in Ian Parker, "Ken Burns's American Canon," *New Yorker*, September 4, 2017.

6. When Freud examined the effects of the uncanny, he analyzed a tale by E.T.A. Hoffman about what happens to children's eyes when they don't go quickly to sleep at night.

From Freud's Ordinary Unhappiness to Winnicott's Good Enough

1. Josef Breuer and Sigmund Freud, *Studies in Hysteria* (1895) (London: Hogarth, 1956).

2. D. W. Winnicott, *Through Paediatrics to Psychoanalysis* (London: Hogarth, 1982).

3. See my BBC Radio3 Free Thinking Lecture, 2012, https://www.youtube.com/results?search_query=susie+orbach+at+st+pauls.

Growing Up Freudian

1. In *Introductory Lectures on Psycho-Analysis*, delivered during World War I.

2. She had a coauthor, an advertising executive named Marvin Small. L. Freeman and M. Small, *The Story of Psychoanalysis* (New York: Pocket Books, 1960).

3. J. Kagan, *An Argument for Mind* (New Haven, CT: Yale University Press, 2006).

4. Lionel Trilling, "The Legacy of Sigmund Freud, Part 2: Literary and Aesthetic," *Kenyon Review* 2, no. 2 (Spring 1940): 152–73.

5. In an essay written to accompany a Library of Congress exhibition on Freud, I imagined a special "Freud Project," an attempt at a rigorous but also sympathetic inventory of Freud's ideas, asking which remained salvageable. P. D. Kramer, "Freud: Current Projections," in M. S. Roth, ed., *Freud: Conflict and Culture* (New York: Knopf, 1998). Some years later, in my brief biography of Freud, I attempted that sort of overview, paying attention also to which ideas and methods Freud introduced and which he had borrowed from others. P. D. Kramer, *Freud: Inventor of the Modern Mind* (New York: HarperCollins, 2006).

6. I would later describe some of my work with him in my first book: P. Kramer, *Moments of Engagement* (New York: W. W. Norton, 1989).

7. I reviewed some of these innovative and highly idiosyncratic therapies in P. D. Kramer, *Should You Leave?* (New York: Scribner, 1997).

8. See my essay "Missing Milton Mazer," in *David's Slingshot: Anti-war Letters from an Island Doctor* (West Tisbury Free Public Library, 2022), 112–15.

9. Empathy is a more complex tool than I am making out here. For my thoughts on its limitations, see "Empathic Immersion," in *Empathy and the Practice of Medicine:*

Beyond Pills and Scalpel, ed. H. Spiro, M.G.M. Curnen, et al. (New Haven, CT: Yale University Press, 1993), 174–89.

10. W. H. Auden, "In Memory of Sigmund Freud," *Selected Poems*, revised ed., ed. Edward Mendelson (London: Faber and Faber, 2009).

11. Is it paradoxical to say that I see my breakthrough effort, *Listening to Prozac*, as Freudian? It is in this sense: it arose from an effort to understand the contemporary sense of self via the reports that patients made to me when they responded to new sorts of antidepressants. The *listening* in the title refers not only to my patients' perceptions but also to my own—to the therapist's ear, the one that Theodor Reik called the third ear. P. D. Kramer, *Listening to Prozac* (New York: Viking, 1993).

12. Regarding the conversational form of psychotherapy, I was especially influenced by the writings of Hellmuth Kaiser. See my foreword to *The Therapist Is the Therapy*, by Louis B. Fierman (Northvale, NJ: Jason Aronson, 1997), xi–xiii.

Psychoanalysis in the Cold War American Race Movie

1. Stanley Kramer with Thomas M. Coffey, *A Mad, Mad, Mad, Mad World: A Life in Hollywood* (New York: Harcourt Brace, 1997), 38.

2. "The Negro in the United States has achieved or been placed in a certain artistic niche. When he is thought of artistically, it is as a happy-go-lucky, singing, shuffling, banjo-picking being or as a more or less pathetic figure. The picture of him is in a log cabin amid fields of cotton or along the levees. Negro dialect is naturally and by long association the exact instrument for voicing this phase of Negro life; and by that very exactness it is an instrument with but two full stops, humor and pathos." James Weldon Johnson, *The Book of American Negro Poetry* (Auckland: Floating Press, 2008), 47. James Edwards's character never speaks in any sort of Black dialect in the film. Kramer writes, "[Edwards] was an intelligent, cultivated actor *with an excellent voice*, and I was lucky to get him." Kramer, *Mad, Mad, Mad, Mad World*, 38 (emphasis mine).

3. Kramer, *Mad, Mad, Mad, Mad World*, 37.

4. Irving Stone, *The Passions of the Mind* (Garden City, NY: Doubleday, 1971), 187 (Stone's emphasis). Charcot acknowledged the power of the idea in the origin of neurosis: "Charcot demonstrated to Freud that ideas, although intangible, could nevertheless be causal agents in neurosis. When a patient developed paralysis, the form that the paralysis took was not determined by the facts of anatomy, but by the patient's faulty idea of anatomy." Anthony Storr, *Freud: A Very Short Introduction* (Oxford: Oxford University Press, 1989), 17.

5. Stone, *Passions of the Mind*, 95.

6. See Kramer's comments at the Turner Classic Movies website, https://www.tcm .com/tcmdb/title/78257/home-of-the-brave#articles-reviews?articleId=1008051.

7. Kramer, *Mad, Mad, Mad, Mad World*, 35.

8. Kramer, *Mad, Mad, Mad, Mad World*, 36.

9. Stanley Kramer also produced the highly regarded 1952 western *High Noon*. "When we used the title of *High Noon* before, to keep *Home of the Brave* secret, it occurred to us that, for the right property, it would be an excellent film title." Kramer, *Mad, Mad, Mad, Mad World*, 67.

10. "Coinciding with and sometimes mirroring major race riots that broke out in several American cities—including New York, Detroit, and Los Angeles—during 1943, extensive race-related disturbances erupted at or near military facilities throughout the United States and in several other countries where American troops were stationed. These disturbances involved greater numbers of people than had earlier ones, took place more often on military property than in surrounding communities, and were more likely than past incidents to feature blacks in the role of aggressors." Sherie Mershon and Steven Schlossman, *Foxholes and Color Lines: Desegregating the U.S. Armed Forces* (Baltimore: Johns Hopkins University Press, 2003), 83. It was also in 1943 that two noted all-Black cast musicals were released: Vincente Minnelli's *Cabin in the Sky*, and Andrew L. Stone's *Stormy Weather*. In January 1944, the Army released *The Negro Soldier*, a documentary produced by famed filmmaker Frank Capra about Black American history seen through the prism of the US military. The film was the direct result of the violence between Black soldiers and civilian police in 1942 at Papago Park, a post outside Phoenix, Arizona, which resulted in fourteen people shot, three killed. See Truman Gibson with Steve Huntley, *Knocking Down Barriers: My Fight for Black America* (Evanston, IL: Northwestern University Press, 2005), 14–15, 148–52.

11. Ralph Ellison, "Harlem Is Nowhere" (1948), in *Shadow and Act* (1964; New York: Vintage Books, 1972), 297.

12. Kramer, *Mad, Mad, Mad, Mad World*, 154. The section epigraph is from Cobbs, *My American Life*, 145.

13. Aram Goudsouzian, *Sidney Poitier: Man, Actor, Icon* (Chapel Hill: University of North Carolina Press, 2004), 202.

14. Quoted in Stephen Farber and Michael McClellan, *Cinema '62: The Greatest Year at the Movies* (New Brunswick, NJ: Rutgers University Press, 2020), 160.

15. Quoted in Farber and McClellan, *Cinema '62*, 160–61.

16. Goudsouzian, *Sidney Poitier: Man, Actor, Icon*, 202.

17. Goudsouzian, *Sidney Poitier: Man, Actor, Icon*, 202.

18. David Evanier, *Roman Candle: The Life of Bobby Darin* (Albany: SUNY Press, 2010), 147.

19. Quoted in Era Bell Thompson and Herbert Nipson, *White on Black: The Views of Twenty-Two White Americans on the Negro* (Chicago: Johnson, 1963), 117.

20. Thompson and Nipson, *White on Black*, 117.

21. Goudsouzian, *Sidney Poitier: Man, Actor, Icon*, 203.

22. Robert Lindner, *The Fifty-Minute Hour: A Collection of True Psychoanalytic Tales* (1955; New York: Other Press, 1982), Kindle version, loc 2602.

23. Lindner, *Fifty-Minute Hour*, Kindle version, loc 2960, 2973.

24. Lindner, *Fifty-Minute Hour*, Kindle version, loc 2678, 2690.

25. Quoted in Farber and McClellan, *Cinema '62*, 160.

26. Price M. Cobbs tells the story of a "severely ill" matronly Black woman named "Emily Thomas," who "suffered several periods of psychotic outburst in which she was barely controllable." The staff at Mendocino State Hospital, where she was a patient, called her Emily. She would not reply. In fact, this seemed to anger her deeply. As Cobbs writes, "In the areas of politesse and basic human regard, Mrs. Thomas was not being well served. . . . Here was a woman who, despite the many difficulties she had had in her life, expected by now to be addressed as 'Mrs. Thomas' not as 'Emily.' Maybe the use of the first name would be appropriate to white people or others, depending upon their upbringing. But in the black, middle-class, church-reared upbringing that Mrs. Thomas had experienced in her life, she was now in a position in which she felt she deserved to be addressed properly, that is, as 'Mrs. Thomas.' Calling her 'Emily' was an insult. Unintended, maybe, since the white staff would have no sense of such a social nuance. But an insult to Mrs. Thomas nonetheless." It took a considerable effort on Cobbs's part to get the staff to call the patient "Mrs. Thomas" instead of "Emily" because they did not understand how she could be insulted in this way. Finally, Cobbs prevailed. This certainly did not cure her but "she was more approachable. . . . She would reply and sometimes even civilly." This became one of the keys to an approach called ethnotherapy, the exact opposite of the color-blind treatment that was valorized in Kramer's *Pressure Point*. Cobbs, *My American Life*, 154–56. Quoted in Farber and McClellan, *Cinema '62*, 160.

Once a Neurologist

1. Sigmund Freud, *The Complete Letters of Sigmund Freud to Wilhelm Fliess 1887–1894*, trans. and ed. Jeffrey Moussaieff Masson (Cambridge, MA: Belknap, 1985), 146.

2. Kenneth R. Lang, *A Companion to Astronomy and Astrophysics* (New York: Springer, 2006), 287.

3. John Daintith and Derek Gjertsen, eds., *A Dictionary of Scientists* (Oxford: Oxford University Press, 1999), 329.

4. Edwin Clarke and L. S. Jacyna, eds., *Nineteenth-Century Origins of Neuroscientific Concepts* (Berkeley: University of California Press, 1987), 389.

5. Clarke and Jacyna, *Nineteenth-Century Origins*, 99.

6. Siegfried Bernfeld, "Freud's Scientific Beginnings," *American Imago* (1949): 181, 182.

7. Siegfried Bernfeld, "Sigmund Freud, M. D., 1882–1885," *International Journal of Psycho-Analysis* (1951): 214.

8. Bernfeld, "Freud's Scientific Beginnings," 171.

9. Ernest Jones, *The Life and Work of Sigmund Freud* (New York: Basic Books, 1953), 1:184; Sigmund Freud, *Collected Papers* (New York: Basic Books, 1959), 182.

10. Freud, *Collected Papers*, 188.

11. Sigmund Freud, *The Standard Edition of the Complete Psychological Works of Sigmund Freud*, trans. and ed. James Strachey (London: Hogarth and the Institute of Psycho-Analysis, 1953–66), 3:185.

12. Sigmund Freud, *The Origins of Psycho-Analysis: Letters to Wilhelm Fliess, Drafts and Notes: 1887–1902*, trans. Eric Mosbacher, ed. James Strachey, Maria Bonaparte, Anna Freud, and Ernst Kris (New York: Basic Books, 1954), 355.

13. Jones, *The Life and Work*, 382.

14. Freud, *The Origins of Psycho-Analysis*, 133.

15. Freud, *The Complete Letters*, 152.

16. Freud, *Beyond the Pleasure Principle*, in *The Standard Edition*, 18:60.

17. Freud, *An Outline of Psycho-Analysis*, in *The Standard Edition*, 23:195.

Tangling with Freud in a Post-Freudian World

1. Sherry Turkle, *Psychoanalytic Politics: Jacques Lacan and Freud's French Revolution* (1978; Guilford, CT: Guilford, 1980).

2. See, for example, Jeffrey Masson, *The Assault on Truth* (New York: Ballantine, 1984).

3. Turkle, *Psychoanalytic Politics*.

4. Sherry Turkle, *The Empathy Diaries* (New York: Penguin Books, 2021).

5. Erik Erikson, *Identity and the Life Cycle* (1952; New York: Norton, 1980).

6. Theodor Adorno, "Die revidierte psychoanalyse," cited in Russell Jacoby, *Social Amnesia: A Critique of Contemporary Psychology* (Boston: Beacon, 1975), 34.

7. This work began when I joined the MIT faculty in 1976. Sherry Turkle, *The Second Self: Computers and the Human Spirit* (1984; Cambridge, MA: MIT Press, 2004).

8. This work began when I joined the MIT faculty in 1976. Turkle, *Second Self*.

9. See Patrick Miller, *Driving Soma: A Transformational Process in the Analytic Encounter* (New York: Karnac, 2014).

10. Gillian Issacs Russell, *Screen Relations: The Limits of Computer-Mediated Psychoanalysis and Psychotherapy* (London: Karnac, 2015).

Freud's First Scientific Publication

1. "Mathematisch-Naturwissenschaftliche Klasse, Section 1," *Sitzungsberichte der kaiserlichen Akademie der Wissenschaften* (Proceedings of the Imperial Academy of Sciences) 75 (April 1877): 419–31.

2. Ernest Jones, *The Life and Work of Sigmund Freud, Vol. 1: The Formative Years and the Great Discoveries, 1856–1900* (London: Hogarth, 1953), 42n1.

3. Philipp Franz von Siebold, *Die Süsswasserfische von Mitteleuropa* (Leipzig: Wilhelm Engelmann Verlag, 1863).

4. Sigmund Freud, "Abstracts of the Scientific Writings of Dr. Sigmund Freud, 1877–1897" (1897), in *The Standard Edition of the Complete Psychological Works of Sigmund Freud*, trans. and ed. James Strachey (London: Hogarth and the Institute of Psycho-Analysis, 1953–66), 3:223–57.

5. The word Freud used, in a letter to Rudolf Brun dated March 18, 1936, was *läppisch*, a pun on *gelappt* ("lobulated"). Sigmund Freud, "Letter to Rudolf Brun (March 18, 1936)," in *Rudolf Brun (1885–1969): Lebens und Werk des Zürcher Neurologen, Psychoanalytikers und Entomologen*, ed. Jürg Aeschlimann (Zurich: Juris, 1980), 67.

6. The Viennese physiologist Joseph Paneth (1857–1890) was a good friend of Freud's.

7. Sigmund Freud, "Letter to Eduard Silberstein (April 5, 1876)," in *The Letters of Sigmund Freud to Eduard Silberstein, 1871–1881*, ed. Walter Boehlich (Cambridge, MA: Harvard University Press, 1990).

Searching for Martha Freud

1. Sources used for this chapter include Lisa Appignanesi and John Forrester, *Freud's Women*; Katja Behling, *Martha Freud: A Biography*; Martin Freud, *Sigmund Freud: Man and Father*; Sophie Freud, *Living in the Shadow of the Freud Family*; Peter Gay, *The Freud Reader*; Peter Gay, *A Godless Jew: Freud and the Making of Psychoanalysis*; Deborah P. Margolis, *Freud and His Mother*; Dale M. Moyer, *The Flash and Outbreak of a Fiery Mind: The Love Letters of Martha Bernays Freud, 1882–1886*; Ankit Patel and Ansh Mehta, editors, *Selected Letters of Sigmund Freud, to Martha Bernays*; Arnold Richards, editor, *The Jewish World of Sigmund Freud: Essays on Cultural Roots and the Problem of Religious Identity*; introduction by Philip Rieff, *Sigmund Freud, Sexuality and the Psychology of Love*; Paul Roazen, *Freud and His Followers*; Marthe Robert, *From Oedipus to Moses: Freud's Jewish Identity*; Nicolle Rosen, *Mrs. Freud: A Novel*; Elisabeth Young-Bruehl, *Anna Freud: A Biography*.

Freud's Dogs

1. Daniel Benveniste, *The Interwoven Lives of Sigmund, Anna and W. Ernest Freud: Three Generations of Psychoanalysis* (Scotts Valley, CA: CreateSpace, 2014).

2. Letter from Sigmund Freud to Kata and Lajos Levy, June 11, 1923.

3. Stanley Coren, *The Pawprints of History: Dogs and the Course of Human Events* (New York: Free Press, 2003).

4. Benveniste, *The Interwoven Lives of Sigmund, Anna and W. Ernest Freud*.

5. Benveniste, *The Interwoven Lives of Sigmund, Anna and W. Ernest Freud*.

6. H.D. [Hilda Doolittle], *Tribute to Freud* (New York: New Directions, 1984).

7. Letter of May 6, 1930, to his wife, Martha.

8. Sigmund Freud, *The Diary of Sigmund Freud, 1929–1939*, trans. Michael Molnar (New York: Scribner, 1992).

9. Freud, *The Diary of Sigmund Freud*.

10. Marie Bonaparte, *Topsy: The Story of a Golden-Haired Chow* (New Brunswick, NJ: Transaction Publishers, 1994).

11. Letter from Sigmund Freud to Marie Bonaparte, December 6, 1936; Freud, *The Diary of Sigmund Freud*, 233.

12. Freud, *The Diary of Sigmund Freud*.

13. Sigmund Freud, *The Interpretation of Dreams* (Oxford: Oxford University Press, 2008).

A Night at the Freud Museum

1. Philip Larkin, interview by Miriam Gross, "A Voice for Our Time," *Observer* (London), December 16, 1979, 35.

2. Marina Warner and Erica Davies, *20 Maresfield Gardens: A Guide to the Freud Museum* (London: Serpent's Tale, 1998), 57.

3. Honore de Balzac, *The Wild Ass's Skin*, trans. Herbert J. Hunt (London: Penguin Classics, 1977), 26, 23, 25.

4. Sigmund Freud, *Letters of Sigmund Freud, 1873–1939*, ed. Ernst L. Freud, trans. James and Tania Stern (New York: Basic Books, 1960), 446.

Playing the Game

1. Sigmund Freud, *Beyond the Pleasure Principle*, in *The Standard Edition of the Complete Psychological Works of Sigmund Freud*, trans. and ed. James Strachey (London: Hogarth and the Institute of Psycho-Analysis, 1953–66), 18:14.

2. Freud, *Beyond the Pleasure Principle*, 18:12–14.

3. Freud, *Beyond the Pleasure Principle*, 18:24.

4. Freud, *Beyond the Pleasure Principle*, 18:16n.

5. Peter Gay, *Freud: A Life for Our Time* (New York: W. W. Norton, 1988), 393.

6. Adam Phillips, *Darwin's Worms: On Life Stories and Death Stories* (New York: Basic Books, 2009), 27.

7. Gay, *Freud*, 391.

8. Sigmund Freud, "Thought for the Times on War and Death," in *Standard Edition*, 14:275.

9. Freud, "Thought for the Times on War and Death," 14:276.

10. Freud, "Thought for the Times on War and Death," 14:281.

11. Freud, "Thought for the Times on War and Death," 14:288.

12. Sigmund Freud, "Mourning and Melancholia" (1917), in *Standard Edition*, 14:246.

13. These are the themes of Michael S. Roth, "Freud's Use and Abuse of the Past," in my *The Ironist's Cage: Memory, Trauma and the Construction of History* (New York: Columbia University Press, 1995), 186–200.

14. Freud, "Mourning and Melancholia," 14:245.

15. Freud's comments on his family's mourning are cited in Gay, *Freud*, 392–93.

16. The "every finding is a re-finding" phrase is from Freud, *Three Essays on the Theory of Sexuality* (1905), *Standard Edition*, 7:222.

Against Interpretation

1. Quoted in "Hook, Line, and Sinker," Erenow, https://erenow.net/ww/operation-mincemeat/23.php.

2. François de La Rochefoucauld, *Collected Maxims and Other Reflections*, trans. E. H. and A. M. Blackmore and Francine Giguère (Oxford: Oxford University Press, 2007), Kindle edition, 151.

3. Ben Macintyre, *Operation Mincemeat: How a Dead Man and a Bizarre Plan Fooled the Nazis and Assured an Allied Victory* (New York: Crown, 2020), Kindle edition.

Freud the Essayist

1. All quotes of Freud in this chapter are taken from *The Standard Edition of the Complete Psychological Works of Sigmund Freud*, trans. and ed. James Strachey (London: Hogarth and the Institute of Psycho-Analysis, 1953–66).

Freud Now?

1. George Dvorsky, "Why Freud Still Matters When He Was Wrong about Almost Everything," *Gizmodo*, August 7, 2013; Benjamin Plackett, "Was Freud Right about Anything?," Live Science, March 21, 2020; Savannah Cox, "What Freud Got Wrong about Psychology (and Your Mother)," *Autism Brain Net*, May 4, 2020.

2. For a feminist critique of the suppression of pregnancy and birth in psycho-analysis and philosophy, see Siri Hustvedt, "Umbilical Phantoms," *International Journal of Psychoanalysis* 103, no. 2 (2022): 368–80.

3. Sander L. Gilman, *Freud, Race, and Gender* (Princeton, NJ: Princeton University Press, 1993).

4. George Prochnik, "The Curious Conundrum of Freud's Persistent Influence," *New York Times*, August 14, 2017.

5. *New York Times* science reporter Nicholas Wade published sixty-eight articles with *gene* in the title, which advertised a gene for a human trait, none of which have held up to scrutiny. See Mark Liberman, "The Hunt for the Hat Gene," *Language Log*, November 9, 2009. Wade left the *Times* two weeks after he published his racist book *A Troublesome Inheritance* in 2014, a work denounced by over a hundred geneticists in a letter. See Michael Balter, "Geneticists Decry Book on Race and Evolution," *Science*, August 8, 2014.

6. Thomas Insel quoted in Andrew Scull, "Thomas Insel and the Future of the Mental Health System," *Mad in America*, April 25, 2022.

7. Sigmund Freud, "On Narcissism: An Introduction" (1914–16), in *The Standard Edition of the Complete Psychological Works of Sigmund Freud*, trans. and ed. James Strachey (London: Hogarth and the Institute of Psycho-Analysis, 1953–66), 16:67; hereafter *SE*.

8. Sigmund Freud, "New Introductory Lectures on Psycho-Analysis," *SE*, 22:95–96.

9. Josef Breuer and Sigmund Freud, *Studies on Hysteria* (1895), *SE*, 2:160.

10. *The Complete Letters of Sigmund Freud to Wilhelm Fliess, 1887–1905*, trans. Jeffrey Moussaieff Masson (Cambridge, MA: Belknap Press, 1985), 152.

11. Sigmund Freud, *Project for a Scientific Psychology* (1895), *SE*, 1:295; hereafter *Project*.

12. Zvi Lothane, "Freud's 1895 *Project*: From Mind to Brain and Back Again," in *Neuroscience of the Mind on the Centennial of Freud's Project for a Scientific Psychology*, ed. R. M. Bilder and F. F. LeFever (New York: New York Academy of Sciences, 1998), 43–65.

13. Manos Tsakiris, "Freud's Theory of Consciousness: From Psychoanalysis to Neuro-Psychoanalysis" (PhD diss., University of London), https://citeseerx.ist.psu.edu.

14. Thomas Insel, *Healing: Our Path from Mental Illness to Mental Health* (New York: Penguin Random House, 2022) 210.

15. Freud, *Project*, 295.

16. John Dupré, "It Is Not Possible to Reduce Biological Explanations in Chemistry and/or Physics," in *Contemporary Debates in Philosophy of Biology*, ed. Francisco J. Ayala and Robert Arp (Malden, MA: Wiley, 2010): 32–47.

17. Pawan Dhar and Alessandro Guiliani, "Laws of Biology: Why So Few?," *Systems and Synthetic Biology* 4, no. 1 (2010): 7–13.

18. See Guiseppe Longo, Maël Montevil, and Stuart Kauffman, "No Entailing Laws, but Enablement in Evolution of the Biosphere," in *Genetic and Evolutionary Computation Conference Companion* (2012): 1379–92.

19. Karl Pribram, "Freud's Project: An Open, Biologically Based Model for Psychoanalysis," in *Psychoanalysis and Current Biological Thought*, ed. Norman Greenfield and William Lewis (Madison: University of Wisconsin Press, 1965). Pribram also published a book with Merton Max Gill, *Freud's Project Reassessed* (Madison: University of Wisconsin Press, 1976).

20. Antonio Damasio, *The Feeling of What Happens: Body and Emotion in the Making of Consciousness* (New York: Harcourt, 1999), 38.

21. Cristina Alberini, François Ansermet, and Pierre Magistretti, "Memory Reconsolidation, Trace Reassociation and the Freudian Unconscious," in *Memory Reconsolidation* (Lausanne: University of Lausanne, 2013), 191.

22. Shaun Raviv, "The Genius Neuroscientist Who Might Hold the Key to True AI," *Wired*, November 13, 2018; Karl Friston, Royal Society, https://royalsociety.org/people/karl-friston-11467/.

23. R. L. Carhart Harris and K. J. Friston, "The Default-Mode, Ego-Functions and Free-Energy: A Neurobiological Account of Freudian Ideas," *Brain* 133, no. 4 (2010): 1265–83.

24. Mark Solms, "New Project for a Scientific Psychology," *Neuropsychoanalysis* 22, no. 1–2 (2020): 5–35. For a critique, see Siri Hustvedt, "Commentary: Mark Solms Project," *Neuropsychoanalysis* 22, nos. 1–2 (2020): 69–72.

25. For an elaboration of transference, see Siri Hustvedt, "Freud's Playground," in *Living, Thinking, Looking* (New York: Picador, 2012), 196–222.

26. *The Freud/Jung Letters: The Correspondence between Sigmund Freud and C. G. Jung*, ed. William McGuire (Princeton, NJ: Princeton University Press, 1974), 12–13.

27. Karl Pearson, *The Grammar of Science* (New York: Cosimo, 2007), 26–27.

28. Linda Gottfredson, "The General Intelligence Factor," *Scientific American* 9 (1998): 25.

29. Ian Deary, "Individual Differences in Cognition: British Contributions over a Century," *British Journal of Psychology* 92, no. 1 (2001): 217.

30. See Richard Lewontin's now classic essay, "The Analysis of Variance and the Analysis of Causes," *American Journal of Human Genetics* 26 (1974): 400–411.

31. There are many papers on the flawed massive modularity thesis. See Jaak Panksepp and Jules B. Panksepp, "The Seven Sins of Evolutionary Psychology," *Evolution and Cognition* 6, no. 2 (2000): 108–131. For a recent paper, see David Pietraszewski and Annie E. Wertz, "Why Evolutionary Psychology Should Abandon Modularity," *Perspectives on Psychological Science* 17, no. 2 (2021): 465–90. For an overall criticism of the field, see Subrena E. Smith, "Is Evolutionary Psychology Possible?," *Biological Theory* 15 (2019): 39–49.

32. Steven Pinker, *The Blank Slate: The Modern Denial of Human Nature* (New York: Penguin, 2002), 308, 374.

33. See Ned Block, "How Heritability Misleads about Race," *Cognition* 56, no. 2 (1995): 99–128.

34. Eric Turkheimer, Erik Petterson, and Erin Horn, "A Phenotypic Null Hypothesis for the Genetics of Personality," *Annual Review in Psychology* 65 (2014): 532.

35. Vidya B. Visvanathan, "Courses Discount Freud's Theories," *Harvard Crimson*, November 30, 2007.

36. Falk Leichsenring, "Are Psychodynamic and Psychoanalytic Therapies Effective?: A Review of Empirical Data," *International Journal of Psychoanalysis* 86, no. 3 (2005): 841–68; Jonathan Schedler, "The Efficacy of Psychodynamic Therapy," *American Psychologist* 65, no. 2 (2010): 98–109; Peter Fonagy, "The Effectiveness of Psychodynamic Psychotherapies: An Update," *World Psychiatry* 14, no. 2 (2015): 137–50; Christiane Steinart et al., "Psychodynamic Therapy: As Efficacious as Other Empirically Supported Treatments? A Meta-Analysis of Outcomes," *American Journal of Psychiatry* 174 (2017): 944–53.

37. Alfred North Whitehead, *Science and the Modern World* (New York: Free Press, 1967), 55.

38. Matteo Colombo and Cory Wright, "First Principles in the Life Sciences: The Free Energy Principle, Organicism, and Mechanism," *Synthese* 198, no. 14 (2021): 3463–88.

39. T. J. Johnson and Oddgeir Friborg, "The Effects of Cognitive Behavioral Therapy as Anti-Depressive Treatment Is Falling: A Meta-Analysis," *Psychological Bulletin* 141, no. 4 (2016): 747–68; Peter Fonagy et al., "Pragmatic Randomized Controlled Trial of Long-Term Psychoanalytic Psychotherapy for Treatment Resistant Depression: The Tavistock Adult Depression Study TADS," *World Psychiatry* 14, no. 3 (2015): 312–21. See also Scott D. Miller, "Swedish National Audit Office Concludes: When All You Have Is CBT, Mental Health Suffers," blog, November 10, 2015.

40. "How *Nature* Contributed to Science's Discriminatory Legacy," *Nature*, September 28, 2022.

41. Valentin Amrhein, Sander Greenland, and Blake McShane, "Scientists Rise Up against Statistical Significance," *Nature*, March 20, 2019.

42. Sigmund Freud, "Remembering, Repeating, and Working-Through," *SE* (1914), 12:154.

CONTRIBUTORS

André Aciman was born in Alexandria, Egypt, and is an American memoirist, essayist, novelist, and scholar of seventeenth-century literature. He is the author of *Call Me by Your Name* and *Find Me*, as well as *Out of Egypt* and other novels, essay collections, and Audible novellas. Aciman is the director of the Writers' Institute and is Distinguished Professor of Comparative Literature at the Graduate Center, CUNY. He has written for the *New York Review of Books*, the *New Yorker*, the *New Republic*, the *New York Times*, the *Wall Street Journal*, and many other magazines and newspapers.

Sarah Boxer, cartoonist, writer, and critic, is the author of two psychoanalytic graphic novels, *In the Floyd Archives*, based on Freud's case histories, and *Mother May I?*, based on the ideas of Melanie Klein, D. W. Winnicott, and Freud. She is also the creator of two Shakespearean tragic-comics, *Hamlet: Prince of Pigs* and *Anchovius Caesar: The Decomposition of a Romaine Salad*. When she was an ideas reporter at the *New York Times* and an editor at the *New York Times Book Review*, Boxer's beats included Freud and psychoanalysis. Her criticism and essays have appeared in the *Atlantic*, the *New York Review of Books*, the *New Yorker*, the *New York Times Book Review*, the *Comics Journal*, *Artforum*, and *Bookforum*.

Jennifer Finney Boylan is the author of eighteen books, including *Mad Honey*, co-authored with Jodi Picoult. She is the Anna Quindlen Writer in Residence at Barnard College of Columbia University and is a trustee of PEN America. In 2022–23 she was a fellow at the Harvard Radcliffe Institute for Advanced Study.

Susie Boyt is the author of seven acclaimed novels as well as the memoir *My Judy Garland Life*, which was serialized on BBC Radio 4 and staged at the Nottingham Playhouse. She recently introduced and edited *The Turn of the Screw, and Other Ghost Stories* by Henry James for Penguin Classics. Her latest novel is *Loved and Missed*, published by New York Review Books in 2023.

Gerald Early is an essayist, cultural critic, and professor of English, African, and African American studies and American culture studies at Washington University in St. Louis. He is the author of several books, including *The Culture of Bruising*.

Esther Freud trained as an actress before writing her first novel, *Hideous Kinky*, which was made into a film starring Kate Winslet. Her other novels include *The Sea House, Lucky Break*, and *Mr Mac and Me*, and most recently, *I Couldn't Love You More.*

Rivka Galchen is a prizewinning author of five books, as well as a staff writer at the *New Yorker* magazine.

Adam Gopnik has been writing for the *New Yorker* since 1986. His books include *Paris to the Moon; The King in the Window; Through the Children's Gate: A Home in New York; Angels and Ages: A Short Book about Darwin, Lincoln, and Modern Life; The Table Comes First: Family, France, and the Meaning of Food; Winter: Five Windows on the Season* (Fiftieth Anniversary Massey Lecture); *At the Strangers' Gate*; and most recently *A Thousand Small Sanities: The Moral Adventure of Liberalism.*

David Gordon was born in New York City. He attended Sarah Lawrence College and holds an MA in English and comparative literature and an MFA in writing, both from Columbia University. His most recent novel is *The Pigeon*. He is also the author of *The Serialist, Mystery Girl, The Bouncer, The Hard Stuff*, and *The Wild Life*, and the story collection *White Tiger on Snow Mountain*. His work has appeared in the *Paris Review, Harper's*, and the *New York Times Magazine*, among other publications.

Siri Hustvedt has a PhD from Columbia University and is a lecturer in psychiatry at Weill Cornell Medical College. She is the author of a book of poetry, seven novels, five collections of essays, and two works of nonfiction. Her work has been translated into more than thirty languages.

Sheila Kohler is the author of eleven novels, three volumes of short fiction, a memoir, and many essays. Her latest novel is *Open Secrets*. Her work has been published in thirteen countries. She has taught at Columbia, Sarah Lawrence, and Bennington, and at Princeton since 2008. Her novel *Cracks* was made into a film directed by Jordan and Ridley Scott. You can find her blog at *Psychology Today* under "Dreaming for Freud."

Peter D. Kramer is the author of eight books, including *Listening to Prozac*, the biography *Freud: Inventor of the Modern Mind*, and, most recently, *Death of the Great Man: A Novel*. Dr. Kramer hosted the nationally syndicated public radio program *The Infinite Mind*, and his essays, op-eds, and book reviews have appeared in the *New York Times, Wall Street Journal, Washington Post*, and elsewhere. For nearly forty years, Dr. Kramer practiced psychiatry in Providence, Rhode Island. He now writes full time and is emeritus professor of psychiatry and human behavior at Brown University.

Phillip Lopate is the author of four essay collections and the editor of *Art of the Personal Essay*. He has also edited a three-volume anthology of the American essay. His other books include studies of Susan Sontag, the New York waterfront, and the photographer Rudy Burckhardt. He is a professor at Columbia University.

Thomas Lynch is the author of five collections of poems, four books of nonfiction, and a book of stories, *Apparition and Late Fictions*. His work has appeared in the *Atlantic, Granta*, the *New Yorker, Esquire, Poetry*, the *Paris Review*, and the *Times* (of New York, Los Angeles, London, and Ireland) and has been the subject of two documentary films, *Learning Gravity* by Cathal Black and *Frontline*'s episode "The Undertaking" on PBS. He has taught at Wayne State University's School of Mortuary Science, the University of Michigan's Graduate Program in Creative Writing, and the Candler School of Theology at Emory University. He keeps homes in Michigan and Moveen, West Clare.

Daphne Merkin is a novelist, memoirist, and literary critic who writes for many publications, including the *New York Times Book Review*, the *Atlantic*, the *New York Review of Books*, and *Airmail*. She is the author of *This Close to Happy: A Reckoning with Depression*, and two collections of essays, *Dreaming of Hitler* and *The Fame Lunches*. Her first novel, *Enchantment*, has been reissued with an introduction by Vivian Gornick and her most most recent book is the novel *22 Minutes of Unconditional Love*. She has taught writing at Marymount Manhattan College, Hunter College, the Ninety-Second Street Y, and the MFA program at Columbia University.

David Michaelis, a contributor to the popular *Central Park* and *Our Boston* anthologies, is the author of three best-selling biographies: *Eleanor, Schulz and Peanuts*, and *N. C. Wyeth*.

Rick Moody is the author of six novels, three collections of stories, two memoirs, and a collection of essays on music. He teaches at Tufts University.

Susie Orbach cofounded the Women's Therapy Centre in London in 1976 and the Women's Therapy Centre Institute in New York in 1981. She has written thirteen books, the most recent *In Therapy: The Unfolding Story*. Her first book, *Fat Is a Feminist Issue*, has been continuously in print since 1978. She continues to help many individuals and couples from her practice in London.

Richard Panek is the author of numerous books on the history and philosophy of science, including *The Invisible Century: Einstein, Freud, and the Search for Hidden Universes*. His most recent book is *The Trouble with Gravity: Solving the Mystery beneath Our Feet*, and his *The Four Percent Universe: Dark Matter, Dark Energy, and the Race to Discover the Rest of Reality* received the American Institute of Physics award for Science Communication. He has also been the recipient of a Guggenheim Fellowship in science writing.

Alex Pheby lives in Scotland and is head of creative writing at the University of Newcastle. His novels include *Playthings*, which fictionalizes the final illness of Daniel Paul Schreber, and *Lucia*, which deals with James Joyce's schizophrenic daughter.

Michael S. Roth is president of Wesleyan University and the author of several books of intellectual history focused on making sense of the past. He curated the exhibition *Sigmund Freud: Conflict and Culture*, which opened at the Library of Congress in 1998, and his most recent books are *The Student: A Brief History* and *Safe Enough Spaces: A Pragmatist's Guide to Free Speech, Affirmative Action, and Political Correctness on College Campuses*.

Casey Schwartz is the author of *In the Mind Fields: Exploring the New Science of Neuropsychoanalysis* and *Attention: A Love Story*. She writes regularly for the *New York Times*.

Mark Solms is a professor at the Neuroscience Institute of the University of Cape Town. He is a member of the South African and American Psychoanalytic Associations and the British Psychoanalytical Society. He has published 350 articles and chapters, and eight books, the latest of which is *The Hidden Spring: A Journey to the Source of Consciousness*.

Colm Tóibín is the author of ten novels, including *The Master, Brooklyn*, and *The Magician*, and two collections of stories. He is the Irene and Sidney B. Silverman Professor of the Humanities at Columbia University.

Sherry Turkle is the Abby Rockefeller Mauzé Professor of the Social Studies of Science and Technology in the Program in Science, Technology, and Society at the Massachusetts Institute of Technology and founding director of the MIT Initiative on Technology and Self. Her most recent books are *Life on the Screen, Alone Together*, and *Reclaiming Conversation*, and a memoir, *The Empathy Diaries*.

CREDITS

INDEX